𝔖elected 𝔑ovels

by

HONORÉ DE BALZAC

𝔇efinitive 𝔗exts

SPLENDORS AND MISERIES
OF COURTESANS

*THE WAY THAT GIRLS LOVE
HOW MUCH LOVE COSTS OLD MEN
THE END OF BAD ROADS
THE LAST INCARNATION OF VAUTRIN*

BY

𝔥onoré de 𝔅alzac

WITH ILLUSTRATIONS

VOLUME I

PRINTED AND PUBLISHED BY
GEORGE BARRIE'S SONS
AT PHILADELPHIA

COPYRIGHTED, 1895, BY G. B.

THE AUTHOR'S PREFACE TO THE HUMAN COMEDY

PREFACE.

In giving the title of THE HUMAN COMEDY to a work in which I have been engaged for nearly thirteen years, I feel it necessary to give a brief explanation of its origin, scope and plan, and to attempt this as impartially as if it had no personal interest for me. This is not so difficult as the public may imagine. There are few works that contribute much to a man's vanity, and much labor adds to his share of modesty. This observation accounts for the careful examination that Corneille, Molière and other great authors made of their own compositions, and if it is impossible for us to equal their lofty conceptions, we may at least strive to imitate them in this characteristic.

The first idea of THE HUMAN COMEDY came to me like a dream, an impossible project which I welcomed and then allowed to escape; it was a charming fancy that showed its smiling face but for an instant, and spreading its wings fluttered back into a visionary heaven. Still, fancy often changes into fact and its tyrannical commands cannot be resisted.

The idea occurred to me, in consequence of a comparison between the human and animal kingdoms.

It would be a mistake to believe that the great

dispute that has recently arisen between Cuvier and
Geoffroy Saint-Hilaire rests upon the ground of a
scientific innovation: *Unity of composition*, expressed
in other terms, occupied the greatest minds of the
two preceding centuries. On reading over the extraordinary works of the mystical writers who have
devoted themselves to the various sciences, considered under their relation to the infinite, such as
Swedenborg, Saint Martin, etc., and the books of
the greatest geniuses in natural history, such as
Leibnitz, Buffon, Charles Bonnet, etc., we find in
the monads of Leibnitz, in the organic molecules of
Buffon, in the vegetative force of Needham, in the
perfect adjustment of similar parts of Charles
Bonnet, who dared to write, in 1760, that an animal
vegetates like a plant; in all these, I say, we find the
rudiments of the great law *of each for himself*, upon
which the *unity of composition* depends. There is but
one single animal. The Creator has employed but
one and the same model for all organic beings. It is
the principle of animal life that each creature should
borrow its external form, or, to speak more exactly,
the differences of its form, from the environment
in which it is destined to become developed. The zoological species result from these differences. The pro-
mulgation and maintenance of this system, that is
moreover in harmony with our ideas of divine power,
will do eternal honor to Geoffroy Saint-Hillaire,

PREFACE

who surpassed Cuvier on this high scientific ground, and whose triumph was acknowledged by the great Goethe in the last article which he wrote.

Far more deeply impressed by this system than by the discussions to which it has given rise, I saw, that, in this respect, society resembled nature. Does not society make of man, in accordance with the environment in which he lives and moves, as many different kinds of men as there are different zoological varieties? The differences between a soldier, an artisan, an administrator, a lawyer, an idler, a scholar, a statesman, a merchant, a sailor a poet, a pauper and a priest, though more difficult to understand, are quite as considerable as those that distinguish the wolf, the lion, the ass, the crow, the shark, the seal and the sheep. There have, therefore, existed, and will always exist, social species, just as there are zoological species. Since Buffon wrote his magnificent work, in which he attempted to include the whole of zoology in the compass of one book, was not there something of the same kind to accomplish in behalf of society? Between the different species of the animal kingdom, nature has set bounds which do not exist in human society. When Buffon described a lion, he needed but few additional words to draw the picture of a lioness; whereas, in society, a woman is not always the female of the male. In one household there can exist two perfectly dissimilar beings. A shop-keeper's wife is sometimes worthy of a prince, while a prince's wife may not be the equal of a poor artist's. The social state is subject to possibilities that are not to be found in nature, for it is nature plus society. The description of social species is, therefore, at least twice as complex as that of animal species, under the aspect of the two sexes alone. Lastly, there is no confusion in the life of animals, and few dramas take place among them; they merely pursue and attack one another. Men also pursue one another, but the greater or less degree of intelligence they possess renders the combat far more complicated. Though some men of science do not as yet admit that a great current of life overflows into humanity from the animal kingdom, it is certain that a grocer may become peer of France, and that a nobleman may sink into the lowest rank of society. Moreover, Buffon has described the life of animals as extremely simple. It needs but few accessories, and they have neither arts nor sciences; whereas man, in obedience to a still undiscovered law, tends to represent his manners, life and thought in all that he appropriates to his needs. Although Leuwenhoëc, Swammerdam, Spallanzani, Réaumur, Charles Bonnet, Muller, Haller, and other patient zoographers have shown us how interesting the habits of animals are, yet, to our eyes at least, the ways of every animal appear to be the same at all periods; whereas the habits, dress, words and houses of a prince, a banker, an artist, a bourgeois, a priest and a pauper are entirely dissimilar and change with each successive civilization.

Thus, the work to be written required a triple form: men, women and things—that is to say, human beings and the material representation they give to their mode of thought; in short, man and his life.

In reading the dry and repellant nomenclatures of facts that are called *histories*, who has not observed that the writers of all times and all countries, in Egypt, Persia, Greece and Rome, have forgotten to give us an account of the customs of the people? The fragment of Petronius on the private life of the Romans does more to irritate than to satisfy our curiosity. The Abbé Barthélemy remarked this immense lacuna in the field of history, and devoted his life to reconstructing the manners of Greece in his *Anacharsis*.

But how could I hope to give interest to the drama of three or four thousand persons that a single society presents? How could I, at the same time, please the poet, the philosopher, and the masses who insist upon receiving their poetry and philosophy through the medium of striking images? I conceived the importance and the poetry of the history of the human heart, but I saw no means of realizing my scheme; for, up to our own time, the most famous story-tellers had lavished their talents upon creating one or two typical characters, and painting one side of life. It was with this thought in mind that I read the works of Sir Walter Scott, the modern troubadour, who was at that time endowing with enormous charm a species of composition that has been unjustly called secondary. Is it not in reality more difficult to compete with nature in drawing such pictures as *Daphnis and Chloe, Roland, Amadis, Panurge, Don Quixote, Manon Lescaut, Clarissa, Lovelace, Robinson Crusoe, Gil Blas, Ossian, Julie d'Etanges, Uncle Toby, Werther, René, Corinne, Adolphe, Paul and Virginia, Jeanie Deans, Claverhouse, Ivanhoe, Manfred and Mignon,* than to marshal an array of facts that are much the same in all countries, to study the meaning of laws that have fallen into disuse, to draw up theories that bewilder nations, or, after the fashion of metaphysicians, to explain the nature of being? In the first place, almost all these characters, whose existence is longer and more real than that of the generations from the midst of which they spring, live only on condition of offering a faithful image of the present. Conceived in the vitals of their century, they are throbbing with the pulsations of the human heart, and often contain a whole system of philosophy.

Sir Walter Scott, therefore, raised the novel to the philosophic value of history; the novel—the branch of literature that, through all the centuries, has incrusted with imperishable diamonds the poetic crown of those countries which have cultivated letters. He infused into it the true spirit of the ancients, combining within its limits drama, dialogue, description, and both portrait and landscape painting; he conferred upon it the two elements of an epic, the true and the marvelous, and gave it poetry in the familiar disguise of the humblest dialects. But as he had not invented a system, but had rather acquired his method in the heat of his inspiration and the logic of his work, it had not occurred to him to bind his stories each to each, so as to make them into one complete history, every chapter of which should be a novel, and every novel an epoch. On observing this want of connection, which, however, robs Sir Walter Scott of nothing of his greatness, I perceived at the same time the system best adapted to the execution of my work, and the possibility of executing it. Although I may say that I was dazzled by the astounding invention of Sir Walter Scott, who is always original, and never falls below his own level, I did not despair, for I discovered that the root of his talent lay in the infinite variety of human nature. Chance is the greatest romancer in the world, and a man has but to study it to be gifted with invention. French society was to be the historian, and I but the secretary. By taking an inventory of virtues and vices, by collecting signal examples of passion, and by painting from life, by making a selection from the chief social events of the time, and by composing types made up of traits taken from several homogeneous characters, I thought I might succeed in writing the history of human manners that has been forgotten by so many historians. Thus, by patience and perseverance, I might be able to realize for France in the nineteenth century, the book we so much regret, that Rome, Athens, Tyre, Memphis, Persia and India have not left us to tell us of their civilizations; the same work as that which, after the example of the Abbé Barthélemy, the brave and patient Monteil attempted, in a less attractive form, on the subject of the Middle Ages.

Still, all this was nothing. By confining himself to the most rigorous reproduction, a writer might be more or less faithful, more or less successful, patient or daring as a painter of human types; he might be the narrator of the dramas of private life, and the archeologist of social furnishings; he might catalogue the various professions and keep a record of good and evil; but to deserve the praise that every artist must be ambitious of receiving, was it not necessary for me to study the cause or causes of social effect, and to apprehend the meaning hidden under this immense mass of figures, passions and events? And after having sought, even if without success, the cause that is the motor of the whole social machine, was I not called upon to consider the principles of nature, and to discover wherein human society approaches the eternal law of beauty and truth, and wherein it strays from it. In spite of the extent of the premises which alone might constitute a work, a conclusion would still be required for the completion of my design. Thus described, society would itself bear witness to the cause of its own advance.

The law that makes a writer what he is, and, as I am not afraid to say, renders him the equal and perhaps the superior of the statesman, is the settled opinion he holds concerning human affairs, and his absolute devotion to fixed principles. Machiavelli, Hobbes, Bossuet, Leibnitz, Kant, and Montesquieu provide the science which statesmen are to apply. "A writer should have decided belief in politics and morals, and should regard himself as a teacher of men; for men have no need of masters to learn how to doubt," said Bonald. I took these great words early for my guide; they are the law of the monarchical writer no less than of the democratic writer. Therefore, when people shall attempt to find me involved in contradictions, it will be discovered that they have misinterpreted some sarcasm of mine, or turned against me the speech of one of my characters, as slanderers are fond of doing. As to the inner meaning and soul of my work, I give its fundamental principles as follows:

Man is neither good nor evil, but is born with instincts and aptitudes; society, far from corrupting him, as Rousseau thought, improves him and makes him better, but self-interest develops his evil as well as his good inclinations. Christianity, and, above all, Catholicism, as I have said in the *Country Doctor*, is a complete system for the repression of the depraved tendencies of man, and the greatest element of social order.

By studying attentively a picture of society, taken as it were from life, with all its good and all its evil, we learn the lesson that if thought, or passion, which includes both thought and feeling, is the social element, it is also the destructive element. In this, the life of society resembles the life of man, inasmuch as a race acquires longevity on condition of moderating its vital action. Instruction, or rather education by means of religious bodies, is consequently the great principle of a people's existence, and the sole means of diminishing the sum of evil and augmenting the sum of good in every society. Thought, the origin of good and ill, can be qualified, ruled and directed by religion alone. The only possible religion is Christianity. (See the letter written from Paris in *Louis Lambert,* in which the young transcendental philosopher explains, with reference to the doctrine of Swedenborg, that there has never been but one religion since the beginning of the world.) Christianity has created the modern nations, and will preserve them. From this the monarchical principle necessarily results. Catholicism and kingship are twin principles, but in regard to the limits within which they should be confined in order to restrain them from absolute development, it is plain that a preface as succinct as the present one, should not become a political treatise. Therefore I shall enter into neither the religious nor political dissensions of the moment. I am writing by the light of two eternal truths, religion and monarchy, which are proclaimed to be indispensable by contemporary events, and toward which every writer of good sense should endeavor to recall our country. Without being an enemy of the elective system, which I regard as an excellent constituent principle of law, I oppose it *considered as the only social method;* above all, when it is as ill-organized as it is to-day, for it does not even represent an imposing minority, the ideas and interests of which a monarchical government would be obliged to respect. The elective system, universally applied, leads to government by the masses, the only government that is irresponsible, and in which there are no bounds to tyranny, for it is called *the law*. For this reason I regard the family and not the individual as the true element of society, and in this respect, at the risk of being considered retrograde, I place myself beside Bossuet and Bonald, instead of allying myself to modern innovators. Since the elective system has become the only social method, if I have recourse to it myself, no contradiction must be inferred between my opinions and my acts. An engineer may announce that a bridge is on the point of breaking down, and that there is danger in crossing it, yet he goes over it himself when it is the only road he can take to town. Napoleon was marvelously successful in adapting the elective system to the genius of our country, and the least important deputies of the legislative body established by him made the most famous orators of the Chambers under the Restoration. No Chamber has been equal to the legislative body, if we compare the members of it separately. The elective system of the Empire was incontestably the better of the two.

This declaration will strike some persons as proud and pretentious; they will quarrel with a novel-writer for aspiring to be an historian, and will ask for an explanation of his scheme. My reply is that I am now fulfilling an obligation. The work I have undertaken will have the length of a history, and I am bound to give a clear interpretation, hitherto unrevealed, of its principles and morals.

I am necessarily forced to suppress those prefaces published for the sake of replying to criticisms of an essentially transient nature, and will quote but one observation from them.

Those writers who have an aim, even if that aim be merely a return to such principles as are to be found in the past by reason of their eternal truth, are always expected to clear the ground. If a man carry a stone into the domain of ideas, if he call attention to an abuse, or if he set a mark on an evil in order to facilitate its removal, he must perforce be regarded as immoral. The reproach of immorality, which a courageous writer has never failed to receive, is moreover the last that remains to be addressed to a poet, when everything else has been said to him. If your pictures of life are true; if, by dint of toiling day and night, you succeed in writing the most difficult language in the world, the imputation of immorality will be cast in your face. Socrates was immoral, Jesus Christ was immoral, and both were persecuted in the name of the societies that they were endeavoring to overturn or to reform. When a man wants to annihilate anybody he taxes him with immorality. This trick, so familiar to rival factions, is the disgrace of those who employ it. Luther and Calvin knew well what they were doing when they injured material interests by using them as a buckler! So it is that their day is past.

By copying the whole of society and reproducing it in all its tumultuous agitation, it must inevitably result that a composition should exhibit more evil than good, and that part of the fresco should represent a group of guilty characters; but the critic immediately cries out on immorality without calling attention to the morality inculcated by another part of the picture, intended as a complete contrast to the first. As my general plan was unknown, however, I could the more readily forgive the criticism I received, especially as it is as impossible to prevent criticism from using its functions, as it would be to stop the workings of sight, speech and judgment. The time of impartiality has not yet come for me. Besides, the author who has not made up his mind to undergo the fire of criticism has no more call to write than a traveler has to set out upon his journey in expectation that the skies will be always clear. On this point I have still to observe that the most conscientious moralists are extremely doubtful whether society can show as many good as bad actions, but in the picture I have drawn of it there are more virtuous than reprehensible characters. I have made all errors, sins and crimes, from the most trifling to the most serious, meet with punishment, human or divine, secret or public. I have done better than the historian, for I am freer than he. Cromwell received no punishment in this world except that inflicted upon him in imagination. He is still the subject of discussion in one school after another. Bossuet himself treated the great regicide with deference. William of Orange, the usurper, and Hugh Capet, also a usurper, died full of days, without being troubled with more doubts and fears than Henri IV. or Charles I. An analysis of the lives of Catharine II. and Louis XIV. would prove them to be utterly destitute of moral principle were they judged from the standpoint of private morality; for, as Napoleon said, for kings and statesmen there is a small and a great code of morals. The *Scenes of Political Life* are based upon this interesting reflection. It is not the law of history to tend toward the ideal as the novel does. History is or should be what it was, whereas *the novel should be a nobler world,* as was said by Madame Necker, one of the most distinguished wits of the last century. But the novel would be of no value if the details of the august falsehood were not correct. Sir Walter Scott was obliged to conform to the ideas of a country that was essentially hypocritical, and his delineation of women was false, as compared with nature, because his models were schismatics. The Protestant woman has no ideal.

She may be chaste, pure and virtuous, but she is reserved in her affections, which are always calm and disciplined as if she were fulfilling a duty. It would seem that the Virgin Mary had chilled the hearts of the sophists who banished her and her treasures of mercy from heaven. In Protestantism there is nothing further for a woman after her fall, but in the Catholic Church she is exalted by the hope of pardon. Consequently there is but one type of woman for the Protestant writer, whereas the Catholic finds a new woman in every new situation. If Sir Walter Scott had been a Catholic, and had set himself to the task of describing truly the different and successive stages of society in Scotland, perhaps he, who drew Effie and Alice—the only characters that, in later life, he regretted having created,—might have admitted the passions, with all the sins and punishments they entail, and all the virtues that repentance teaches. Human nature is made up of passion, without which religion, history, romance, and art would be useless.

On seeing that I made a true picture of the many facts I had collected, some people have been so mistaken as to imagine me a votary of the Pantheistic school, with its two aspects of sensuality and materialism. But they may be, nay, must be, mistaken. I do not believe in the indefinite progress of society; I believe in the individual progress of man. Those who maintain that I consider man as a finite creature are strangely deceived. *Seraphita*, that shows the workings of the doctrine of the Christian Buddha, seems to me to furnish a sufficient answer to this trifling accusation formerly advanced against me.

In some portions of my long work I have attempted to bring to popular notice the amazing facts, or, I might say, the marvels of electricity, that exerts so incalculable an effect upon man; but how should those cerebral and nervous phenomena, proving the existence of a new moral world, disturb the sure and certain relations between God and his worlds? How should the Catholic dogmas be shaken by them? If, by indisputable fact, thought is one day classed among those fluids which are known only through their effects, and the substance of which evades our senses, however intensified by mechanical contrivances, it will be the same thing as when Christopher Columbus observed that the earth was round, or when Galileo demonstrated that it moved upon its axis. Our future cannot be affected by it. Animal magnetism and its miracles, with which I have been familiar since 1820; the interesting researches of Gall, the successor of Lavater; and all those who, for the last fifty years, have been studying thought as the opticians have been studying light, that may be called akin to it, are conclusive in favor of the mystics, who are the disciples of Saint John the Apostle, and in favor of the great thinkers who have established the spiritual world, in which the relations between man and God are revealed.

If the meaning of my composition be well understood, it will be acknowledged that I accord to indubitable facts of every-day life, whether secret or open, to the acts of individual existence, and to their origin and cause, the same importance that, up to this time, historians have attached to the public life of nations. The unknown struggle between Madame de Mortsauf and her passion, in a valley of the Indre, is perhaps as great as the most glorious of battles (*The Lily of the Valley*), for in the battle it is only the fame of a conqueror that is at stake, whereas, with Madame de Mortsauf it is heaven itself. The misfortunes of the *Birotteaus*, the priest and the maker of perfumes, seem to me the type of those of humanity. La Fosseuse (*The Country Doctor*) and Madame Graslin (*The Village Priest*) are like all women. We all have the same troubles every day. I have had to do a hundred times what Richardson did only once. Lovelace has a thousand forms; for social corruption borrows the colors of the environment in which it is developed. On the other hand, Clarissa, that lovely picture of impassioned virtue, is drawn in lines of hopeless purity. A man must be a Raphael to draw many Virgins, and perhaps, in this respect, literature is beneath the level of painting. It may, therefore, be allowed me to draw attention to the many characters of irreproachable virtue in the published portions of my work: Pierrette Lorrain, Ursule Mirouët, Constance Birotteau, la Fosseuse, Eugénie Grandet, Marguerite Claës, Pauline de Villenoix, Madame Jules, Madame de la Chanterie, Eve Chardon, Mademoiselle d'Esgrignon, Madame Firmiani, Agathe Rouget, Renée de Maucombe; also many less important characters, who, though thrown into less conspicuous relief than those mentioned above, offer the reader the same example of domestic virtue. Do not Joseph Lebas, Genestas, Benassis, the priest Bonnet, the doctor Minoret, Pillerault, David Séchard, the two Birotteaus, the priest Chaperon, the judge Popinot, Bourgeat, the Sauviats, the Tascherons, and many others resolve the difficult literary problem of making a virtuous character interesting?

It was no trifling task to paint the two or three thousand salient figures of the age, for, after all, that is the number of types presented by every generation, and contained in THE HUMAN COMEDY. This multitude of figures, characters and existences required frames, and, if the expression may be forgiven me, galleries. Hence, as is known, I naturally divided my work into SCENES OF PRIVATE LIFE, PROVINCIAL LIFE, PARISIAN LIFE, POLITICAL LIFE, MILITARY AND COUNTRY LIFE. In these six books are classified all the STUDIES OF MANNERS AND MORALS that make up the general history of society, or, as our ancestors would have said, the collection of its deeds and exploits. The six books correspond, moreover, to general ideas. Each has its own sense and meaning, and formulates an epoch of human life. I shall now repeat briefly what was written after an inquiry into my plan by a young genius too early lost to the world of letters, Félix Davin: The SCENES OF PRIVATE LIFE represent childhood and youth with the failings peculiar to those two periods of life, and the SCENES OF PROVINCIAL LIFE represent the age of passion, calculation, self-interest and ambition. The SCENES OF PARISIAN LIFE give a picture of the tastes, vices and all the unbridled tendencies called into being by the customs peculiar to a great capital, in which the extremes of good and evil meet. Each of these three parts has its local color: the social antithesis of Paris and the provinces furnished me with immense resources. Not only men, but also the chief events of life are expressed by types. There are situations and typical phases represented in every existence, and I have tried to be especially exact in this branch of my subject. I have attempted to give an idea of the different parts of my beautiful country. My book has its geography as well as its genealogy and its families, its places and its things, its people and its facts; as it has its heraldry, its nobles and its bourgeois, its artisans and its peasants, its politicians, its dandies, and its army—in fact, its own world.

After having portrayed social life in these three books, it still remained for me to describe the exceptional existences that resume the interests of some or all of those who are in any respect outside of the ordinary law of life; hence the SCENES OF POLITICAL LIFE. Having achieved this vast picture of society, was not I called to represent it also in a state of warfare, bursting its bounds either for defence or conquest? Therefore I wrote the SCENES OF MILITARY LIFE, still the least complete portion of my work, but a place for which will be reserved in this edition, so that it may be included in it when it is finished. Finally, the SCENES OF COUNTRY LIFE are, so to speak, the evening of the long day, if the social drama may be so named. In this last book are to be found the purest characters, and the application of the great principles of order, wisdom and morality.

Such is the foundation of tragedy and comedy and their *dramatis personæ* that underlies the PHILO-SOPHIC STUDIES, the second part of this work, in which the social means to every end are discussed, and the ravages of thought described, sentiment by sentiment. The first book of this series, *The Skin of the Wild Ass*, connects the STUDIES OF MANNERS AND MORALS with the PHILOSOPHIC STUDIES by the link of an Oriental fancy, in which Life itself is represented in a deadly struggle with Desire, the first principle of every passion.

Above these are the ANALYTICAL STUDIES, but I shall say nothing about them, as but one single one has been published, *The Physiology of Marriage.*

Later, I mean to add to this two other works of the same character. First, *The Pathology of Social Life;* then *The Anatomy of Universities* and the *Monograph of Virtue.*

On seeing all that there remains for me to do, some one may say of me what my editors said: "May God grant you a long life!" I pray only that I may not be so tormented by men and things as I have been since I embarked in this terrific undertaking. It has been in my favor, and I thank God for it, that the greatest geniuses and noblest characters of the time, and with them sincere friends, as great in private life as the former are in public life, have shaken me encouragingly by the hand. And why should not I acknowledge that friendship such as theirs, and the testimonies received from time to time from strangers, have sustained me in my career, protecting me against myself and against the unjust attacks of others, against calumny that has too often pursued me, against despondency and against the too sanguine hope that is so often taken for inordinate vanity. I had resolved to meet all attacks and insults with impassive stoicism, but on two occasions I have been compelled to defend myself against cowardly slander. If those persons who believe that all injuries should be forgiven regret that I showed my powers in literary fencing, there are some Christians who think that, in the time we live in, it is well to point out the generosity of silence.

In this connection, I should like to observe that I acknowledge as my works only those that bear my name. Besides the HUMAN COMEDY, there is nothing of mine except the *Hundred Comic Tales*, two plays, and some separate articles, all signed. I am now availing myself of an incontestable right, but my disavowal, even if it should include those works in which I have had some share, is due less to vanity than to a regard for truth. If people persist in attributing to me books which, from a literary point of view, I do not acknowledge as mine, but with the copyright of which I have been entrusted, I shall allow them to say what they please, for the same reason that I leave the field free to calumny.

The immensity of a scheme that embraces at once the history and the criticism of society, the analysis of its evils and the discussion of its principles, authorized me, I believe, to give my work the title of THE HUMAN COMEDY, under which it appears to-day. Whether it is too ambitious, or only just, the public must decide when the work is finished.

PARIS, July, 1842.

THE WAY THAT GIRLS LOVE

*TO HIS HIGHNESS THE PRINCE ALFONSO
SERAFINO DI PORCIA:*

Permit me to place your name before a work essentially Parisian, and contemplated in your house during the past weeks. Is it not natural to offer you flowers of eloquence which have sprouted in your garden and been watered by regrets which brought on homesickness that you have soothed, when I wandered beneath the *boschetti* whose oaks brought back to my mind the Champs-Élysées? Perhaps by this means I may redeem the crime of having dreamed of Paris before the Duomo, of having longed for our muddy streets on the clean and neat pavements of Porta Renza. When I shall have several volumes ready to publish, which can be dedicated to certain of the Milanese, I shall be glad to find names already dear to the old Italian story-tellers among those of persons whom we love and in memory of whom I ask you to recall

    Yours with sincere affection,

July, 1838.   DE BALZAC.

PART FIRST

THE WAY THAT GIRLS LOVE

*

In 1824, at the last ball of the Opera, many masqueraders were struck with the beauty of a young man who was walking up and down the corridors and foyer, with the appearance of a person in search of some woman, whom unforeseen circumstances had kept at home. The secret of his motions, lazy and hurried by turns, is known only to some old women and to a few habitual loafers. In this vast meeting ground the crowd pays little heed to the crowd: interests are intense; idleness itself is preoccupied. The young dandy was so completely absorbed in his restless search that he did not perceive his success; the exclamations of sarcastic admiration from some masqueraders, marks of genuine surprise, gestures of derision, soft words, he heard them not, he saw them not. Although his beauty classed him among those exceptional persons who come to the ball of the Opera in search of adventure, and who wait for it as people used to wait for a lucky stroke at roulette, while Frascati was alive, he appeared to be vulgarly confident of his evening's success. He was evidently the hero of one of those dramas of three characters which compose the entire masked ball at the Opera and are known only to such persons as play their parts; since, for young women who go simply in order to say "I have seen it," for country folk, for unsophisticated young people, and for foreigners, the Opera must be the palace of weariness of body and mind. To them this black throng, slow and crowded, which goes, comes, twines, turns, returns, mounts, descends, and which can be compared only to ants on a wood-pile, is no more comprehensible than the Exchange is to a Breton peasant who has never heard of a ledger. With rare exceptions men in Paris do not mask themselves. A man in a domino looks absurd. Here the character of the nation is strikingly shown. People who are anxious to hide their happiness can go to the ball at the Opera without making their appearance public, and the masks necessary at the door disappear at once within. A most amusing sight is the confusion at the door after the ball has begun: the mass of people making their exit at odds with the new-comers. Then the masked men are jealous husbands come to spy upon their wives, or lucky husbands not caring to be spied upon by them; two situations equally ridiculous. But, though he knew it not, the young man was followed by a fellow in a murderous-looking mask, fat and short, and lumbering along like a barrel. To the habitué of the Opera, this domino betrayed a manager, an agent on Change, a banker, a notary, some bourgeois

suspicious of his unfaithful wife. In truth, in the
highest society, nobody courts humiliating evidence.
Several masqueraders had already pointed mock-
ingly at this monstrous-looking personage; others
had called out to him; some youngsters had jeered
at him. His bearing and demeanor showed marked
contempt for these random shots. He followed
wherever the young man led, like a hunted boar
who cares not for the bullets that whistle past his
ears nor the dogs that bark upon his trail.

Although, upon their first arrival, pleasure and
anxiety had donned the same livery, the famous
black gown of Venice, and in spite of the confusion
of the Opera ball, the different cliques of which
Parisian society is composed, met, greeted one another and looked about. For the initiated there are
inferences so accurate that this magic volume can
be read as easily as an amusing novel.

The habitués would never have thought this man
in luck; he would surely have worn some significant
favor—red, white, or green, the sign of some former
success in love. Was he in pursuit of revenge?
As they watched the masked figure dogging the
steps of the lucky man, several idlers gave heed
once more to the handsome youth about whose face
joy had spread her divine halo. The young man
attracted more and more attention; the more he
walked, the more he aroused the general curiosity.
Everything about him displayed habits of refinement. In accordance with a fatal law of our
epoch, there was little difference, physical or moral,

between the most distinguished the most well-bred son of a duke or peer, and this attractive boy who had but yesterday been clutched by the iron hand of poverty in the midst of Paris. With him, youth and beauty could hide deep gulfs as they can with many young men who are ambitious to play a part in Paris without possessing the capital necessary to support their pretensions, and who every day risk all for all, making sacrifice before the god most worshiped in this royal city, Chance—yet his dress and manner were faultless. He trod the classic floor of the foyer like a man accustomed to the Opera from his youth. Who has not noticed that here, as in every zone of Paris, there is a method which reveals who you are, what you are doing, whence you come, and what you wish?

"How handsome he is! I can turn here to look at him," said a masquerader in whom the habitués recognized a woman of fashion.

"Don't you remember him?" answered her cavalier. "Yet Madame du Châtelet introduced him to you——."

"What, the little apothecary whom she was in love with, who turned journalist, Mademoiselle Coralie's lover?"

"I thought he had fallen too deep ever to climb up again, and I can't understand how he can appear once more in Paris society," said Count Sixte du Châtelet.

"He has the air of a prince," said the domino, "and that actress with whom he lived never gave it to him; my cousin, who found him out, could never have scrubbed him so clean. I should like to know this Sargine's mistress. Tell me something about her life which can help me to her acquaintance."

This couple, which followed the young man, whispering as they went, were carefully noted by the masquerader with the square shoulders.

"Dear Mr. Chardon," said the prefect of Charente, taking the dandy's arm, "allow me to present you to a lady who wishes to renew her acquaintance with you."

"Dear Count Châtelet," answered the young man, "this lady herself has taught me the absurdity of the name by which you address me. A royal prescript has restored to me the name of my mother's ancestors, the Rubemprés. Though the newspapers have announced the fact, it concerns such a humble person that I do not blush to recall it alike to friends, enemies and mere acquaintances. Class yourself where you will, but I am sure that you will not disapprove a step to which I was advised by your wife when she was as yet simply Madame de Bargeton."

This delicate epigram, at which the lady smiled, made the prefect of Charente feel a nervous chill.

"Tell her," added Lucien, "that I bear *gules, with a mad bull of silver in a field sinople.*"

"Mad for silver," repeated Châtelet.

"Madame la Marquise will explain to you, if you do not know, why this ancient crest is somewhat better than the chamberlain's key and the golden bees of the Empire which may be found in yours to the great despair of Madame Châtelet, *née Nègrepelisse d'Espard,*" said Lucien sardonically.

"Since you have recognized me, I can puzzle you no further, and I can't tell you how much you puzzle me," said the Marquise d'Espard in a low tone, amazed at the impertinence and cleverness of a man whom she had formerly despised.

"Allow me then, madame, to preserve the sole chance I have of holding your attention by remaining in this mysterious shadow," said he with the smile of a man who does not care to imperil happiness that is assured.

The marquise could not repress a slight start on feeling herself (to use an English expression) *snubbed* by Lucien's conciseness.

"I congratulate you on your change of position," said the Count du Châtelet.

"And I accept your compliment in the spirit in which you make it," answered Lucien, bowing to the marquise with surpassing grace.

"The coxcomb!" said the count in a low tone to Madame d'Espard, "he has ended by outdoing his ancestors."

"When fatuity falls upon us young people it means almost invariably good fortune in some high place: but with the rest of you it means bad luck. Besides I should like to know which of our friends has taken this pretty bird under her protection; perhaps I might then find the chance of amusing myself to-night. Of course, my anonymous note is a spiteful trick arranged by some rival, for it concerns this young man; his impertinence has been dictated to him. Watch him. I am going to take the Duke de Navarreins' arm; you will know where to find me."

Just as Madame d'Espard was about to speak to her relative, the mysterious masquerader stepped between her and the duke to whisper in her ear:

"Lucien loves you. He it is who wrote the note. Your prefect is his worst enemy. How could he explain before him?"

The stranger moved away, leaving Madame d'Espard prey to a double surprise. The marquise knew nobody in the world who could play the part of this unknown mask. Fearing a trap, she walked away to find a seat and disappeared. Count Sixte du Châtelet, whose ambitious purpose Lucien had cut short with an affectation which betrayed long contemplated vengeance, followed the consummate dandy, and soon met a young man with whom he thought he could speak freely.

"Ah, Rastignac, have you seen Lucien? He has shed his skin. He's completely transformed."

"If I were as good-looking as he, I should be richer than he," answered the young swell in a flippant but shrewd tone, that gave token of attic sarcasm.

"No," whispered the big masquerader, paying back his sarcasm with interest by the manner in which he accented the monosyllable.

Rastignac, who was not the man to swallow an insult, stood as if struck by lightning, and allowed himself to be led into the embrasure of a window by an iron grasp which he could not shake off.

"You young cock, fresh from mother Vauquer's chicken-coop, you who dared not seize old Taillefer's millions when the hardest part of the work was done, know, for your own safety, if you don't treat Lucien like a brother that you love, that you are in our hands, though we are not in yours. Silence and devotion, or I'll join your game and knock over your nine-pins. Lucien de Rubempré is protected by the greatest power of to-day, the Church. Choose between life and death. Your answer?"

Rastignac felt his head swim, like a man who has gone to sleep in a forest and wakes up to find himself beside a hungry lioness. He was afraid: there were no witnesses; at times like this, the bravest men give themselves up to fear.

"Only *he* could know—and dare—," he said to himself half aloud.

The mask squeezed his hand to prevent his finishing his sentence.

"Act as if it were *he*," said he.

Then Rastignac did as does a millionaire when he is held up on the highroad by a brigand; he surrendered.

He stepped toward du Châtelet and said: "My dear count, if you value your position, treat Lucien de Rubempré as a man whom, some day, you'll find in a much higher place than yours."

The black figure allowed an imperceptible gesture of satisfaction to escape him, and walked off after Lucien.

"Well, my friend, you have changed your opinion

of him rather speedily," answered the prefect, naturally astonished.

"As speedily as those who sit in the centre and vote with the right," retorted Rastignac to this deputy-prefect whose vote had been lost to the ministry during the past few days.

"Are there any honest opinions nowadays? There are only self-interests," said des Lupeaulx, who was listening to them. "What is it all about?"

"About Monsieur de Rubempré. Rastignac wants me to think that he is rather important," said the deputy to the general secretary.

"My dear count," returned des Lupeaulx gravely, "Monsieur de Rubempré is a young man of the greatest merit and so well backed that I should be very pleased to be able to renew my acquaintance with him."

"There he goes tumbling into the wasp-nest of the rakes of the day," said Rastignac.

The three speakers turned toward a corner where stood several wits, men more or less famous, and several swells. These gentlemen shared their observations, their jokes and their scandals, trying to amuse themselves or waiting for some amusement to turn up. In this strangely mingled group were persons with whom Lucien had had varied relations: connections outwardly pleasant and ill-turns glossed over.

"Well, Lucien, my boy, here we are again, all cleaned and mended. Whence do we come? So we've remounted our steed by dint of the presents dispatched from Florine's boudoir?" "Bravo, my boy!" exclaimed Blondet, dropping Finot's arm in order to grasp Lucien familiarly by the waist and press him to his heart.

Andoche Finot was the owner of a review for which Lucien had worked almost gratis, and which Blondet was enriching by his collaboration, the wisdom of his advice and the depths of his opinions. Finot and Blondet personified Bertrand and Raton, with this simple difference that la Fontaine's cat eventually woke up to the fact that he was being duped, while Blondet, though aware all along of the imposture, kept on toiling for Finot. This brilliant *condottiere* of the pen was, in fact, destined to a long slavery. Beneath a heavy exterior, beneath the dulness of a surly impertinence, Finot concealed a brutal will sprinkled with cleverness as a laborer's bread is spread with garlic. He knew how to gather in the harvest of thoughts and of money which he reaped from the fields of the dissolute lives led by men of letters and men of politics. To his misfortune, Blondet had sold his strength to his vices and to his idleness. Constantly overtaken by want, he belonged to the unfortunate band of clever people who can do everything for the fortunes of others and nothing for their own: Aladdins who lend their lamps. These admirable counselors have minds that are clear and just when they are not perverted by self-interest. With them it is the head and not the hand that acts. Thence comes the looseness of their manners, and thence it is that weaker minds load them with contumely. Blondet shared his

purse with the comrade he had wounded the night
before; he dined, drank, slept with the man he
would throttle on the morrow. His amusing para-
doxes justified everything. He took the whole
world as a joke, and he did not wish to be taken in
earnest. Young, popular, almost famous, happy,
he did not, like Finot, spend his time in acquiring
the fortune that his old age would need. The rarest
kind of courage, perhaps, is that which Lucien needed
at this moment, to snub Blondet as he had just
snubbed Madame d'Espard and Chatelet. Unfortunately, with him, the pleasures of vanity interfered
with the exercise of pride, which surely is the beginning of many great things. His vanity had triumphed in the last encounter; he had shown himself
rich, happy and disdainful toward two persons who
had disdained him when he was poor and wretched.
But as a poet, could he, like a hardened diplomat,
break from two self-styled friends who had received
him in his poverty and given him a bed in the days
of his distress? Finot, Blondet and he had debased
themselves together, they had revelled in orgies
which had swallowed only the gold of their creditors.
Like soldiers who do not know how to use their
courage, Lucien did what many people in Paris do.
He compromised his character afresh by accepting
Finot's handshake without discarding Blondet's
caress. Whoever has dipped into journalism or
is still in it, lies under the hard necessity of
bowing to men he despises, smiling upon his worst
enemy, consorting with the rankest baseness, and

dirtying his fingers in his struggle to pay his adversaries in their own coin. He grows accustomed to seeing evil, to letting it pass; he begins by sanctioning it, he ends by doing it. As time goes on, the soul, spotted continually by shameful dealings, decays, the spring of noble thoughts rusts, the hinges of low standards swing and turn of themselves. Alceste becomes Philinte; characters weaken, talents deteriorate, high ideals of work disappear. The man who was wont to pride himself on his paragraphs wastes his energies on wretched articles which, sooner or later, his conscience points at as if they were so many sins. Some have tried, like Lousteau, like Vernou, to be great authors. They become nerveless writers of reviews. We cannot honor too highly writers whose character is as lofty as their talent, men like d'Arthez, who can walk with firm step across the quicksands of literary life. Lucien knew not what to answer to the wheedling of Blondet, whose mind exercised over him an irresistible fascination—the ascendant of the corruptor over his pupil. Besides Blondet had a recognized position in the world through his *liaison* with the Countess de Montcornet.

"Has an uncle left you his fortune?" asked Finot in a sarcastic voice.

"I have been bowling down fools, after your fashion," answered Lucien in the same tone.

"Possibly monsieur has a review, some journal?" answered Andoche Finot with all the conceited impertinence that the sharper shows toward his victim.

"Better still," replied Lucien, whose vanity, wounded by the affected superiority of the editor, gave him the spirit his new position warranted.

"And what may that be, my friend?"

"I have a purpose."

"Lucien has one of his purposes," said Vernou smiling.

"This fellow has beaten you, Finot; I told you he would. Lucien has talent. You have mismanaged him and spoiled him. Think it over, you great blockhead!", exclaimed Blondet.

Penetrating as musk, Blondet discerned more than one secret in Lucien's gesture, accent and manner. Even as he soothed him, he was able to tighten the curb by his words. He wanted to know the reasons for Lucien's return to Paris, his projects and his means of livelihood.

"Down on your knees before a superiority that you shall never reach, whoever you are, Finot," he went on. "Admit this gentleman on the instant, to the number of those to whom the future belongs; he is one of us. Witty and handsome, as he is, must not he succeed by your *quibuscumque viis*. Here he stands in his good Milanese armor, with his strong dagger half drawn and his banner flying. In heaven's name, Lucien, where did you steal that charming waistcoat? Love alone can discover cloth like that. Have we a home? Just now I need to know my friends' addresses. I have nowhere to sleep. Finot has turned me out for to-night on the common pretext of pleasure."

"My boy," said Lucien, "I have put into practice an axiom which assures me a quiet life: *Fuge, late, tace.* I must go."

"But I won't let you go until you pay me a sacred debt—that little supper, hey?" said Blondet, who was rather too much given to good cheer and liked to be treated when his pockets were empty.

"What supper?" demanded Lucien with a hasty gesture of impatience.

"Don't you remember? This is the way I recognize a friend's prosperity: his memory is gone."

"He knows what he owes us. I'll stand surety for his heart," broke in Finot, who understood Blondet's joke.

"Rastignac," said Blondet, taking the young swell by the arm as he came to the column above the foyer, where the three friends were grouped, "there's a supper stirring; you'll make one of us. At least, unless this gentleman persists in denying a debt of honor; he may."

"Monsieur de Rubempré is incapable of it, I'll warrant him," said Rastignac, who was thinking of something very different from a jest.

"There's Bixiou," cried Blondet, "he'll make one. Nothing is complete without him. When he's away, champagne sticks to my tongue and I find everything tasteless even to the spice of epigrams."

"Friends," said Bixiou, "I see that you are crowded round the wonder of the day. Our dear

Lucien brings back the metamorphoses of Ovid. Just as the gods used to change into peculiar vegetables and other things to seduce women, he has changed Le Chardon into a gentleman to seduce, what? Charles X! My dear Lucien," said he, holding him by a button of his coat, "a journalist who goes about dressed like a lord deserves a pretty reception. If I were in their place," said the pitiless jester, pointing towards Finot and Vernou, "I should slander you in their paper; you would bring them in a hundred francs, ten columns of jokes."

"Bixiou, a host is sacred for twenty-four hours before and a dozen more after dinner; our distinguished friend invites us to supper."

"What! what!" exclaimed Bixiou; "but can there be anything more necessary than to save a great name from oblivion or to endow a needy aristocracy with a man of genius? Lucien, the press esteems you; you have been its brightest ornament, and we will uphold you. Finot, a filet, the best in Paris! Blondet, a sugared sweetmeat on the fourth page of your paper. Let's advertise the appearance of the finest book of the age, *The Archer of Charles IX!* Beg Dauriat to give us *The Marguerites* at once, those divine sonnets of the French Petrarch; carry our friend on the shield of stamped paper which makes and unmakes reputations."

"If you care to sup," said Lucien to Blondet, endeavoring to rid himself of the throng which threatened to increase, "it seems to me that you have no need of making use of parables and hyperbole with an old friend as if he were an idiot. Tomorrow evening at Lointier's," said he, darting forward at the sight of a woman.

"Oh! oh! oh!" cried Bixiou, in three distinct keys and with a scoffing air as he appeared to recognize the domino before which Lucien was walking, "this deserves to be looked into."

And he followed the handsome couple, passed them, scrutinized them carefully and returned, much to the satisfaction of the envious group who were eager to know the source of Lucien's altered fortunes.

"My friends, you have long since known Monsieur de Rubempré's good fortune," said Bixiou. "It's des Lupeaulx' old rat."

One of the evils, forgotten nowadays, but common at the opening of this century, was the luxury of *rats*. "A rat"—the word is already antiquated—was applied to a girl of ten or eleven years, attached to some theatre, or more often to the Opera, and educated by libertines in a life of vice and infamy. A rat was a kind of devil's page, a girl transformed into a street arab who enjoyed freedom from punishment. The rat could steal everything; people had to look out for it as a dangerous animal. It brought into life an element of gayety, the part played in the old comedy by the Scapins, the Sganarelles and the Frontins. A rat was too expensive; it brought neither honor, nor profit, nor pleasure. The fashion of rats passed away so completely that few people of to-day knew this intimate detail of high life before the Restoration until the moment when several writers seized upon the rat as though it were a new subject.

"What, would Lucien rob us of La Torpille after he has had Coralie killed under him?"

On hearing these words the broad-shouldered looking masquerader made an involuntary motion which, slight as it was, did not escape Rastignac's notice.

"That's impossible," answered Finot, "La Torpille hasn't a farthing to give him. Nathan told me that she borrowed a thousand francs of Florine."

"Gentlemen, gentlemen!" said Rastignac, seeking to defend Lucien against these odious imputations.

"Well," cried Vernou, "has the gentleman, after having been kept by Coralie, turned into an old prude?"

"Oh," said Bixiou, "those thousand francs make me quite sure that our friend Lucien lives with La Torpille."

"What an irreparable loss to the choice spirits of literature, science, art and politics!" exclaimed Blondet. "La Torpille is the only woman who has the making of a perfect courtesan. Teaching has not spoiled her; she can neither read nor write: she would have understood us. We should have adorned our time with one of those splendid Aspasia-like figures without which a century cannot be great. See how du Barry decorates the 18th century, Ninon de Lenclos the 17th, Marion de

Lorme the 16th, Impérce the 15th, Flora the Roman republic, which she made her heir and which was able to pay the public debt with this inheritance! What would Horace be without Lydia, Tibullus without Delia, Catullus without Lesbia, Propertius without Cynthia, Demetrius without Lamia, whose glory she is to-day?"

"Blondet, talking of Demetrius in the foyer of the Opera, seems to me rather too much like copy for the *Debats*" whispered Bixiou in his neighbor's ear.

"And without all these queens what would the empire of the Cæsars be?" went on Blondet; "Lais, Rhodope are Greece and Egypt. Besides they are the poetry of the centuries in which they lived. This poetry which Napoleon lacked, for the widow of his great army is a barrack-room joke, was not wanting to the Revolution with its Madame Tallien. And now in France, where it is undecided who shall elect a queen, surely there is a vacant throne. It was our chance. We might have made a queen. I should have given la Torpille an aunt, for it is too well known that her mother died on the field of dishonor; du Tillet would have bought her a house; Lousteau, a carriage; Rastignac, footmen; Lupeaulx, a cook; Finot, bonnets;"—Finot could not withhold a start as he smarted beneath this joke—; "Vernou would have puffed her; Bixiou would have made his wittiest speeches for her. The aristocracy would have sought their amusements at our Ninon's, and we should have summoned the artists thither under pain of death. Ninon II. would have been superbly impertinent, crushingly luxurious. She would have had her own ideas. At her house some forbidden masterpiece of drama would have been read, or might at need have been written to order. She would not have been democratic; a courtesan is monarchical by nature. Ah, what a loss! She, who should love her generation, adores one small man! Lucien will make a hunting-dog of her."

"Not one of the royal women you have named has ever grubbed in the street," said Finot, "and this charming rat has wallowed in the mire."

"Like the seed of a lily in its earth," replied Vernou, "she has grown more beautiful and has bloomed in her dirt. Thence comes her superiority. Mustn't one know all things in order to create laughter and joy which belongs to all things?"

"He is right," said Lousteau, who, until then, had looked on in silence; "La Torpille can laugh and make others laugh. This knowledge of great authors and great actors belongs to those who have penetrated to the depths of social life. At eighteen this girl has known already the height of wealth, the abyss of poverty and men of every class. She holds, as it were, a magic wand wherewith she unchains the brutal appetites so violently compressed within the minds of men who still have some heart though they are busied with the world of politics or of science, of literature or of art. There is no woman in Paris who can say to the brute, as she can: 'Up!' And the brute leaves his lair and goes out to revel in debauchery. She seats you at her table, she helps you to drink, to smoke. In short this woman is the salt sung of by Rabelais which, when it is cast on matter, kindles a soul and raises it to the marvelous regions of art. Her gowns display unheard-of splendor. At times, her fingers drop their jewels as her mouth its smiles. She gives to everything the spirit of the hour. Her talk sparkles with brilliant sallies. She has the secret of the brightest and most effective onomatopœia; she—"

"You are wasting columns of newspaper," said Bixiou, interrupting Lousteau; "La Torpille is immeasurably better than all that. You have all of you been her lovers more or less; not one of you can say that she has been his mistress. She can have you all at any time; you will never have her. You force her door; you have a favor to beg of her."

"Oh, she's more generous than a bandit chieftain on the crest of the wave, and more devoted than the best college friend," said Blondet. "You may trust her with your purse and your secrets. But the reason that makes me vote for her as queen is her Bourbon indifference to the fallen favorite."

"Like her mother, she's much too dear," said des Lupeaulx. "The Dutch beauty would have swallowed the revenues of the Archbishop of Toledo. She has devoured two notaries—"

"And reared Maxime de Trailles when he was a page," said Bixiou.

"La Torpille is too dear, as Raphael, as Carême, as Taglioni, as Lawrence, as Boulle, as all artists of genius were too dear," said Blondet.

"Esther never had that look of a woman dressed to perfection," said Rastignac, pointing toward the domino to whom Lucien was offering his arm. "I'll bet on Madame de Sérizy."

"There's no doubt about it," cried du Châtelet. "Monsieur de Rubempré's good fortune is explained."

"Ah! The Church knows how to choose her levites. What a charming secretary to an embassy he will make!" said des Lupeaulx.

"And all the more," replied Rastignac, "as Lucien is a man of talent. These gentlemen have more than one proof of it," added he, turning toward Blondet, Finot and Lousteau.

"Yes. That fellow's cut out to get on in the world," said Lousteau, who was bursting with jealousy, "and all the more because he has what we call *independence of mind*."

"It was you that moulded him," said Vernou.

"Very well," answered Bixiou, looking at des Lupeaulx, "I appeal to the memory of the general secretary and master of requests. That domino is La Torpille, I'll bet a supper on it."

"I'll take the bet," said du Châtelet, eager to learn the truth.

"Come, des Lupeaulx," said Finot, "see whether you can't recognize your old rat's ears."

"There's no reason for committing treason against

the masquer," answered Bixiou, "La Torpille and Lucien will pass us as they walk back across the foyer, and then I'll prove that it is she, I promise you."

"So our friend Lucien has come to the surface?" said Nathan, who had joined the group. "I supposed that he had gone back to Angoumois for the rest of his days. Has he discovered some secret against the English?"

"He has done what you won't do in a hurry. He has paid everything."

The broad masquerader nodded his head in assent.

"In settling down," said Nathan, "a man always unsettles himself. He loses all his spirit; he becomes a bondholder."

"Oh! He'll always be high and mighty. He'll always have a loftiness of mind that will raise him above his so-called superiors," answered Rastignac.

At this minute journalists, dandies, idlers, all scanned the fascinating object of their bet, like jockeys examining a horse on sale. These judges, hardened among scenes of Parisian depravity, all of excellent minds and each in a different path, corruptors alike, alike corrupt, all devoted to unchecked ambition, accustomed to take everything for granted and to leave nothing undiscovered, had their eyes excitedly fastened upon a masked woman, a woman who could be identified by them alone. Only they and some few habitués of the Opera ball could recognize, beneath the long shroud of the black domino, beneath the hood, beneath the falling cape which hides a woman so completely, the curves of form, the individualities of presence and gait, the movement of the waist, the carriage of the head, the things least noticeable to the common eye and the most easy for them to discern. In spite of the shapeless exterior they could recognize that most moving sight that the eye can see: a woman moved by true love. Whether she were La Torpille, the Duchess of Maufrigneuse or Madame de Sérizy, the last or the first round of the social ladder, this creature was an admirable creation, the light of a happy dream. These old young men and young old men alike felt a sensation so poignant that they envied Lucien the exalted privilege of this transformation of a woman into a goddess. The masked figure walked as if she were alone with Lucien. For this woman there were no longer ten thousand people, an atmosphere heavy and thick with dust. No, she was beneath the heavenly vault of love, as Raphael's Madonnas are beneath their oval fillets of gold. She did not feel the press of the throng; the flame of her glance shot from the twin holes in her mask and darted into Lucien's eyes; the very quivering of her frame seemed to have for its motive the corresponding movement of her lover. Whence comes this flame which sheds its light about a woman in love, which marks her from the crowd? Whence comes this fairy lightness which seems to change the laws of weight? Is it the soul escaping? Has happiness bodily virtues? The simplicity of a girl, the graces of childhood show forth from beneath the domino. Though they are separate and in motion, these two beings resemble those groups of Flora and Zephyrus cunningly intertwined by the cleverest sculptors. But this was greater than sculpture, the greatest of arts. Lucien and his lovely domino brought to mind those angels playing with birds and flowers which Jean Bellini's brush has placed beneath his pictures of the Virgin mother. Lucien and this woman belonged to the imagination which is above art as cause is above effect.

When this woman, forgetful of everything, was at a single step from the group, Bixiou cried out: "Esther!"

The unfortunate woman turned her head quickly as if she had heard her name, then, recognizing the malicious figure, she hung her head like a dying man as he breathes his last. There was a shrill burst of laughter, and the group melted into the midst of the crowd as frightened field-mice scuttle from the roadside to their holes. Rastignac alone did not go farther than was necessary, in order to avoid the appearance of shrinking before the angry glance of Lucien. He could wonder at two sorrows equally deep although hidden; one, poor Torpille stricken down as if by lightning, the other, the unknown masquerader, the only person in the group who had not stirred. Esther whispered one word in Lucien's ear, her knees trembled beneath her, and Lucien disappeared supporting her. Rastignac

THE WAY THAT GIRLS LOVE 27

looked after the handsome couple and stood buried in his thoughts.

"Whence came this name of Torpille?" said a gloomy voice which went through him like a knife, for it was no longer disguised.

"It is *he*. He has escaped again," said Rastignac aside.

"Silence or I'll throttle you," answered the masquerader, assuming a different voice. "I am satisfied with you; you have kept your word. You have more than one arm to help you. Henceforth be silent as the grave, and before that silence answer my question."

"This girl is so fascinating that she could have bewitched the Emperor Napoleon, and she can bewitch somebody still more difficult to seduce, you!" replied Rastignac, moving away.

"One moment," said the masquerader. "I am going to show you that you have never seen me before."

The man unmasked. Rastignac hesitated a moment as he recognized nothing of the hideous creature he had formerly known in the Maison Vauquer.

"The devil has let you change everything but your eyes, and those no one can ever forget."

The iron hand clenched his arm to enjoin an eternal silence.

At three o'clock in the morning des Lupeaulx and Finot found the elegant Rastignac resting against a column on the spot where the terrible masquerader had left him. Rastignac had confessed to himself. He had been the priest and the penitent, the judge and the accused. He allowed them to take him away and give him a breakfast and went home completely drunk but silent.

*

The Rue de Langlade, as well as the adjacent streets, abuts into the Palais Royal and the Rue de Rivoli. This portion of one of the most brilliant quarters of Paris will long preserve the stains left by those heaps of filth which marked the unlawful haunts and "*mills*" of old Paris. These streets, narrow, sombre and muddy, where business gives little heed to appearances, assume at night a mysterious look that is full of contrasts. In going from the brilliantly lighted districts of the Rue Saint-Honoré, of the Rue Neuve-des-Petits-Champs, and of the Rue de Richelieu, where presses a ceaseless crowd, where glitter the masterpieces of industry, fashion and art, any man unfamiliar with the nights in Paris would feel a gloomy dread as he turned into the network of alleys which encircle that brightness that is reflected to the sky. Thick darkness succeeds to torrents of gas. Here and there a pale lamp throws its uncertain and smoky rays which light only a few black obstacles. The few passers-by walk quickly. The shops are closed; those which are open are of a bad character; a bar-room dirty and dark, a linen-draper's selling cologne. A noxious chill spreads its mantle over your shoulders. Few carriages pass. There are sinister-looking places, among them the Rue de Langlade, the entrance of the Passage Saint-Guillaume, and several winding streets. The city council has as yet been able to do nothing toward cleansing this vast leprosy, for prostitution has long since established her headquarters there. Perhaps it is for the best interests of Paris to allow these alleys to retain their foul appearance. Passing by in the light of day, it is impossible to imagine what these streets become at night. They are strewn with strange-looking figures—people without a caste. White, half-naked forms lean against the walls. The darkness is alive. Between the houses and the roadway flows a stream of gaudily dressed women walking and chattering. Several half-open doors give forth loud peals of laughter. Words fall upon the ear such as Rabelais asserted are frozen and melt. Snatches of song rise from between the paving-stones. The sound is not uncertain; it means something: when it is hoarse it is a voice, but if it sound like a chant it loses all kinship with the world; it is a wild, strident noise. Shrill whistles sound constantly; the very boot-heels have something maddening and derisive about their creak. Everything together makes a man dizzy. The atmospherical conditions are altered: it is hot in winter and cold in summer. But whatever the weather, this strange place offers the same spectacle. The fantastic world of Hoffman of Berlin is there. The most mathematical accountant believes nothing he has seen there after he has passed back through the districts that lead to respectable streets where there are passers-by and shops and gaslights. More disdainful or more modest than the kings and queens of old, who were not ashamed to be seen with courtesans, modern policy and government dare not face this plague of great cities. Surely laws must change with time; and those which govern individuals and their liberty are of nice adjustment; but perhaps society should show itself liberal and bold in such matters purely material, as air, light and streets. The moralist, the artist and the wise official alike will lament those ancient wooden galleries of the Palais Royal where those sheep used to wander who will never cease to follow the pleasure-seekers. Is it not better that the pleasure-seekers should follow them? What has happened? To-day, the most brilliant quarters of the boulevards are forbidden to the family in the evening. In this respect the police has not made the most of its resources. A few crooked alleys might have saved the public highway.

The girl, heart-broken by a single word at the Opera ball, had lived for the past month or two in a house of mean appearance on the Rue de Langlade. Propped against the wall of an enormous building, this construction, badly plastered, without depth but of tremendous height, receives its light from the street and bears some resemblance to a parrot's perch. A suite of two rooms is on every story. This house is provided with a slender staircase fitted closely to the wall and curiously lighted by window frames which mark the outline of the stair on the exterior of the house, and where every landing is indicated by a sink, one of the worst of Parisian peculiarities. The shop and the ground floor were inhabited at this time by a tinsmith. The proprietor lived on the first floor, and the other four stories were occupied by very respectable grisettes who obtained a discount and favorable terms from the owner and the porter on account of the difficulty of renting a house so singularly built and situated. The uses of this quarter are sufficiently explained by the presence of a number of houses like this, unsuitable for business and which can be devoted only to employments unlicensed, precarious or disreputable.

At three o'clock in the afternoon the janitress, who had seen Mademoiselle Esther brought back fainting by a young man at two o'clock in the morning, consulted the grisette on the floor above, who, before getting into her carriage on her way to a party, had declared her uneasiness on Esther's account: she had not heard a sound. No doubt Esther was still asleep, but this sleep seemed suspicious. Alone in her lodge the janitress felt sorry that she could not go and see what was going on in the fourth story where were Mademoiselle Esther's lodgings. Just as she had determined to entrust to the tinsmith's son the care of her lodge, a sort of niche arranged in a corner of the ground floor, a cab stopped in front of the house. A man wrapped from head to foot in a cloak, with the evident purpose of concealing his dress or his rank, stepped out and asked for Mademoiselle Esther. The janitress felt entirely reassured. The silence and tranquillity of the recluse seemed quite explained. As the stranger ascended the stairs above the lodge, the janitress noticed the silver buckles which decorated his shoes, and she thought that she could detect the black fringe of the sash of a cassock. She went out and questioned the coachman. He replied without giving an answer, and she understood still better. The priest knocked; no answer came other than faint sighs from within. Then thrusting his shoulder against the door, he burst it open with a vigor lent him by charity no doubt, but which in another would have appeared the result of habit. He rushed into the inner room and saw, before a Virgin of colored plaster, with her hands clasped together, poor Esther on her knees, or rather lying in a heap.

The grisette was senseless. A chafing-dish of burned charcoal told the story of the awful morning. The hood and the cloak of the domino lay on the floor. The bed was undisturbed. The poor girl, cut to the heart by a deadly wound, had, no doubt, arranged everything after her return from the Opera. The wick of a candle stuck in a socket full of melted wax showed how deeply Esther had been absorbed in her last meditations. A handkerchief steeped in tears proved a sincerity of despair like that of Magdalen, whose classic pose was the same as that of this unholy courtesan. This perfect repentance brought a smile to the priest's face. Not clever at dying, Esther had left her door open without thinking that the air of the two rooms would require a great quantity of charcoal before it could become impossible to breathe. The vapor had merely stifled her. The fresh air from the stairs restored her by degrees to the consciousness of her ills. The priest stood wrapt in gloomy thought, untouched by the heavenly beauty of the girl and watching her first movements as though she had been some animal. His eyes wandered from the prostrate body to the different objects scattered about the floor, with apparent indifference. He looked at the furniture of the room, at the red-tiled rough, cold floor, ill concealed by a threadbare carpet. A small bed of painted wood canopied by yellow calico curtains spotted with roses; a single armchair and two chairs, also of painted wood and covered with the same calico, which curtained the window as well; a wall-paper of a gray background flecked with flowers, but blackened by time and grease; a mahogany work-table; a fire-place littered with kitchen utensils of the meanest description; two bundles of kindling-wood; a stone mantel-piece strewn with glasses, ornaments and scissors; a dirty pincushion; gloves white and perfumed; a charming bonnet tossed on a water-pitcher; a shawl from Ternaux which stopped a hole in the window; an elaborate gown hung from a nail; a small sofa, bare, without cushions; old and broken sandals; fascinating slippers; boots to make a queen jealous; plates of chipped crockery stained with the traces of the last repast and heaped up with covers of nickel-plate, the silverware of Parisian poor; a great basket full of potatoes and soiled linen, with a fresh gauze bonnet on top; a bad wardrobe, with a looking-glass, wide open and empty except for a few pawn-tickets from the mont-de-piété which lay on the shelves; such was the collection of things, sad and gay, poor and rich, which met the eye.

These traces of luxury in broken fragments, this room so perfectly appropriate to the Bohemian life of this girl fallen amongst her unwashed linen like a horse dead in his harness, entangled in his reins beneath the broken shaft—did this strange spectacle cause the priest to reflect? Did he say to himself that at least this erring woman must be disinterested, to live in such penury and love a rich young man? Did he attribute the disorder of furniture to disorder of life? Did he feel pity? horror? Was his charity aroused? One who had seen him thus, his arms crossed, his forehead contracted, his lips compressed, his eye fierce, would have thought him filled with gloomy and malignant thoughts, opposing projects, sinister designs. Surely he was blind to the lovely curves of a breast flattened beneath the weight of her bended figure and to the graceful lines of limbs that could be traced beneath the folds of her black skirt, as she knelt crouched upon the floor. The careless pose of the head, which, viewed from behind, revealed the white neck, soft and flexible, and the fair, ripe shoulders did not move him. He did not raise Esther. He seemed to be deaf even to the tortured gasps which betrayed the return of consciousness. It was not until she heaved a dreadful sob and cast her startling glance upon him that he deigned to lift her and to place her on the bed with an ease that betokened immense strength.

"Lucien!" she murmured.

"Love returns; the woman is not far away," said the priest with a kind of bitterness.

Then the poor victim of Parisian debauchery noticed the costume of her saviour and said with the smile of a child that seizes some longed-for object.

"Then I shall not die without a reconciliation with Heaven."

"You can atone for your sins," said the priest, moistening her forehead with water and holding beneath her nostrils a cruet of vinegar which he had found in a corner.

"I feel that life, instead of leaving me, flows more strongly than ever," said she when she had received the priest's care, and expressed her gratitude by gestures full of naturalness.

This charming pantomime, that the graces themselves might have copied for the destruction of mankind, was a perfect justification of the surname of this strange girl.

"Do you feel better?" asked the priest as he handed her a glass of sugar and water to drink.

This man seemed perfectly accustomed to places such as this; he knew them through and through. He felt completely at home. This privilege of feeling at home everywhere belongs only to kings, to girls and to thieves.

"When you feel quite yourself," went on this

singular man after a pause, "you will tell me the motives which have brought you to commit your latest crime, this attempted suicide."

"My story is very simple, father," answered she. "Three months ago I was living in the vice in which I was born. I was the last of human beings and the most vile, now I am only the most unhappy. Don't make me tell you of my poor mother, murdered—."

"By a captain in a disreputable den," said the priest interrupting his penitent. "I know your birth, and know that if a person of your sex can be pardoned for living a life of shame it is you who have never had a good example."

"I have never been even baptized, nor have I ever been taught the precepts of any religion."

"All can be forgiven," answered the priest, "if only your faith and your repentance be sincere and without regret."

"Lucien and God fill my heart," said she with touching simplicity.

"You should say God and Lucien," replied the priest smiling. "You recall to me my reasons for coming. Leave nothing unsaid which concerns this young man."

"Have you come for his sake?" she asked with a tender glance which would have softened any priest but him. "Oh! he suspected what might happen."

"No," answered he, "it is not on account of your death, but for your life, that I come here. Come, tell me your relations."

"In one word," said she.

The poor girl trembled at the harsh tone of the ecclesiastic, but like a woman whom brutality has long ceased to surprise, she answered:

"Lucien is Lucien, the loveliest and the best man in the world. But if you know him you cannot think my love unnatural. Three months ago I met him by chance at the Porte Saint Martin, where I had gone for an outing. For we were given one day a week at the house of Madame Meynardie, where I was. The next day, you see, I ran away without permission. Love had entered into my heart and had changed me so perfectly that when I came back from the theatre I scarcely felt the same person. I loathed myself. Lucien could never find out about me. Instead of telling him where I lived I gave him the address of this lodging. A friend of mine was living here then and she was kind enough to move out for me. I give you my sacred word."

"You must not swear."

"Is it swearing simply to give your sacred word? Well, then, since that day I have toiled in this room like a lost soul, making chemises at twenty-eight sous apiece, in order to gain my bread honestly. For a month I have eaten nothing but potatoes, just in order that I might be respectable and worthy of Lucien, who loves and respects me as the purest of the pure. I have made my formal declaration to the police in order to recover my rights and I have been placed under surveillance for two years. It is very hard to get those who are so ready to write your name on the registers of vice, to scratch it off again. The only prayer that I asked of Heaven was to protect my resolution. I shall be nineteen in the month of April, at that age there is hope. It seems as if I were three months old. I prayed to God every morning and implored Him never to allow Lucien to know my former life. I bought this Virgin that you see, and I have prayed to her in my own way, for I don't know any prayers. I can't read or write. I have never entered a church. I have never looked at the Host, except out of curiosity when it is carried in processions."

"What do you tell the Virgin?"

"I talk to her as I talk to Lucien, with those bursts of feeling that make him cry."

" Ah, he cries?"

" From joy," she answered quickly. " Poor boy! We know each other so well that we have the same soul. He's so sweet, so caressing, so tender-hearted, so witty, so graceful. He says that he is a poet; I say that he is God. Pardon me, but you priests don't know what love is. There are no others save such as I, who know men well enough to appreciate a Lucien. A Lucien, you see, is as rare as a woman without sin. When you meet him you can love nobody else; that is all. But such a man must have a woman worthy of him. It was for this that I wished to become fit to be loved by my Lucien, and thus came all my misfortune. Yesterday at the Opera I was recognized by some men who have no more heart than tigers have compassion; I should sooner expect sympathy from a tiger. The veil of innocence that I wore is fallen from me; their laughter pierced my head and my heart. Don't think that you have saved me; I shall die of sorrow."

"Your veil of innocence?" said the priest. "Then you have always been cruel to Lucien?"

"Oh! father, you who know him, how can you ask me such a question. How can a woman resist a god?"

"Do not blaspheme," said the ecclesiastic in a gentle voice. "Nobody can be like to God. Exaggeration does not beseem real love. You have not a pure, true love for your idol. Had you felt the change which you boast has come over you, you would have acquired the virtues that belong to youth. You would have known the joy of chastity, the delicacy of shame, those two glories of a girl. You do not love."

Esther made a gesture of horror which the priest saw, but which did not disturb the rigid calm of the confessor.

"Yes, you love him for your own sake and not for his; for the pleasures of this world which delight you, and not for love itself. If you have loved thus, you have never felt that holy tremor the which inspires a creature on whom God has set seal of exquisite perfection. Have you considered that you were degrading him by your past impurity, that you were going to corrupt a child by those hideous delights that have brought you your cognomen, notorious in infamy? You have been inconsistent with yourself and with your passion of a day—"

"Of a day!" repeated she, raising her eyes.

"What name can I give to a love that is not eternal, which does not unite us, even to the end of a Christian's future, with the person that we love?"

"Oh, I want to be a Catholic," cried she in a deep, strong voice which would have won her pardon from our Saviour.

"Is a girl who has received neither the baptism of the Church nor of knowledge; who knows not how to read nor write nor pray; who cannot make one step without the stones rising up to accuse her; worthy of notice only through the fleeting privilege of a beauty that sickness may carry away to-morrow, perhaps; is this creature, vitiated, degraded, knowing her degradation—had you been more ignorant and less loving, you had been more excusable— is this future victim of suicide and of hell, the woman who could be the wife of Lucien de Rubempré?"

Each sentence was a dagger-thrust piercing to the bottom of her heart. At each phrase the rising sobs, the fast-flowing tears of the hopeless girl bore witness with what strength the light poured at once into her mind, simple as that of a savage; into her soul, awakened at length; into her nature, over which depravity had spread a cloak of muddy ice that melted in the sun of faith.

"Why am I not dead?" was the one thought that she gave utterance to in the midst of the torrent of ideas which rushed madly through her brain.

"My daughter," said the awful judge, "there is a love which is hidden before men, and the knowledge of it is welcomed by the angels with smiles of joy."

"What?"

"Love without hope, when it inspires life and instils into it the principle of unselfishness, when it ennobles every act by the thought of attaining an ideal perfection. Yes, the angels commend that love; it leads to the knowledge of God. To perfect, to hide from him even the knowledge of the terrible jealousy that kindles in your heart, to give him everything that he wishes were it to your own hurt, to love what he loves, to have your face turned towards him unceasingly, to make yourself worthy of him you love, to make for him a thousand secret sacrifices, to worship him from afar, to give your blood drop by drop, to sacrifice your self-love for his sake, to have no more pride nor anger with him, toward him, to follow him though he knows it not: this love, religion would have pardoned; it would have offended neither the laws of men nor of God and would have led into a different path from that of your filthy pleasures."

As she heard this dreadful judgment pronounced in these words—and what words they were and with what accent spoken!—Esther felt a natural distrust. This speech was like a peal of thunder that presages the bursting of the storm. She looked at the priest and felt that cold sinking of the heart which the boldest feel in the presence of imminent and sudden danger. No look could have read what was passing within this man, but for the bravest there was more to dread than to hope in the aspect of his eyes, clear and yellow as the eyes of tigers and over which austerity and fasting had spread a veil like to that which rests on the horizon through the dog-days: the earth is hot and dazzling, but the mist renders it indistinct and vaporous; it is almost invisible. A severity quite Spanish: deep furrows, made hideous and like to deep ruts by the thousand scars of a frightful attack of small-pox, ploughed his olive, sunburned face. His stern features were set off by the frame of the stiff wig of a priest who cares not how he looks, a wig close cut and of a black that reddened in the light. His athletic chest, his soldier-like hands, his carriage, his powerful shoulders were those of the caryatides which architects of the Middle Ages have employed in some palaces of Italy and which recall vaguely the figures on the façade of the theatre of the Porte Saint Martin. The least clear-sighted people might have known that burning passions or strange accidents had thrown this man into the bosom of the Church. Surely the most astounding thunderbolts alone could have changed him, if such a nature could be changed. Women who have led the life so violently repudiated by Esther arrive at a complete indifference to the outward forms of man. They resemble the literary critic of to-day who can be compared to them in several ways, and who becomes absolutely indifferent to the rules of art. He has read so many works, he has seen so many pass away, he is so accustomed to written pages, he has witnessed the unraveling of so many plots, he has seen so many dramas, he has written so many articles without saying what he thinks, he has betrayed the cause of art so often for the sake of his own likes and dislikes, that he comes to feel disgust for everything, and yet he continues to pass judgment. There is need of a miracle to enable this writer to produce a great work; just as pure, noble love is only by a miracle born in the heart of a courtesan. The tone and the manner of this priest, who might have stepped from a canvas of Zurbaran, seemed so hostile to this poor girl that, little as exteriors meant for her, she felt herself less an object of the shepherd's care than the central subject of some scheme. Unable to distinguish between the wheedling of self-interest and the holy grace of charity, for only doubled care can detect the false money of a friend, she felt herself, as it were, between the claws of some fierce and monstrous bird which had swooped down on her after circling for some time overhead, and in her terror she said these words in a frightened voice:

"I thought that priests were bidden to comfort us, and you are killing me!"

At this cry of innocence the ecclesiastic made a gesture and said nothing; he was collecting his thoughts before answering. During this instant these two persons so singularly brought together scrutinized each other furtively. The priest understood the girl, but the girl could not understand the priest. Doubtless he gave up some design which threatened poor Esther and returned to his first plan.

"We are the healers of souls," said he gently, "and we know what medicines suit their maladies."

"Much must be forgiven misery," said Esther.

She thought herself mistaken, and slipping down from her bed she flung herself at the man's feet, kissed his cassock with the deepest humility, and lifted toward him her eyes filled with tears.

"I thought that I had done much," said she.

"Listen, my child. Your fatal reputation has plunged Lucien's family into mourning. They are afraid, and with some justice, that you will drag him into dissipation, into a world of follies."

"It is true; I myself took him to the ball to entrap him."

"You are so beautiful that he wishes to glory in you before the eyes of the world, to display you proudly and exhibit you like a horse. If it were only money that he wasted! But he will waste his time, his strength; he will lose his desire for the high destinies which they wish to be his. Instead of being some day ambassador, rich, admired, famous, he will become, like many another libertine who has drowned his talents in Paris mud, the lover of an impure woman. As for you, you will later take up your former life, after having risen for a moment to a lofty sphere, for you have not in you; that which a sound education gives—strength to resist evil and to think of the future. You will never break loose from your companions any further than you have broken loose from those people who shamed you at the Opera this morning. The true friends of Lucien, alarmed by the love which you have inspired in him, have dogged his steps, have learned all. Full of consternation they have sent me to you to sound your feelings and to decide your fate. But although they are strong enough to rid this young man's path of a stumbling-block, they are merciful. Know this, my daughter: a woman whom Lucien loves has a right to their regard, for a true Christian worships the mire where perchance has strayed a ray of the divine light. I have come as the agent of their kindness; but had I found you wholly obstinate and armed with effrontery and cunning, corrupt to the marrow and deaf to the voice of repentance, I would have abandoned you to their anger. This civil and political freedom, so hard to get, which for society's sake the police are loath to give, and which I have heard you long for with all the ardor of true repentance—here it is," said the priest, drawing from his belt a paper of official appearance. "They saw you yesterday; this notification is dated to-day: you see the power of the persons who are interested in Lucien."

At the sight of this paper, that convulsive tremor which is caused by an unexpected joy moved Esther so sincerely that she had on her lips a smile such as an idiot wears. The priest paused, looked at the child to see whether, deprived of that hideous force which sinful people draw even from their sin and restored to her original frail and delicate nature, she would resist her strongest impulses. Deceitful courtesan, Esther had played the comedy; but become once more innocent and true she might die as a blind man suddenly cured may lose his sight afresh if he be struck by too brilliant light. This man at this moment saw human nature to its bottom, but he remained in a calm terrible from its fixity. He was a frozen Alp, white and near to heaven, immovable and disdainful, with sides of granite and yet beneficent. Women of the streets are essentially emotional creatures; they pass from the most obstinate distrust to the most perfect confidence. In this respect they are below the animal. Excessive in everything, in their joys, in their despairs, in their religion, in their irreligion, almost all go mad if death, which has a high rate among their kind, did not decimate them, and if lucky chances did not raise some of them above the mire in which they live. He who would penetrate to the depths of misery of this horrible life must see how deep a woman can sink into madness without resting there by gazing in wonder at the wild ecstasy of La Torpille on her knees before the priest. The poor girl looked at the redeeming paper with an expression which Dante forgot, and which surpassed the inventions of his hell. But with the reaction came the tears. Esther rose, threw her arms about this man's neck, laid her head on his breast, let her tears trickle down, kissed the coarse cloth that covered this heart of steel, and seemed to wish to reach the heart itself. She seized this man, covered his hands with kisses, in a holy burst of gratitude she used all her softest caresses. Lavishing upon him the sweetest names, in the midst of her sugared words she whispered: "*Give it to me,*" a thousand times and with a thousand intonations. She folded him in her tender embraces, covered him with her glances with a rapidity which left him defenceless; at length she succeeded in allaying his anger. The priest knew how well this girl had deserved her surname; he knew how hard it was to resist this fascinating creature. All at once he understood Lucien's love and what it was that had seduced the poet. Passion like this hides, beneath a thousand allurements, a barbed hook which soonest pierces the lofty soul of the artist. These passions, unintelligible to the crowd, are perfectly explained by that thirst for the ideal which characterizes creative minds. Does it not bring us near to the angels charged to bring back the erring into the path of right, to purify a creature such as this —is it not to create? What an incentive, to unite moral beauty to physical beauty! What proud happiness to succeed! What an ideal task is that which needs no weapon but love! These connections, illustrated besides by the example of Aristotle, of Socrates, of Plato, of Alcibiades, of Cethegus, of Pompey, and so monstrous in the eyes of the multitude, are founded upon the sentiment which led Louis XIV. to build Versailles, which drives men to all ruinous ventures: to convert the miasmas of a morass into a sweet smelling hill surrounded by running waters; to place a lake upon a hill, as the Prince of Conti did at Nointel, or Swiss landscapes at Cassan, like Bergeret, the farmer of the revenue. In short it is art making incursions into the domain of morality.

The priest, ashamed of having yielded to this affectionate demonstration, pushed Esther from him sharply. She sat down ashamed too, for he said to her:

"You are still a courtesan."

He coolly placed the letter in his belt. Like a child with but one desire in its mind, Esther did not take her eyes from that part of his girdle which covered the paper.

"My child," went on the priest after a pause, "your mother was a Jewess and you have never been baptized, but you have never been taken to the synagogue. You are within the religious limbo of little children."

"Little children," repeated she in a pathetic voice.

"Just as on the police charts you are a figure beyond the pale of society," continued the priest unmoved. "If some chance love has made you believe, three months ago, that you were born again you should feel that since that day you are become a child. Thus you must be guided as though you were a child; you must change absolutely, and it is my duty to make you unrecognizable. First of all, you must forget Lucien."

The poor girl felt her heart breaking at this word.

She looked into the priest's face and made a sign of refusal. She felt that her saviour was her executioner, and could not speak.

"At least, you will give up seeing him," he went on. "I will take you to a convent where young girls of good family receive their education. You will become a Catholic, you will be instructed in the practice of Christian rites, you will learn religion; you will come away a girl, accomplished, chaste, pure, well-educated, if—"

The man raised his finger and paused.

"If," he continued, "you have the strength to leave La Torpille behind."

"Ah," cried the poor child, for whom every word had been a note of music at whose sound the gates of paradise were slowly opening, "ah, if I could spill all my blood here and be made anew!"

"Listen."

She was silent.

"Your future depends upon your power of forgetting. Think of the obligations you are under. A word, a gesture which should betray La Torpille kills the wife of Lucien; a syllable spoken in a dream, an involuntary thought, an unchaste look, an impatient movement, a recollection of your dissolute past, a duty left undone, a motion of the head which should reveal what you know or what has been known to your misfortune—"

"Go on, my father," said the girl with the exaltation of a saint, "to walk in shoes of red-hot iron and smile, to live clad in a corset armed with teeth and preserve the grace of a dancing girl, to eat bread sprinkled with ashes, and drink wormwood, all will be sweet, easy."

She fell on her knees, she kissed the priest's shoes, she wet them with her tears, she seized his legs and embraced them, muttering incoherent words through her tears of joy. The fair locks of her wonderful hair streamed down and rested like a carpet beneath the feet of this heavenly messenger, yet when she arose and looked at him she saw him gloomy and severe.

"In what have I offended you?" said she in alarm. "I have heard of a woman like myself who bathed in perfumes the feet of Jesus Christ. Virtue has made me so poor that I have nothing but tears to offer you."

"Did you not hear me?" answered he in a cruel voice. "I tell you that you must come out of the house where I shall take you, so changed in body and soul that not a man or woman who has known you can cry out 'Esther' and make you turn your head. Yesterday love did not give you the strength to bury the prostitute too deep to rise again; she appears afresh in worship that is not addressed to God."

"Was it not he that sent you to me?" she said.

"If during your education you were even seen by Lucien, all would be lost," replied he. "Remember that."

"Who will comfort him?" she asked.

"In what would you comfort him?" demanded

the priest in a voice which for the first time during the scene betrayed a nervous tremor.

"I don't know. He is often sad."

"Sad!" replied the priest. "Did he tell you why?"

"Never," answered she.

"He was sad because he loved a girl such as you," cried he.

"Ah, yes, he must have been," she replied with deep humility. "I am the most despicable creature of my sex, and I could only find favor in his eyes by the force of my love."

"That love should give you courage to obey me blindly. If I were to take you at once to the house where you are to be educated, everybody here would tell Lucien that you had gone away to-day, Sunday, with a priest; he would be on your track. In a week, the janitress, not seeing me return, will take me for that which I am not. Then, in the evening seven days from to-day, at seven o'clock, you will slip out quietly and get into a cab which will be in waiting for you below the rue des Frondeurs. During the week, shun Lucien; contrive excuses, put him off, and when he comes, go upstairs to some friend's room. I shall know if you have seen him, and in that case everything would be ended; I should not even return. You need this week in order to buy yourself decent gowns and to lay aside your wanton appearance," said he, placing a purse on the mantel-piece. "There is something about your manner and your clothes which Parisians know well and which tells them what you are. Have you never, on the streets or boulevards, met a modest and pure girl walking with her mother?"

"Oh, yes. It always hurts me. To see a mother with her daughter is one of our worst punishments. It awakens the remorse hidden within the folds of our hearts, which eats into us. I know only too well what it is I need."

"Very well, then, you know what you are to be next Sunday," said the priest rising.

"Oh," said she, "teach me a real prayer before you go, so that I may pray to God."

It was a touching sight to see this priest making this girl repeat the *Ave Maria* and the *Pater Noster* in French.

"They are very beautiful!" said Esther, after she had twice and without a mistake repeated these two splendid and familiar expressions of the Catholic faith.

"What is your name?" she asked of the priest when he bade her good-bye.

"Carlos Herrera. I am a Spaniard and banished from my country."

Esther took his hand and kissed it; she was no longer a courtesan; she was an angel rising from a fall.

*

In a house celebrated for the religious and aristocratic training which it gave, one Monday morning early in the month of March of this year, the scholars saw their pretty group increased by a newcomer, whose beauty triumphed undisputed not only over her comrades, but even over those especial and perfect details of beauty which were found among them. In France it is excessively rare, not to say impossible, to find the thirty famous graces described in Persian verses—carved, they say, within the seraglio—, and which a woman must have to be wholly beautiful. In France, although few are combined, there are exquisite details. The imposing whole, which sculpture seeks to attain and which it has attained in a few rare works like the Diana and the Calypso, is the privilege of Greece and of Asia Minor. Esther had come from this cradle of the human race, the native land of beauty: her mother was a Jewess. The Jews, although so often degraded by their contact with other peoples, offer amongst their many tribes certain strains which still preserve the sublime type of Asiatic beauty. When they have not a repulsive ugliness they bear the magnificent stamp of Armenian faces. Esther would have borne off the prize at the seraglio; she possessed the thirty beauties harmoniously intermingled. Far from injuring the finished loveliness of her figure or the freshness of her complexion, her strange life had imparted to her something womanly. Her skin had no longer the polished firmness of green fruit, nor yet the mellowness of the overripe: there were still years for her to bloom. A little while more of license would have made her too stout. This richness of health, this perfection of animal life in a woman in whom sensuality usurped the place of thought, must seem extraordinary to the eyes of physiologists. By a circumstance rare, almost impossible among very young girls, her hands, of an admirable mould, were soft, transparent and white as those of the young mother of a second child. She had exactly the foot and the hair, so justly famous, of the Duchesse de Berri, hair that no maid-in-waiting could hold, so abundant was it, and so long that it fell to the floor and lay there in coils; for Esther was of that middle height which allows a woman to be made a sort of plaything to take up, to lay down, to take once more and to carry without fatigue. Her skin, fine as rice-paper and of a warm amber color, shaded by red veins, was radiant without dryness, soft without moisture. Nervous to excess, but delicate in appearance, Esther attracted instant attention by a feature prominent in the faces which Raphael's pencil has best portrayed, for Raphael, of all painters, has studied most and rendered best the Jewish beauty. This wonderful characteristic was formed by depth of the arch beneath which the eye rolled as though it were separate from its frame, and whose sweep, in its clear outlines, resembled the inner curve of an archway. When youth, with its clear translucent tints, paints the lovely arc crowned by thick eyebrows; when the light falls upon the delicate curves below and rests there in its roseate brilliance, there are there treasures of tenderness to satisfy a lover, beauties to make a painter despair. This is the finishing touch of nature, these bright curves where the very shadow is golden, this tissue which has the consistency of a nerve, the flexibility of the most delicate membrane. The eye at rest within is like a magic eye in a nest of silken threads. But later this marvel is filled with a fearful sadness, when passion has darkened these delicate outlines, when sorrow has scarred this network of fibres. Esther's birth betrayed itself in this oriental contour of her eyes with their Turkish lashes and their gray slate-color which changed in the light to the bluish black of a raven's wing. The gentle tenderness of her look could alone soften its dazzling brightness. It is only the races sprung from the desert that hold within their eyes the power of fascinating every one. For a woman can always fascinate some one. Doubtless, their eyes keep something of the infinite which they have contemplated. Has nature, in her foresight, provided their retinas, with a reflecting curtain that enables them to retain the image of the sands, the floods of sunlight, the burning cobalt of the atmosphere? Or do human beings, like the other things of nature, take something from their environment and keep through all the centuries the qualities which they draw from it? This great solution of the race problem is perhaps hidden within the question itself. Instincts are living facts, of which the cause lies in necessity that has been undergone. The animal species are the results of the use of these instincts. To be convinced of this truth so long sought, it suffices to extend to bodies of men the experiment recently made upon flocks of English and Spanish sheep, which, in the meadows of valleys where grass abounds, graze close together, while they scatter on the mountains, where grass is rare. Take these two varieties of sheep away from their respective countries and transport them to Switzerland or to France, the mountain sheep will graze apart though the meadow be low and covered with luxuriant grass; the meadow sheep will feed rubbing against one another though they be on an Alp. Many generations hardly alter instincts acquired and transmitted. After a hundred years the character of the mountain breed reappears in an obstinate sheep, just as after eighteen hundred years of banishment the east glowed in Esther's eyes and face. This look had no terrible fascination; it cast a gentle warmth, a natural tenderness, and the hardest wills melted beneath its flame. Esther had conquered hate; she had amazed the licentious youth of Paris, yet this look and the softness of her velvet skin had won for her the terrible surname which had almost brought her to the grave. Every part of her was in harmony with the character of the fairy of the blazing sands. Her forehead was strong and proudly moulded. Her nose, like an Arab woman's, was delicate and tender, with oval nostrils well placed and somewhat exposed to view. Her mouth, red and fresh, was a rose unstained by trace of orgy. Her chin, modeled as if some loving sculptor had polished its curve, was white as milk. One thing alone, for which she had no remedy, betrayed the fallen courtesan: torn fingernails which needed time before they could look like a lady's, so much had their shape been injured by the lowest cares of housework. Her schoolmates began by envying these miracles of beauty, but their jealousy turned to admiration. The first week did not pass before they were devoted to the simple Esther, for they were interested in the secret misfortunes of a girl of eighteen who could neither read nor write, who had never learned nor even been taught, and who would bring to the archbishop the glory of the conversion of a Jew to Catholicism, and to the convent the fête of a baptism. They felt the superiority of their education and pardoned her beauty. Esther soon acquired the manners, the softness of voice, the bearing and the attitudes of these high-born girls; in short she found once more her earlier nature. The change became so complete that at his first visit, Herrera, who seemed incapable of surprise, was amazed, and the sister superior complimented him on his ward. The teachers had never in their career met with a disposition more lovely, gentleness more Christian, modesty more sincere, nor a greater desire to learn. When a girl has suffered the ills that had been heaped upon this poor scholar, and while she awaits a reward such as the Spaniard had promised Esther, it is not hard for her to realize those miracles of the early Church which the Jesuits repeated in Paraguay.

"She is edifying," said the sister superior, kissing her forehead.

This word, so thoroughly Catholic, told all.

During the time for recreation, Esther asked her companions modestly about the simplest things in the world, and for her they were what the first surprises of life are for a baby. When she learned that on the day of her baptism and of her first communion she would be dressed in white, that she would have a bonnet of white satin, white ribbons, white shoes, white gloves, and that her hair would be tied with white bows, she burst into tears in the midst of her amazed companions. It was the scene of Jephtha on the mountain reversed. The courtesan was afraid of being understood; she cast off her terrible sorrow in the joy that the anticipation of this ceremony caused her. As there is surely as great a gulf between the manners she had left behind and the manners she had assumed, as there is between the savage state and civilization, she had the grace, the simplicity, the depth which distinguish the wonderful heroine of the Puritans of America. She had also, though she herself knew it not, a love gnawing at her heart, a strange love, a longing more intense in her who knew everything than it could be in a virgin who knows nothing, even though these two desires had the same cause and the same goal. During the first months the novelty of a secluded life, the surprises of study, the occupations she was taught, the practices of religion, the fervor of a holy purpose, the tenderness of the affection she inspired, and most of all the exercise of the faculties of awakened intelligence—everything helped her to forget the past, even the fresh efforts of memory which she made: for she had as much to unlearn as to learn. There are, in us, many memories: the body, the mind, each has its own. Homesickness, for example, is a disease of physical memory. During the third month the strength of this virgin soul, which stretched its wings toward heaven, was, not conquered, but shackled by a secret resistance, the cause of which Esther herself did not know. Like the sheep of Scotland, she wished to graze apart; she could not overcome the instincts developed by license. Were the muddy streets of Paris, which she had renounced, calling her to come back? Did the broken chains of her evil habits still hold her by forgotten links? Did she still feel them, as, according to doctors, old soldiers still suffer in the limbs which they have lost? Had vice and its excesses eaten to the marrow of her bones where the holy water could not reach the devil lurking within? Was the sight of him, for whose sake these angelic efforts were made, necessary to her whom God would pardon for mingling human love with love divine? One had led to the other. Had there taken place in her an upheaval of the vital force which entailed this inevitable suffering? All is doubt and darkness in a situation that science has disdained to examine, finding the subject too immoral and too compromising, as if the physician, the writer, the priest and the statesman were not above suspicion. In spite of this a physician has had the courage to begin these studies, left incomplete. He was overtaken by death. Perhaps the black melancholy which preyed upon Esther and cast a shadow over her happy life was made up of all these reasons: and, unable to comprehend them, perhaps she suffered as the sick suffer who have never known medicine or surgery. It is a strange thing. Abundant and healthful food instead of the hateful food of excitement could not sustain Esther. A pure and regular life, divided between tasks designedly moderate and amusements, substituted for an ill-ordered life where the pleasures were as horrible as the pains, saddened the poor girl. The sweet repose, the quiet nights which replaced exhausting fatigues and cruel emotions, gave her a fever which escaped the practiced eye of the matron. In short, good and happiness, succeeding to ill and misfortune, the security following unrest, were as painful to Esther as her miserable past would have been to her young companions. Planted in corruption, she had grown up in its midst. The hellish rule of her early home swayed her still in spite of the sovereign commands of an absolute will. That which she hated was her very life, that which she loved was killing her. Her faith was so strong that her piety delighted everybody. She loved to pray. She had opened her soul to the light of the true faith, and she received it without effort, without doubt. The priest who guided her was enraptured; but with her the body thwarted the soul at every turn. Once carp were taken from a muddy pond and placed in beautiful clear water in a marble basin, in order to satisfy a wish of Madame de Maintenon, who fed them with fragments from the royal table. The carp slowly died. Animals may be devoted, but man will never taint them with the leprosy of flattery. A courtier noticed this silent protest in Versailles. "They are like me," said the unacknowledged queen; "they mourn the dirty pools which they have lost." This sentence is the whole story of Esther. At times the poor girl felt driven to run about the splendid gardens of the convent, she rushed quickly from tree to tree, she flung herself desperately down in the dark corners, seeking what? She knew not, but she yielded to the demon, she coquetted with the trees, she spoke to them in words she did not pronounce. Sometimes in the evening she glided along the walls like a snake, without a shawl, her shoulders bare. Often at chapel, during the services, she knelt with her eyes fastened on the cross, and everybody marveled at her as her tears ran; but she wept for vexation; in place of the sacred images she longed to see, the dazzling nights when she had led the orgy, as

Habeneck leads a symphony of Beethoven at the Conservatory, those nights filled with mirth and wantonness, quivering with frantic life and laughter, arose before her wild, savage, brutal. Without, she was tranquil as a virgin held to earth by her woman's form alone; within, she was an imperial Messalina. She alone knew this secret combat of devil against angel. When the sister superior reproved her for doing her hair more elaborately than the rules allowed, she altered it with sweet and ready obedience. She was willing to cut it off, if the sister had ordered it. This homesickness had a touching grace in a girl who had rather die than return to her impure home. She grew pale, changed, thin. The sister superior lightened her tasks and took the interesting girl to her room to question her. Esther was happy; she was delighted with her companions; she did not feel wounded in a vital spot, and yet her vitality was deeply wounded. She regretted nothing; she wished for nothing. The sister, amazed by her scholar's answers, knew not what to think as she saw her drooping beneath this overpowering languor. When the young girl's condition looked grave the doctor was called, but the doctor knew nothing of Esther's former life and could not suspect it. He found life everywhere, suffering nowhere. The malady upset all hypotheses. There remained one way of casting light upon the physician's doubts which entailed a terrible idea. Esther refused obstinately to submit to an examination by the doctor. In this difficulty, the sister called upon

CARLOS HERRERA VISITS ESTHER

the Abbé Herrera. The Spaniard came, saw Esther's desperate condition, and talked for a moment in secret with the doctor. After this confidence, the man of science announced to the man of faith that the only hope was a journey to Italy. The priest did not wish this journey to be made before Esther's baptism and first communion.

"How much time is needed?" asked the doctor.

"One month," answered the sister.

"She will be dead," replied the doctor.

"Yes, but in a state of grace, and saved," said the priest.

In Spain the religious problem takes precedence of all other problems, be they political, civil, vital. The doctor did not reply to the Spaniard; he turned toward the sister, but the terrible priest held his arm to stop him.

"Not a word," said he.

The doctor, pious and monarchical as he was, cast upon Esther a look full of tender compassion. This girl was lovely, a lily bending from its stalk.

"For the love of God!" cried he as he went out.

The same day Esther was taken by her protector to the *Rocher de Cancale*, for in his desire to save her the priest had recourse to the strangest expedients. He tried a double excess: an excellent dinner to bring back to the poor girl the remembrance of her orgies; the Opera to give her again some glimpses of the world. There was need of all his crushing authority to reconcile the young saint to such worldliness. Herrera disguised himself so completely in a soldier's uniform that Esther could scarcely recognize him. He took care to provide a veil for his companion, and placed her in a box where she was hidden from the public gaze. This half-way remedy, that would not endanger an innocence so perfectly regained, was soon exhausted. Esther felt disgust for the dinners of her protector, a religious aversion for the theatre, and soon fell back into her melancholy.

"She is dying of love for Lucien," thought Herrera, who wished to sound the depth of this soul, and to know what could be exacted of it.

Thus there would come a time when this poor girl would no longer be upheld by her moral strength and when her body must yield. The priest calculated this moment with that horrible sagacity which in former times executioners employed in their art of putting a victim to the torture. He found his pupil in the garden, seated on a bench against an arbor caressed by the April sun; apparently she was cold and trying to warm herself. Her comrades were looking compassionately at her ashen paleness, her eyes like those of a dying doe, and her sad attitude. Esther rose to meet the Spaniard with a movement which showed how little she had of life, and, let us say it, how little taste she had for life. This poor vagabond girl, this poor wounded swallow excited for the second time the pity of Carlos Herrera. This gloomy minister, whom God should use only to fulfill His vengeance, received the sick girl with a smile as bitter as it was tender, as revengeful as it was kind. Accustomed, during her semi-monastic life to meditation and to self-questioning, Esther for the second time felt a thrill of distrust at the sight of her protector; but, as at the first time, she was reassured instantly by his words.

"My dear child," said he, "why have you never spoken to me about Lucien?"

"I have promised you," answered she, trembling from head to foot with a convulsive shiver, "I have sworn to you never to pronounce that name."

"And yet you have never ceased to think of him."

"That, sir, is my only fault. I think of him at every hour. As you appeared I was saying that name to myself."

"Is it absence that is killing you?"

For answer, Esther bowed her head after the manner of the sick who already feel the air of the grave.

"To see him again?" said he.

"Would be to live," she answered.

"Is it your soul alone that thinks of him?"

"Ah, sir, love cannot be divided in two."

"Girl of the accursed race! I have done everything to save you. I give you back to your destiny; you shall see him again!"

"Why do you hurt my happiness? Can I not love Lucien and be faithful to virtue, which I love as I love him? Am I not as ready to die for her as I should be to die for him? Shall I not die for these two gods, for virtue which should make me worthy of him, for him who has thrown me into the arms of virtue? Yes, ready to die without seeing him again, ready to live as I see him once more. God will be my Judge."

Her color had returned, her pallor was tinged with gold. Yet again Esther awakened his pity.

"On the morrow of that day when you shall be washed in the waters of baptism, you shall see Lucien and if you believe that in living for him you can live virtuous, you shall never be separated from him."

Esther's knees gave way and the priest was obliged to lift her. The poor girl had fallen as though the earth had slipped from beneath her feet; the priest seated her on the bench, and as soon as she could speak she said:

"Why not to-day?"

"Do you wish to rob his reverence of the triumph of your baptism and conversion? You are too near Lucien not to be far from God."

"Yes, I forgot everything else."

"You will never belong to any religion," said the priest, with a gesture of deep irony.

"God is good," she answered, "He reads my heart."

Captivated by the enchanting simplicity which broke forth in Esther's voice and look, attitude and gesture, Herrera kissed her for the first time upon her forehead.

"The libertines have chosen your name well; you would beguile God the Father Himself. You must wait a few days more and then you shall both be free."

"Both?" repeated she in ecstasy.

Viewed from a distance this scene amazed both scholars and teachers. They thought that they had witnessed some magical transformation, as they compared Esther with her former self. The girl, quite changed, lived once more. She reappeared in her true loving nature, sweet, coquettish, impulsive, gay. In a word, she came to life again!

Herrera lived in the rue Cassette, close to Saint-Sulpice, the church to which he was attached. This church, built in a severe barren style, suited this Spaniard, whose religion was derived from the Dominicans. A forlorn hope of the crafty policy of Ferdinand VII., he opposed the constitutional party though he knew that this devotion could never be rewarded but by the re-establishment of "*rey netto.*" And Carlos Herrera gave himself body and soul to the "*Camarilla*" at a time when the Cortes seemed in no danger of being overthrown. For the world this conduct bore witness of a lofty soul. The expedition of the Duc d'Angoulême had taken place, King Ferdinand was on the throne, and Carlos Herrera did not go to Madrid to claim the price of his services. Protected from public curiosity by a diplomatic silence, he gave, as reason for his prolonged stay at Paris, his warm affection for Lucien de Rubempré, and it was to this that the young man owed already the royal grant relative to his change of name. Besides Herrera lived a very retired life after the traditional fashion of priests employed on secret missions. He performed his religious duties at Saint-Sulpice, went out only on business and then at night in a carriage. His day was taken up by the Spanish siesta, which sleeps away the hours between the two meals, the time when Paris is most crowded and busy. The Spanish cigar played its part too and consumed as much time as tobacco. Idleness is a mask as well as gravity, for gravity itself is idleness. Herrera lived on the second story of a house in one wing while Lucien occupied the other wing. These apartments were separate and at the same time united by a large reception room, whose antique splendor was equally suited to the grave ecclesiastic and the young poet. The courtyard of this house was gloomy. Tall trees shaded the garden with their thick foliage. Silence and discretion meet in dwellings chosen by priests. Herrera's lodging can be described in two words: a cell. Lucien's suite, resplendent with luxury and furnished with refinements of comfort, contained all the requisites of the elegant life of a dandy, poet and author, ambitious, dissolute, at once proud and vain, neglectful in the extreme yet desirous of order; one of those imperfect geniuses, who have some power of desiring and conceiving (which are perhaps the same thing), but who lack the power of doing. Of themselves Lucien and Herrera formed a complete political combination. There, no doubt, lay the secret of this alliance. Old men, in whom the motive of life has changed its place and settled within the sphere of interest, often feel the want of a pretty toy, of a young and impassioned actor to accomplish their ends. Richelieu found too late a handsome, fair, mustachioed face to toss to the women whom he thought fit to amuse. Misunderstood by young simpletons he was obliged to banish his master's mother and to overawe the queen; for he had labored to ingratiate himself first with one and then with the other, although his was not a nature to attract the love of queens. Whatever road he take across an ambitious life, a man must brush against a woman at the time he least expects the encounter. However powerful a government be, it needs a woman to play against a woman, just as the Dutch cut diamond with diamond. Rome at the height of her power bowed to this necessity. Remember too, how differently the lives of Mazarin, the Italian cardinal, and Richelieu, the French cardinal, became supreme: Richelieu meets with opposition amongst the great lords; he lays the axe to the root; he dies at the apex of his power, worn out by this duel in which he had only a Capuchin for a second. Mazarin is repulsed by the united burghers and nobles who, armed and sometimes victorious, make royalty itself flee before them; but the servant of Anne of Austria cuts off no heads, conquers all France, and moulds Louis XIV., who finished the work of Richelieu by strangling the nobility with silken cords in the great harem of Versailles. Madame de Pompadour once dead, Choiseul is lost! Had Herrera discovered these deep maxims? Had he done justice to himself earlier than Richelieu had done? Had he chosen a

Cinq-Mars, and a faithful Cinq-Mars, in Lucien? No one could answer these questions nor measure the ambition of this Spaniard, as no one could foresee what should be his end. These questions, asked by such as could steal a glance at this long-secret union, sought to pierce a horrible mystery that Lucien had only known for a few days. Carlos was ambitious for both: this is what his conduct meant to persons who knew him and who believed, every one, that Lucien was the natural son of the priest.

Fifteen months after his appearance at the Opera which had thrown him too soon into a society where the priest had no wish to see him until he had finished arming him against the world, Lucien had three handsome horses in his stable, a coupé for the evening, a chaise and a tilbury for the morning. He took his meals at restaurants. Herrera's expectations were fulfilled: dissipation had engrossed his pupil; but he had thought it necessary to leave an outlet for the mad love which Lucien felt for Esther. After spending some forty thousand francs, every adventure brought back Lucien more completely to La Torpille. He sought her stubbornly, and as he failed to find her, she became for him what the game is for the hunter. Could Herrera know the nature of a poet's love? When once this sentiment has gained a foothold in the head of one of these little great men, as surely as it has secured his heart and pierced his senses, this poet becomes as far above humanity by the strength of his love as he is by the power of his fancy. Indebted to the caprice of an intellectual birth for the rare faculty of painting nature by images which express both sentiment and thought, the poet gives to his love the wings of his fancy. He feels and he paints; he acts and he thinks; he multiplies his feelings by his thought; he triples present happiness by hopes for the future and recollections of the past; he intermingles those fine delights of the soul which make him the prince of artists. The passion of a poet becomes a mighty poem wherein often the measure of man is surpassed. Does not the poet place his mistress far higher than the region where women like to dwell? Like the sublime cavalier of la Mancha he transforms a workwoman of the fields into a princess. He waves for himself the wand whose touch transforms everything by magic, and thus he increases his happiness by the divine world of the ideal. And this love is a model of passion. It is intemperate in all things: in its hopes, in its despair, in its anger, in its sadness, in its joy; it flies, it leaps, it climbs; it is not like the excitements of ordinary men; it is to common love what the eternal torrent of the Alps is to the brooks of the plain. These splendid geniuses are so rarely understood that they waste themselves in false hopes: consume themselves in searching for their ideal mistresses. They die almost always like beautiful insects, that are carefully decked by the most poetic of natures for the feasts of love, and, still virgins, are trodden upon by the foot of a passer-by. But there is another danger, when they meet the woman who appeals to their souls, and who is often a baker's daughter, they do as Raphael did, as the beautiful insects do, they die beside the *Fornarina*. Lucien was one of these. His poet's nature, of need extreme in all things, good and evil alike, divined the angel in the woman rather spotted by corruption than corrupt. He saw her always white-winged, pure, mysterious, as though she had made herself for him knowing that he wished her thus.

Toward the end of the month of May, 1825, Lucien had lost all his vivacity. He stayed at home, dined with Herrera, thought, worked, read the collection of diplomatic treaties, sat cross-legged on a divan, and smoked three or four hookahs a day. His groom was more busied in polishing and perfuming the stems of this beautiful instrument than in currying the horses' coats and in decking their heads with rosettes for a drive in the Bois. On the day that the Spaniard noted Lucien's pale forehead, and traced the germs of illness in the frenzy of hidden love, he wished to penetrate to the heart of this man on whom he had built his life.

One lovely evening when Lucien, stretched in an armchair, was watching mechanically the setting of the sun behind the garden trees, and was blowing a cloud of his perfumed smoke in equal and prolonged puffs, as thoughtful smokers do, he was awakened from his revery by a deep sigh. He turned and saw the priest standing near him with crossed arms.

"Have you been standing there?" asked the poet.

"For a long time," answered the priest, "my thoughts have been following the compass of yours."

Lucien understood.

"I never claimed for myself an iron nature such as yours. For me life is by turns a heaven and a hell; but when by chance it is neither one nor the other, it wearies me and I grow weary of myself."

"How can a man be weary of life with such splendid hopes before him?"

"When he ceases to believe in these hopes or when they are too thickly veiled."

"No nonsense," said the priest; "it is much worthier of you and of me that you should open your heart to me. There lies between us what there ought never to be—a secret. This secret has lasted for sixteen months. You love a woman."

"What then?"

"A disreputable woman, named La Torpille."

"Well?"

"My son, I have given you leave to take a mistress, but a woman of the court, young, beautiful, influential, a countess at the least. I picked out Madame d'Espard for you, in order to use her, without scruple, as a tool; for she would never have perverted your heart, she would have left you free. To love a prostitute of the lowest kind, when you cannot, as kings can, make her noble, is a cardinal sin."

"Am I the first to throw ambition to the winds and rush down the path of an unbridled love?"

"Good," ejaculated the priest, as he picked up the *bocchinetto* of the hookah, which Lucien had let fall, and handed it to him; "I understand the epigram. Is it impossible to unite ambition and love? Son, you have in old Herrera a mother whose devotion is perfect."

"I know it," said Lucien, taking his hand and shaking it.

"You wished for the toys of riches. You have them. You wish to shine; I guide you in the path of success, I kiss unclean hands that you may rise, and you rise. A little more time and you shall lack nothing that men and women delight in. Your caprices have made you effeminate; you are manly at heart. I know you thoroughly and I pardon everything. You have only to speak, to satisfy your passions of a day. I have enriched your life, by giving it that which makes it worshiped by the crowd, the seal of government and power. You shall be as great as you are little; but we must not break the die with which we stamp our coin. I grant you everything except the errors that would ruin your future. When I throw open for you the doors of the Faubourg Saint-Germain, I forbid you to wallow in the gutters. Lucien, on your behalf, I will be like a bar of iron; I will suffer all things for you, for your sake. It is thus, then, that I have transformed your clumsiness in the game of life into the craft of a cunning player."

Lucien tossed his head back with an angry jerk.

"I have carried away La Torpille!"

"You?" shrieked Lucien.

In a burst of wild rage the poet leaped to his feet, threw the golden jeweled *bocchinetto* into the priest's face, and hurled him, athlete as he was, to the ground.

"I," said the Spaniard, as he rose, still keeping his awful gravity. The black wig had fallen. A skull smooth as a death's-head gave the man his true expression. It was dreadful. Lucien sat on his divan, his arms hanging loosely at his sides. Overwhelmed, he gazed stupidly at the priest.

"I have carried her away," repeated the ecclesiastic.

"What have you done with her? You took her off on the day after the masked ball."

"Yes. On the day after I had seen a human being who belonged to you insulted by fools whom I would not deign to kick."

"Fools!" cried Lucien, interrupting him. "Call them monsters beside whom the victims of the guillotine are angels. Do you know what poor Torpille has done for three among them? One of them had been her lover for two months. She was poor and picked up her crusts from the gutter. He hadn't a cent. Like me, when first you found me, he was very close to the river. The fellow used to get up at night, and go to the cupboard where were the remnants of the girl's dinner, and eat them. Eventually she discovered this. She understood his sense of shame; took care to leave plenty of remnants and was very happy. She told it only to me, in her cab, coming back from the Opera. The second had stolen; but before his theft was discovered she lent him the money, thus he was enabled to refund it, but he never remembered to repay the poor child. As for the third, she made his fortune in playing a comedy that displayed all the genius of Figaro: she passed for his wife and became the mistress of an influential man who thought her a most ingenuous and respectable woman. To one life, to another honor, to the last fortune, which to-day is worth them all. And this is how she has been rewarded by them!"

"Do you wish them to die?" said Herrera, who had a tear in his eye.

"I know you now. I understand you."

"No, learn the whole truth, mad poet," said the priest. "La Torpille is no more."

Lucien sprang so violently at Herrara's neck that another man would have lost his balance; but the Spaniard's arm held the poet firm.

"Listen," said he coldly, "I have made of her a woman, chaste, pure, well brought up, religious, everything that a woman should be. She is being taught. She can, she must become, beneath the mastery of your love, a Ninon, a Marion Delorme, or a DuBarry, as that journalist said at the opera. You shall acknowledge her as your mistress, or if you follow wiser counsel you shall remain hidden behind a curtain of your own creation. Either course will bring you profit and pride, pleasure and advancement; but if you are as great a statesman as you are a poet, Esther will never be more than your amusement. In time, perhaps, she may be of great use to us, for she's worth her weight in gold.

Drink, but do not drink too deep. If I had not curbed your passions, where would you be to-day? You would have sunk with La Torpille into the slough of misery, whence I dragged you.—Take this, read it," said Herrera, with as much directness as Talma in "Manlius," whom he had never seen.

A paper fell into the poet's lap and drew him from the utter amazement into which the priest's terrible answer had plunged him. He took it and read the first letter written by Mademoiselle Esther:

"To Father Carlos Herrera:

"My dear guardian, will you not think that my gratitude surpasses my love when you see that I make use of the faculty of expressing my thoughts for the first time in giving thanks to you instead of consecrating it to painting a love that Lucien has perhaps forgotten. To you who are a holy man I can tell what I could not confess to him who still wishes to attach my happiness to this earth. Yesterday's ceremony has poured its wealth of grace upon me and I place my destiny in your hands. If I be called upon to die far from my beloved, I shall die purified, like the Magdalen, and my soul shall become, for his sake, the rival of his guardian angel. Shall I ever forget yesterday's fête? How can I wish to step down from the glorious throne where I have climbed? Yesterday I washed away all my sins in the waters of baptism, and I received the sacred body of our Saviour. I have become one of His temples. At that moment I heard the songs of angels; I was more than a woman; I was born to a life of light, attired like a virgin for a heavenly bridegroom, amidst an intoxicating cloud of incense and prayers, while the earth rejoiced and the world was glad. When I felt myself worthy of Lucien, though I had never dared hope it before, I cast away every impure love and I will not walk in other paths than those of virtue. If my body is more feeble than my soul, let it perish. Be the ruler of my destiny, and, if I die, tell Lucien that I died for him as I was born unto God.

"*Sunday evening.*"

Lucien, with tears in his eyes, looked toward the priest.

"You know the lodgings of big Caroline Bellefeuille in the Rue Taitbout," said the Spaniard. "This girl, who was left uncared for by the police magistrate, was in frightful want; she was going to be arrested. I bought her rooms outright and she went out with her effects. Esther, the angel who wished to climb to heaven, has come down and is awaiting you there."

Just then Lucien heard his horses prancing in the courtyard below. He had no strength to show his admiration for devotion that he alone could appreciate. He threw himself into the arms of the man whom he had outraged, and made amends by a single look in which he silently expressed his gratitude; then he leapt down the staircase, shouted Esther's address to his "tiger," and the horses dashed away as if their legs were animated by their master's passion.

*

On the following day, a man, who by his dress might have been a disguised gendarme, was pacing the street before a house in the Rue Taitbout, as though he were expecting somebody to come out. His gait betokened anxiety. In Paris it is not uncommon to meet with such excited persons; real gendarmes watching for some refractory soldier of the National Guard; bailiffs taking measures for an arrest; creditors contemplating some insult on the debtor who has securely locked his door; jealous lovers; suspicious husbands; friends busied in a friend's business; but it is very rare to come upon a face darkened by the stern and cruel thoughts which animated the gloomy features of a powerfully built man as he walked to and fro beneath Mademoiselle Esther's windows with the blind haste of a caged bear. At twelve o'clock a window opened and allowed a chambermaid's hand to push back the carefully padded shutters. A few moments later, Esther, clad in her dressing-gown, and leaning upon Lucien's arm, came to breathe the air. An observer would have taken them for the original of a pretty English vignette. Suddenly Esther caught sight of the basilisk eyes of the Spanish priest. The poor girl gave a startled cry as though she had been struck by a bullet.

"There's the terrible priest," she whispered, pointing him out to Lucien.

"He!" said Lucien with a smile, "He's no more priest than you."

"What is he then?" she asked fearfully.

"Oh, he's an old lascar, who only believes in the devil," replied Lucien.

Had Esther been less absolutely devoted, this light cast upon the secrets of the false priest might have ruined Lucien forever. As they walked from the bedroom to the dining-room where their breakfast had just been served, the lovers met Carlos Herrera.

"What have you to do here?" demanded Lucien shortly. "To bless you," answered the undaunted priest as he stopped the couple and obliged them to halt in the little parlor of the suite. "Listen, my dears. Have a good time, be happy. All that is very well. Happiness at any price is my motto. But you," said he to Esther, "you whom I raised from the mire and whom I cleansed body and soul, you can have no claim to block Lucien's path. As for you, my boy," said he turning to Lucien after a pause, "you are no longer poet enough to run a steeplechase after a new Coralie. It is prose that we are writing. What can become of Esther's lover? Nothing. Perhaps Esther can become Madame de Rubempré? No,—well the world, my love," said he laying his hand on Esther's fingers which quivered as though a snake were coiled about them, "the world must not know that you exist, the world, above all things, must never know that a Mademoiselle Esther loves Lucien and that Lucien is in love with her. This apartment shall be your prison, my girl. If you wish to go out and if your health require it, you must walk during the night at hours when you cannot be seen; for your beauty, your youth and the distinction you have gained at the convent, would be too quickly noticed in Paris. The day that the world shall know," he went on with terrible earnestness and a still more terrible look, "that Lucien is your lover or that you are his mistress, that day shall be the beginning of your end. Though Lucien is a younger son, permission has been obtained for him to carry the arms of his mother's line. But this is not all. The title of marquis has not been granted him, and to secure this, he must marry the daughter of some noble family in whose favor the King will confer this honor upon him. This marriage will place Lucien in the court world. This boy whom I have made a man, shall first become secretary of an embassy; later he shall become minister in some German court and aided by God or by me, whichever best serves his turn, he shall sit some day on the benches of the peerage—"

"Or on the benches of—" cried Lucien, interrupting the priest.

"Silence," cried Carlos, covering Lucien's mouth with his large hand. "Such a secret to a woman!—" whispered he in his ear.

"Esther, a woman?" exclaimed the author of "Marguerites."

"More sonnets and nonsense," said the priest. "All angels become women again sooner or later. But there are times when a woman is at once child and monkey: two creatures who kill us for a joke. Esther, my jewel," said he to the frightened girl, "for your waiting maid, I have found a woman as much bound to me as if she were my daughter. For cook, you shall have a mulatto woman who will give your house an aristocratic air. With Europe and Asia, you can live here, everything included, on a thousand francs a month and live like a queen—of the stage. Europe has been seamstress, dressmaker and chorus girl. Asia has cooked for a gluttonous *milord*. These two creatures shall serve you like fairies."

As she saw how small and young Lucien looked beside this being who was capable of falsehood or sacrilege, or worse, this woman, sanctified as she was by love, felt cold terror in her heart. Without a word she drew Lucien aside into the next room. Then she said to him:

"Is it the devil?"

"Much worse,—for me!" answered he quickly. "But, if you love me, try to imitate his devotion and obey him on pain of death—"

"Of death?" said she, still more alarmed. "Of death," repeated Lucien. "Ah, dear heart, no death could compare with the fate which would be mine if—"

Esther turned pale and faint as she heard these words.

"Well," cried the priestly forger "haven't you finished plucking the leaves of your Marguerites?"

Esther and Lucien reappeared, and the poor girl who dared not raise her eyes to the mysterious priest, answered: "You shall be obeyed, as God is obeyed, sir." "Good!" he answered. "For some time you can be very happy and—since you have to provide toilets only for the night and the morning, you can be very economical."

The lovers turned toward the dining-room but Lucien's protector beckoned the charming couple to stop. They obeyed him.

"I have just spoken to you of your servants, my child," said he to Esther. "I ought to introduce them."

The Spaniard rang twice, and the two women whom he called Europe and Asia appeared. It was easy to see the cause of their cognomens.

Asia who seemed to be a native of the island of Java, offered to the astonished beholder the copper-colored countenance peculiar to the Malays, flat as a board. The nose looked as if it had been knocked in by a violent blow, and the strange position of the maxillary bones gave the lower portion of her face a resemblance to that of a large monkey. The forehead, although low, did not lack a certain look of intelligence produced by habitual cunning. The two small shining eyes were calm as those of a tiger's, but they never looked you in the face. Asia seemed afraid of frightening those about her. Her pale blue lips were slightly parted, showing irregular teeth of dazzling whiteness. The dominant expression of her animal physiognomy was cowardice. Her hair sleek and oily, like the skin of her face, rose in two black bands on either side of a richly colored silk handkerchief. Her ears, which were extraordinarily pretty, were ornamented with two large black pearls. Small, short, thick-set, she looked like one of those preposterous creations that the Chinese allow on their screens—or rather, like those Hindoo idols of a scarcely believable type which have been discovered by travelers. Esther shuddered as she saw this monster stand before her dressed in a stuff gown and white apron.

"Asia," said the Spaniard, toward whom this woman raised her head with a motion like that of a dog as he watches his master, "this is your mistress."

He pointed toward Esther as she stood there in her wrapper. Asia looked at the young sylph with a half-melancholy expression, but simultaneously a stifled flame from beneath her short quivering lashes shot like a spark of fire toward Lucien who, with his gorgeous dressing-gown thrown open, his shirt of fine linen, his red trousers and his loose fair curls escaping from beneath a Turkish fez, looked like a young god. The genius of Italy can invent the story of Othello; the genius of England can adapt it to the stage; but nature alone has the power of being more splendid and more perfect than England and Italy in the expression of jealousy. Esther saw the look, and seizing the Spaniard's arm dug her nails into it like a cat clinging to the edge of a precipice, the depth of which it cannot see. The Spaniard spoke three or four words in an unknown tongue to the strange Asiatic monster who instantly crouched before Esther's feet and kissed them.

"It is not," said the Spaniard to Esther, "a woman but a man, whose gift for cooking would make Carême madly jealous. Asia can accomplish anything in a kitchen. She will prepare a simple dish of beans that will make you doubt whether the angels have not intermingled herbs from heaven. Every morning she will go to market, and will fight like the devil she is, in order to get everything at the lowest price; she will weary the curious with her discretion. As you will be supposed to have been in the Indies, Asia will do much to make the story credible, for she is one of those Parisian women who can appear to belong to any country they wish. But my advice is that you do not pass for a foreigner. Europe, what say you?"

Europe formed an absolute contrast to Asia, for she was as neat a soubrette as ever Monrose could have wished for a rival on the boards. Slender, and giddy-looking, with little ferret features and turned-up nose, Europe offered to view a face worn by the dissipations of Paris, the pale face of a girl fed on raw potatoes, at once flaccid and firm, pliant and obstinate. With one small foot advanced and her hands in the pockets of her apron, her animation was so great that she never ceased to fidget, although she did not move from her place. Grisette and ballet-dancer as well, she had worked at many trades in spite of her youth. Perverse as all the women of a penitentiary put together, she might have robbed her parents and been acquainted with the benches of the police court. Asia was frightful to look upon, but she could be understood in a moment; she was a lineal descendant of Locuste; whereas Europe inspired an uneasiness which could not but increase in proportion as she was employed. Her depravity seemed boundless. She could sow discord in heaven, as they say.

"Perhaps the lady comes from Valenciennes," said Europe, in a small shrill voice. "I do, myself, sir," she added in an affected tone, turning to Lucien. "Will you tell me the name by which I must know Madame?"

"Madame von Bogseck," answered the Spaniard, giving this assumed name without hesitation. "She is a Jewess, a native of Holland, a merchant's widow, and sick with some liver trouble that she has brought back with her from Java. Not a large fortune—in order not to arouse curiosity."

"What income? Six thousand francs, and shall we complain of her meanness?" asked Europe.

"That's it," said the Spaniard, nodding, "you crafty devils!" he added in a terrible voice as he noticed Europe and Asia exchange glances that he did not like. "You know my orders? You serve a queen. You owe her the respect that a queen is entitled to. You will nurse her as you would nurse revenge. You must be as devoted to her as to me.

Not the janitor, nor the neighbors, nor the lodgers, nobody in the world must know what goes on here. It is your duty to divert any curiosity that may be excited. And this lady," continued he, laying his large hairy hand upon Esther's arm, "must not commit the slightest imprudence. If need be you must prevent her, but—always respectfully. Europe, it will be your task to make arrangements for Madame von Bogseck's dresses, and you will do the sewing yourself for economy's sake. Above all, no outsider, however insignificant, must set foot in the apartment. You two must be able to do everything. My love," said he to Esther, "when you wish to drive in the evening, you will tell Europe. She knows where to find your servants, for you are to have a groom—of my choice, like these two slaves."

Esther and Lucien could not answer a word. They listened to the Spaniard and gazed at the two priceless servants to whom he gave his orders. To what secret did he owe the obsequious devotion written upon those two faces, one so wickedly rebellious, the other so utterly cruel? The priest divined the thoughts of Esther and Lucien as they stood stupefied as Paul and Virginia would have stood at the sight of two horrible serpents, and whispered to them in his softest voice:

"You can count on them as you can on me. Keep no secret from them. That will please them— go to your work, little Asia," said he to the cook— "and you, my pet, set one more place at the table," added he to Europe. "The least that these children can do is to invite their papa to breakfast."

When the two women had closed the door behind them and the Spaniard could hear Europe running to and fro, he said to Lucien and the girl, as he opened his great hand.

"I have them."

Word and gesture were alike terrible.

"Where did you find them?" cried Lucien. "The deuce!" he answered, "I did not look for them at the foot of thrones! Europe has been drawn from the mire and is afraid of falling into it again. When they do not satisfy you, threaten them with '*the priest*' and you shall see them shake like mice before a cat. I am a tamer of wild beasts," he added smiling.

"I think you are a demon!" cried Esther prettily, pressing closer to Lucien.

"My daughter, I have tried to give you to Heaven; but the church always finds a repentant woman a fiction and if there were one she would turn courtesan again in Paradise. You have succeeded in making yourself forgotten and in becoming outwardly a respectable woman; for at the convent you have learned what you never could have discovered in the infamous world in which you lived. You owe me nothing," said he as he saw a lovely look of gratitude come over Esther's face. "I did everything for his sake," he added pointing at Lucien: "You are a courtesan, you will live a courtesan, and will die a courtesan. In spite of all the attractive theories of trainers, here on earth, an animal remains what it is. The phrenologist is right, you have the bump of love."

The Spaniard was evidently a fatalist, as Napoleon, Mohammed and many great statesmen have been fatalists. It is a strange fact that almost all men of action incline toward fatalism, and most thinkers toward Providence.

"I don't know what I am," answered Esther with heavenly sweetness; "but I love Lucien and shall love him till I die."

"Come to breakfast," said the Spaniard shortly, "and pray God that Lucien does not marry soon, for if he does, you will never see him again."

"His marriage would be my death," she said.

She allowed the counterfeit priest to pass in first, in order that she might raise her lips unseen to Lucien's ear.

"Is it your will," said she, "that I remain under the power of this man who guards me with these two hyenas?"

Lucien inclined his head. The poor girl hid her misgivings and tried to seem happy, but she felt terribly ill-at-ease. More than a year of constant and devoted care was needed to accustom her to these two frightful creatures that Carlos Herrera named the "two watch dogs."

*

Lucien's conduct, since his return to Paris, was marked by an impenetrable reserve which was well calculated to arouse and did arouse the jealousy of all his old friends, upon whom he took no revenge except by exciting their envy by his success, his irreproachable appearance and his manner of holding them at a distance. This poet, who had been so talkative and familiar, became cold and circumspect. De Marsay, the mirror of the Parisian youth, affected no more punctilio in speech or manner than Lucien. As to wit, the journalist had long ago given ample proof of that. De Marsay, to whom many people were pleased to oppose Lucien, giving the preference to the poet, had the littleness to be vexed. Lucien, who was in high favor with men who stood behind the seats of power, gave up all thoughts of literary glory so entirely that he was indifferent to the success of his romance, published under its true title, "The Archer of Charles IX.," and to the burst of applause which greeted his book of sonnets entitled "Marguerites," that was sold by Dauriat in a single week.

"It is a posthumous success," he answered laughingly to Mademoiselle des Touches, who complimented him upon it.

The terrible Spaniard held his creature with an

iron grasp in the path toward the goal where trumpet blasts and spoils of victory await the patient politician. Lucien had taken Beaudenord's bachelor apartment on the Quai Malaquais, in order to be near the Rue Taitbout. His adviser was lodged in three rooms on the fourth story of the same house. Lucien had now but a single horse for riding and driving, one servant and a groom. When he did not dine out, he dined with Esther. Carlos Herrera watched the household on the Quai Malaquais so carefully that Lucien did not spend in all ten thousand francs a year. Ten thousand francs supplied Esther's wants, thanks to the constant, inexplicable devotion of Europe and Asia. Lucien employed the greatest precautions in going to and from the Rue Taitbout. He never went there, unless in a cab with drawn curtains, and always made the cabman drive into the courtyard. His passion for Esther, and the existence of the household in the Rue Taitbout, absolutely secret from the world, harmed none of his prospects or connections. Not a word escaped him on this delicate subject. His mistakes in a similar affair with Coralie at the time of his first sojourn in Paris, had taught him his lesson. Besides, his life wore the air of respectable regularity beneath which mysteries are so often hidden. People saw him abroad every evening until one hour after midnight; they found him at home every morning from ten until an hour after noon. Then he went to the Bois de Boulogne and made calls until five o'clock. He was seldom afoot and thus avoided meeting his old acquaintances. Whenever some newspaper man or one of his former comrades bowed to him, he returned the courtesy by an inclination of the head, polite enough to avoid giving offence, yet betraying a deep disdain that was death to French familiarity. Thus he quickly disembarrassed himself of any acquaintance he did not wish to prolong. A long cherished hatred prevented him from going to see Madame d'Espard, who had often asked him to her house. If he met her at the Duchess of Maufrigneuse's, at Mademoiselle des Touches', at the Countess de Montcornet's or elsewhere, he treated her with the most exquisite politeness. The hatred that Madame d'Espard warmly reciprocated obliged Lucien to be prudent, and we shall see how he had roused it by allowing himself the pleasure of revenge, which cost him a severe admonition from Carlos.

"You are not strong enough yet to revenge yourself on anybody whomsoever," the Spaniard had said to him. "When a man is journeying beneath a hot sun, he does not stop to pluck the prettiest flower that grows."

Lucien's prospects were so bright, his real superiority so strongly marked that young men, who felt their fortunes dimmed or eclipsed by his return to Paris and his extraordinary good luck, were all delighted to pay him an ill turn. Lucien, who knew that he had many enemies, was well aware of the unfavorable temper of his friends, and Herrera showed admirable caution in constant warnings to his adopted son against the treachery of the world and the fatal imprudence of youth. Every evening Lucien was questioned by the priest and told him the most minute details of the day. Thanks to the counsel of his mentor he eluded the most inquisitorial curiosity that exists—the curiosity of society. Protected by a gravity that was wholly English, and hedged in by diplomatic caution, he gave to no one either the right or the opportunity to meddle in his affairs. His handsome young face became as impassive in society as the face of a princess at a public ceremony.

Toward the middle of the year 1829 everybody talked of his approaching marriage with the eldest daughter of the Duchesse de Grandlieu, who had no less than four girls to provide with husbands. Nobody doubted that in case the match took place, the King would grant Lucien the title of Marquis. This marriage was to decide Lucien's political career, for he would probably be named minister at some German court. For three years Lucien's life had been unswervingly prudent, and it was concerning him that de Marsay had made the singular remark, "That fellow must have some strong power behind him."

Thus Lucien was almost famous. His devotion to Esther had been of great service to him in playing his part as a man of sober life. A habit of this kind saves an ambitious man from many foolish ventures. By holding himself aloof from women, he never allows his physical nature to react upon his moral nature. Lucien's happiness realized the dreams of penniless poets starving in a garret. Esther, the very ideal of a loving courtesan, while she recalled to Lucien's mind the actress Coralie, with whom he had lived for a year, effaced her memory completely. All affectionate and devoted women dream of seclusion and incognito, and the life of the pearl at the bottom of the sea; but with most of them it is only an attractive fancy, a subject of conversation, or a proof of love which they think of giving and yet never give; but Esther, always living in the delights of her first joy, feeling herself constantly beneath Lucien's first tender glance, lived for four years without feeling an impulse of curiosity. She gave her whole mind to obeying the letter of the law laid down by the fatal hand of the Spaniard. Far more than that! In the midst of the most intoxicating delight, she did not make use of that limitless power which the ever re-awakening desires of a man lend to the woman he adores, to ask Lucien a single question in regard to Herrera. The very name of the priest never ceased to alarm her; she dared not think of him. The wise benefits of this man to whom Esther certainly owed her education, her respectability and her regeneration seemed to the poor girl to be the wages of hell.

"I shall pay dear for it all some day," she said to herself in terror. On every clear night she went out to drive in a cab. She drove about with a speed no doubt enjoined by the priest, in some charming forest in the neighborhood of Paris; at Boulogne, Vincennes, Romainville or Ville d'Avray, frequently with Lucien, and sometimes alone with Europe. She went without fear, for whenever Lucien was not by her side, she was accompanied by a mounted groom dressed in the most approved style, armed with a real knife, whose physiognomy and gaunt muscular figure gave the impression of great strength. This additional protector was provided, after the English-fashion, with a cane, known technically as the "bâton de longueur" a quarterstaff that can keep many assailants at a distance. Obedient to an order of the priest, Esther had never spoken a word to this attendant. Whenever she wished to turn back, Europe called out and the groom then whistled to the coachman, who was never very far away. When Lucien walked with Esther, Europe and the groom kept at a distance of a hundred yards, like two of those infernal pages that the magician lends to his favorites in the "Thousand and One Nights."

Parisian men, still more often Parisian women, do not know the charms of a wooded path on a lovely night. Silence, moonlight, and solitude calm the body like a bath. Ordinarily, Esther left her house at ten o'clock, walked from midnight until one, and returned by half after two. She never arose before eleven o'clock, and then she took her bath and dressed with that elaborate care, which demands too much time to be employed by Parisian women in general and is only to be found among courtesans, and women of fashion who have their whole day at their disposal. She was never ready until Lucien came and then she went to meet him like a flower that has just blossomed. Her only care was her poet's happiness. She gave herself up to him absolutely and allowed him the most complete liberty. She never tried to look beyond the house whose light she was. The priest had cautioned her in this regard for it was part of his deep laid scheme that Lucien should make love to others. Happiness has no story, and the story-tellers of all countries have recognized that the words "they lived happily" end all the adventures of love. Nothing beyond the reasons for this fanciful happiness in the midst of Paris, can be told. It was happiness in its loveliest guise: a poem, a symphony of four years. Every woman will say "That is a great deal." Neither Esther nor Lucien had said "It is too much." For them the formula "They lived happily" was still more explicit than in the fairy tale, for they had no children. Thus Lucien could flirt with whom he liked, give way to every poet's caprice, and, let us say it, to the necessities of his position. While he was slowly climbing the ladder, he executed secret missions for certain statesmen, co-operating with them in their several schemes. In this service he was singularly discreet. He paid great attention to Madame de Sérizy in whose favor, as social gossip said, he stood very high. Madame de Sérizy had torn Lucien away from the Duchesse de Maufrigneuse, who as people said "had lost her hold," one of those phrases which women use to revenge themselves on fortunate rivals. Lucien was, so to speak, in the bosom of the Grand Almonry and in the confidence of several women who were friends of the Archbishop of Paris. Prudent and unassuming he waited with patience. Thus the speech of de Marsay, who at this time was married and was obliging his wife to lead a life as retired as Esther's, embodied more than one keen observation. But the submarine dangers of Lucien's situation will be brought to light during the course of this story.

In these circumstances on a beautiful night in the month of August, the Baron de Nucingen was driving back to Paris from the estate of a foreign banker established in France at whose house he had been dining. This estate was in Brie at eight leagues from Paris. But as the baron's coachman had boasted that he could drive his master thither and back with his own horses, the man took the liberty of going slowly after night had fallen. As they enter the wood of Vincennes, the situation of horses, servants, and master was as follows: After liberal potations in the pantry of the illustrious autocrat of the exchange, the coachman, completely intoxicated, slept, still holding the reins in order to deceive the passers-by. The groom behind, snored as loud as a top that has been brought from Germany, the country of tiny figures of carved wood, of great "Reinganum" and tops. The baron was inclined to reflection, but when the bridge of Gournay was passed, the soothing influence of digestion closed his eyes. The slackness of the reins told the horses of the coachman's condition; they heard the deep bass of the groom perched on the dicky, and feeling themselves their own masters, they made use of their short period of liberty to move leisurely on at their own sweet wills. Like intelligent slaves, they offered to robbers the opportunity of rifling one of the richest capitalists of France, the most profoundly cunning of all that class which eventually acquired the significant name of "lynxes." In short, now that they were under no control, and attracted by that curiosity which everybody has noticed among domestic animals, they stopped at a turn in the road in front of another pair of horses, to whom they were doubtless saying in brute-language: "Whom do you belong to? What are you doing? Are you happy?" When the carriage stopped moving, the drowsy baron waked up. At first, he thought that he had not left his friend's park; then he was astonished by a heavenly vision which surprised him without his accustomed weapon, calculation. The moonlight was so brilliant that it was possible to read even a newspaper. In the silence of the woods and in this pure light the baron saw a woman, alone, who was just stepping into her cab watching the extraordinary spectacle of his sleeping carriage. At the sight of this lovely being the Baron de Nucingen felt as though a light had been kindled within him. Perceiving that she was admired, the girl lowered her veil with a frightened gesture. The mounted groom uttered a hoarse cry. Its significance was well understood by the coachman, for the cab darted off like an arrow. The old banker felt excessively excited. The blood rushed from his feet to his brain and set that on fire, and then the flames turned back to his heart. His throat contracted, and the wretched man feared an attack of indigestion; yet in spite of this supreme apprehension, he sprang to his feet.

"Hi! Du pig plockhead. After! after!" he screamed. "Ein hundert franc eef du gatch dat garriage."

At these words, "a hundred francs," the coachman started up and the groom heard them no doubt in his sleep. The baron repeated the offer; the coachman lashed his horses into a gallop and near the Barrière du Trône succeeded in catching up with a cab that bore some resemblance to that in which Nucingen had seen the heavenly stranger. It was occupied, however, by the commission agent of some large firm and a well-dressed woman of the rue Vivienne. This mistake dismayed the baron.

"Ef I had taken Chorge—meaning George—in your stead, du pig prute, he vud haf gaught ze vooman," said he to his servant while the officers examined the carriage.

"Oh, sir, I think the devil was in that footman's livery, and changed his carriage into this one."

"Zere ees no tefil," ejaculated the baron.

The Baron de Nucingen at this time admitted himself to be sixty years of age. Women had come to be perfectly indifferent to him, and for the strongest of reasons, the woman's. His boast was that he had never known the love that leads to folly. He looked upon his emancipation from women as a blessing and said, calmly, that the most heavenly of them all was not worth her cost even if she gave herself for nothing. People said that he was so surfeited with pleasure that he no longer spent a couple of thousand francs a month for the pleasure of being duped. As he sat in his box at the Opera, his indifferent eye wandered tranquilly over the ballet dancers. No bright glance shot toward the capitalist. From out this dangerous band of old young girls and young old women—the delight of Paris pleasure-seekers—natural love, false love, self-love, love of respectability and of vanity, love of elegance, virtuous love, married love, whimsical love, the baron had bought them all, had known them all except true love. This love now swooped upon him as a bird on his prey, as it once swooped upon Gentz, the confidant of his Highness, the prince of Metternich. Everybody knows the absurdities that this old diplomat was guilty of for the sake of Fanny Elssler and how he cared far more to see her dance than to listen to the interests of Europe. The woman who had overturned the iron-bound chest, called Nucingen, seemed to him like a woman unique in her generation. We cannot be sure that Titian's mistress, Leonardo da Vinci's Mona Lisa, Raphael's Fornarina were as beautiful as the majestic Esther in whom the most carefully practiced eye in Paris could not have recognized the faintest trace of the courtesan. Besides, the baron was overpowered by that fine aristocratic air of womanhood, which Esther, beloved and surrounded by luxury, refinement and devotion, had in the greatest perfection. Happy love is the consecrated oil of woman's life. With it they become proud as empresses.

For a week the baron drove every night in the wood of Vincennes, then in Bois de Boulogne, then in the wood of Ville-d'Avray, then in the wood of Meudon, and finally through every environ in Paris in a vain search for Esther. Her splendid Jewish face, which he called "a vace of ze piple," was always before his eyes. At the end of a fortnight he lost his appetite. Delphine de Nucingen and her daughter Augusta, whom the baroness was just introducing into society, did not perceive at first the change that was wrought in the baron. The mother and daughter never saw him except in the morning at breakfast, and in the evening, at dinner, whenever they all dined at home, which was only on the days when Delphine had company. But at the end of two months, seized by feverish impatience and a prey to a trouble closely akin to homesickness, the baron, amazed at the uselessness of his money bags, grew thin and appeared so ill that Delphine had secret hopes of becoming a widow. She mourned hypocritically over her husband and kept her daughter at home. She overwhelmed her husband with questions; he answered as the English do when they are provoked, scarcely at all. Delphine de Nucingen gave a great dinner every Sunday. She had chosen to receive on that day because she had noticed that in good society nobody went to the theatre on that day, so that it was ordinarily left quite without engagements. The invasion of shop-keepers or country people makes Sunday almost as dull in Paris as in London.

Thus the baroness invited the famous Desplein to dine, in order to have a consultation, in spite of the sufferer's protestations that he had never felt better in his life. Keller, Rastignac, de Marsay, du Tillet, all friends of the family, had given the baroness to understand that a man like Nucingen must not die suddenly. His vast business demanded precautions; it was essential to know what enterprises should be continued. These gentlemen were asked to dinner and together with them the Comte de Gondreville, François Keller's father-in-law, the Chevalier d'Espard, des Lupeaulx, Doctor Bianchon, Desplein's favorite pupil; Beaudenord and his wife, the Comte and Comtesse de Montcornet, Blondet, Mademoiselle des Touches and Conti, and lastly, Lucien de Rubempre, for whom, five years since, Rastignac had conceived the most enthusiastic friendship—but "per order," as they say on placards.

"We sha'nt get rid of him too easily," remarked Blondet to Rastignac, as he saw Lucien enter the drawing-room, handsomer than ever, and dressed with admirable effect.

"It were better to make a friend of him, for he's to be feared," said Rastignac.

"He?" interposed de Marsay. "Nobody's position

is to be feared unless it be clearly defined. His is rather unattacked than impregnable! What do you suppose he lives on? Whence comes his fortune? I'm sure that he's some sixty thousand francs in debt."

"He has found a very rich protector in a Spanish priest who is devoted to him," answered Rastignac.

"He's marrying the eldest Mademoiselle de Grandlieu," said Mademoiselle des Touches.

"Yes," returned the Chevalier d'Espard, "but they require him to buy an estate with an income of thirty thousand francs to insure the fortune that his bride will bring him. He needs a million, and a million isn't to be found in the pocket of any Spaniard."

"That's dear, for Clotilde is very plain," said the baroness.

Madame de Nucingen habitually called Mademoiselle de Grandlieu by her Christian name, as if she, born a Goriot, were accustomed to such society.

"No," replied du Tillet, "the daughter of a duchess never looks ugly to our eyes, above all when she brings the title of marquis and a diplomatic position. But the greatest stumbling-block in the way of the marriage is Madame de Sérizy's mad love for Lucien. She probably loads him with money."

"I'm not surprised to see Lucien so serious; for Madame de Sérizy will not be likely to give him a million to help him marry Mademoiselle de

Grandlieu. Doubtless he's at a loss what to do," said de Marsay.

"Yes, but Mademoiselle de Grandlieu worships him," said the Comtesse de Montcornet, "and with her aid perhaps he will get better terms."

"What will he do with his sister and his brother-in-law, d'Angoulême?" asked the Chevalier d'Espard.

"But the sister's rich," replied Rastignac, "and now he thinks her certain to become Madame Séchard de Marsac."

"Difficulties or none, he's a handsome man," added Bianchon, as he rose to greet Lucien.

"How are you, my boy?" said Rastignac, shaking Lucien warmly by the hand.

De Marsay returned Lucien's bow with cold politeness.

Before dinner, Desplein and Bianchon, while they laughed and joked, examined the Baron de Nucingen and perceived that his trouble was entirely mental. Nobody, however, could divine its cause, for nobody dreamed that this lynx of the Stock Exchange could be in love. Bianchon, divining that nothing except love which could explain the pathological condition of the banker, spoke a word or two to Delphine de Nucingen, who smiled like a woman who has long since guessed her husband's trouble. After dinner when the company went out into the garden, the closer friends of the family scrutinized the banker, trying to comprehend his extraordinary case by listening to Bianchon's opinion that Nucingen must be in love.

"Are you aware, baron," said de Marsay to the banker, "that you've grown very thin, and that people suspect you of breaking the laws of nature's economy?"

"Nefer," protested the baron.

"But they do," insisted de Marsay, "they dare to pretend that you're in love."

"Eet's drue," answered Nucingen, piteously, "I zigh vor zometing unknown."

"You, in love, you? You're a fool!" said the Chevalier d'Espard.

"To pe in luff, at my age, I know vel dat notting ees more riteeculous. But id's drue."

"Is she a woman in society?" inquired Lucien.

"But," said de Marsay, "the baron would never waste away if his love were not hopeless. He can afford to buy any woman who needs money or who is on sale."

"I to nod know her ad all," answered the baron, "ant I can say eet now, for Matame ti Nucingen ees in ze salon; I haf nefer known what luff vas bevore. Luff? I tink it ees to vaste avay."

"Where was it that you met this guileless creature?" asked Rastignac.

"In ze garriage ad mitnight, in ze vood of Fincennes."

"Describe her," said de Marsay.

"Ein vite cauze vrill, pink tress, vite shawl, vite veil. Druly a vace of ze piple. Eyes like vire. A complexion of ze East."

"You were dreaming!" said Lucien smiling.

"Eet's drue; I vas zleeping like a log, a pig log," he continued, "for it happenet as I vas coming pack from ze country-blace of mein frient."

"Was she alone?" demanded du Tillet, interrupting the lynx.

"Yez," said the baron in a dejected tone, "exzept ein vootman ant eine vaiting vooman."

"Lucien looks as if he had his suspicions," cried Rastignac, as he noticed a smile on the face of Esther's lover.

"Who is there who does not know women that might meet Nucingen at midnight?" said Lucien twirling round.

"Then it isn't a woman who goes into society?" asked the Chevalier d'Espard, "for the baron would have recognized the footman."

"I haf nefer seen her any vare," replied the baron, "ant for forty tays I haf hat ze bolice looking for her ant they to nod fint her."

"It is better that she should cost you a few hundred thousands of francs than that she should cost you your life, and at your age an unfed passion is dangerous," said Desplein. "You might die of it."

"Yes," answered the baron, turning to the last speaker, "ze tings I ead to nod nourish me. Ze air zeems teatly. I go to ze vood at Fincennes to zee ze blace where I zaw her. Ach, ze life zat I leat! I haf nod peen able to attent to ze last loan. I haf asked ze advize of my bartners, ant zey have bitied me. I would gif ein million to know zat vooman.

Ich will fint her, for now I nefer go to ze Exchanghe. Ask ti Dilet."

"Yes," answered du Tillet. "He has lost all taste for business; he is changing his nature, and that is a symptom of approaching death."

"A zympdom of luff," continued Nucingen, "ant mit me zat is ze same ting."

The simplicity of this old man, who was a lynx no longer, now that for the first time in his life he had found something more holy and more sacred than gold, touched this group of worldly people. Some looked at one another and smiled, others looked at Nucingen, plainly thinking: "A man as strong as he to come to this!" Then everybody went back to the drawing-room discussing what had happened. It was certainly an event of a nature most likely to create a great sensation. Madame de Nucingen laughed when Lucien disclosed the banker's secret, but, noticing his wife's derision, the baron took her by the arm and led her into the embrasure of a window.

"Matame," said he in a low tone, "haf I efer uttered ein zyllaple of mockery in regart to all your lufs zat you should zneer ad mine? Eine gut vife vud dry to help her husband mitout zneering ad him as you to."

By the old banker's description, Lucien had recognized Esther. Already troubled that his smile had been noted, he profited by a moment's general conversation while the waiters were passing the coffee about, to disappear.

"What has become of Monsieur de Rubempré?" asked the Baronne de Nucingen.

"He is faithful to his motto: *"Quid me continebit,"* answered Rastignac.

"That means 'Who can keep me,' or 'I am invincible,' as you will," remarked de Marsay.

"At the moment that the baron described his vision, Lucien's face relaxed into a smile that made me think the woman must be an acquaintance of his," said Horace Bianchon, not thinking of the danger of so natural an observation.

"Gut!" said the banker to himself.

Like all hopeless invalids, the baron grasped at anything which bore the semblance of hope, and he determined to have Lucien watched by other spies than those of Louchard, the cleverest commercial detective in Paris, with whom he had been in communication for the past fortnight.

*

Before he went to Esther, it was Lucien's duty to pass at the Grandlieus' house the two hours which were to make Mademoiselle Clotilde-Frédérique de Grandlieu the happiest girl in the Faubourg Saint Germain. The prudence which characterized the conduct of this young and ambitious man counseled him to lose no time in telling Carlos Herrera of the effect which his smile at the baron's description of Esther had produced. Nucingen's love for Esther and his intention of setting the police on the track of his unknown idol were themselves of enough importance to communicate to a man who had sought beneath the cassock the sanctuary which criminals of old found in the church. Besides Lucien's road from the Rue de Saint Lazare, where the banker lived at this time, to the Rue Saint Dominique, where the Grandlieus' house was situated, led directly past his own apartment on the Quai Malaquais. Lucien found his grim friend smoking his breviary, that is to say, puffing a pipe before going to bed. The man's tastes were not so foreign as his nature, and he had given up the Spanish cigars which he found too mild for him.

"This is growing serious," answered the Spaniard when Lucien had told him all. "Since the baron employs Louchard to hunt down the girl, he may be shrewd enough to have you tracked, and if he does, everything will come to light. I have none too much of the night and morning left to arrange my plans for the game that I shall play against the baron. First of all I shall show him the impotence of the police. When our lynx has lost all hope of finding his lamb, I agree to sell her to him for what she is worth."

"Sell Esther!" screamed Lucien, whose first impulse was always excellent.

"So, you forget our position," returned Carlos Herrera.

Lucien hung his head.

"Money gone," the Spaniard went on, "and sixty thousand francs of debts to pay. If you wish to marry Clotilde de Grandlieu you must buy an estate worth a million to insure the fortune that goes with her ugly face. So you see Esther is the hare and I am coursing her with this lynx, and hope to fleece him of a million. That is my business."

"Esther would never—"

"That is my business."

"She will die."

"That is the funeral's business. Besides afterwards?," cried the brutal priest with a manner that checked Lucien's remonstrances.

"How many generals died in the prime of their lives for the Emperor Napoleon?" he asked of Lucien after a moment's silence. "A man never wants for women! In 1821, in your eyes, Coralie had

not her peer: then you had not yet met Esther.
After this girl will come, do you know who? The
undiscovered woman! Of all women she shall be
the most beautiful and you shall seek her in that
capital where the son-in-law of the Duc de Grandlieu
represents the king of France as minister. And
tell me, foolish boy, do you think Esther will die?
Can the husband of Mademoiselle de Grandlieu still
keep Esther? So let me have my way. You
haven't the worry of thinking about everything.
That's my business. You must do without Esther
for a week or two, but you shall go to the Rue
Taitbout all the same. Walk your safe path, bill
and coo, play your part carefully, slip into Clotilde's
hand the burning letter that you wrote this morning
and bring me back a note that has some passion in it.
Writing will console her for her troubles. That girl
suits me. You will find Esther a little sad, but tell
her to obey. We need our liveries of virtue, our
cloaks of honesty, the screens behind which great
men hide their infamy; my present character is at
stake, and so is yours, which must never be doubted.
Chance has served us better than I calculated,
though for the past two months my brains have been
busy enough." As Carlos Herrera uttered these
terrible sentences, which came out, one by one,
with the effect of pistol shots, he was dressing
and making ready for a walk.

"I can see your delight," cried Lucien; "you
never loved poor Esther, and you watch in ecstasy
for the moment that you can rid yourself of her."

"You are never tired of loving her, are you? Just so, I am never tired of hating her. But haven't I always acted as if I were sincerely devoted to the girl, I, who through Asia held her life in my hands? A few poisonous mushrooms in a stew, and all would have been over. And yet Mademoiselle Esther lives! She is happy! Do you know why? It's because you love her. Don't be a child. For four years we have waited to see whether the cards were for or against us; you see we must use something more than skill to pluck the fruit that fate hangs over our path. In every stroke of fortune there is good and ill, and so there is in this. Do you know what I was thinking of as you came in?"

"No."

"Of making myself, here, as at Barcelona, the heir of a devout old woman by Asia's help."

"A crime?"

"It is my only chance to make your happiness certain. The creditors are growing uneasy. Once pursued by officers and chased from the Grandlieus' house, what would become of you? The devil would demand his due."

Carlos Herrera described with a gesture the suicide of a man leaping into the water; then he fixed his penetrating gaze upon Lucien, such a look as forces the will of a strong mind to enter the soul of a weaker man. This fascinating look overcame the last traces of resistance and betrayed the existence not only of secrets of life and death between Lucien and his mentor, but also of passions as far above the ordinary passions of life as the priest was above the baseness of his position.

Condemned to live apart from society and forbidden by law ever to return; worn by vice, by anger and by fearful struggles against himself, but endowed with a consuming strength of intellect, this man who was at once mean and great, obscure and famous, burning with a life-long fever of ambition, lived once more in the graceful person of Lucien, whose soul he had made his own. He was represented in society by this poet to whom he gave his character and his iron will. To him Lucien was more than a son, more than a beloved wife, more than a family, more than life itself; he was his revenge. Thus as strong minds cling more closely to an idea than to reality, he was bound to him by indissoluble ties.

He had bought Lucien's life just as the despairing poet was on the verge of suicide, and then he had made with him one of those hellish compacts, which are never seen except in novels, but whose awful possibility has often been shown in court in the famous dramas of the law. Heaping upon Lucien all the pleasures of Parisian life, convincing him that a triumphant future was still possible, he had made him his tool. From the moment that he revived in a second self, no sacrifice was too bitter for this strange man. With all his strength he was so feeble against the whims of his creature that he had eventually entrusted him with all his secrets. Perhaps this complicity, entirely moral though it was, made one more bond between them. From the day that La Torpille had been carried away, Lucien knew the horrible pedestal on which his happiness stood.

The cassock of a Spanish priest hid Jacques Collin, a notorious criminal, who ten years before had lived under the ordinary name of Vautrin in the Vauquer boarding-house where Rastignac and Bianchon were quartered at the time. Jacques Collin, surnamed "Trompe-la-Mort," escaped from Rochefort almost immediately after he had been sent back there, and turned to good account the example given by the famous Comte de Sainte-Helene, while he modified the more criminal portions of Coignard's plan. To go about in the guise of an honest man, and still to lead the life of a galley-slave, is a proposition, in terms so contradictory that eventual detection is inevitable, especially at Paris; for, when a criminal enters a household, he increases tenfold the dangers that surround his imposture. To be beyond pursuit, must not a man reach a level above the commonplace incidents of life? In society a man runs risks which come but rarely to men who have no dealings with society. Then, too, the cassock is the most secure of all disguises, when the counterfeit priest can support it by an exemplary, solitary and inactive life.

"I will turn priest," thought this dead layman, who longed to live once more as a member of society and to satisfy passions as strange as himself.

The civil war, which the Constitution of 1812 had kindled in Spain, where this man of passionate energy had gone, enabled him to have the real Carlos Herrera killed in a secret ambush. Natural son of a noble lord, long since abandoned by his father, ignorant even of her to whom he owed his existence, this priest, at the recommendation of a bishop, was entrusted by King Ferdinand VII. with a secret mission to France. The bishop, who was the only man who felt an interest in Carlos Herrera, died while this forlorn hope of the church was making the journey from Cadiz to Madrid and from Madrid to France. After his fortunate meeting with a man whose personality was so well adapted to his schemes, Jacques Collin cut gashes in his own back in order to efface the fatal letters, and altered his face by means of chemical processes. Before destroying the priest's body, he transformed his own into the closest possible imitation of it, and succeeded in giving himself some resemblance to his Tosia. To complete a metamorphosis almost as marvelous as that which is told in the Arabian story, where the dervish in his old age acquires the power of entering a youthful body by the aid of magic spells, the galley-slave, who was already familiar with Spanish, picked up as much Latin as an Andalusian priest would be likely to know. Banker in three prisons, Collin had enriched himself by the deposits which the prisoners had entrusted to his honesty that was well known and also enforced; for in business like his, dagger-thrusts wipe out mistakes. To these funds he added the money given by the bishop to Carlos Herrera. Before his departure from Spain he was able to secure the treasure of a conscience-stricken woman of Barcelona. He had given her absolution and at the same time promised to effect the restoration of sums which his penitent had stolen after committing a murder, and which were the source of all her fortune. Now that he was a priest, entrusted with a secret mission which was to secure for him the most powerful patronage in Paris, Jacques Collin resolved to do nothing to compromise the character he had assumed, and abandoned himself to the chances of his new life. On the road from Angoulême to Paris he fell in with Lucien, who seemed to the false priest to furnish a weapon of extraordinary power. Having saved him from suicide he said to him: "Give yourself up to a priest of God as a man gives himself up to the devil, and you shall have all the opportunities of a new destiny. You shall live as in a dream and the worst awakening you can have is the death that you have already tried to give yourself."

The union of these two beings who became as one rested on this forcible argument, and in addition Carlos Herrera cemented it by a cunningly contrived complicity in crime. Gifted with a genius for corruption he destroyed Lucien's honesty by plunging him into cruel necessities and rescuing him from them only on his tacit acquiescence in ignoble and shameful actions. Thus still pure, loyal, noble in the eyes of the world, Lucien formed the social splendor in whose shadow the forger wished to dwell.

"I am the author; you shall be the play. If you fail it is I who shall be hissed," he said to Lucien the day on which he avowed his sacrilegious disguise.

Carlos moved prudently from confession to confession, apportioning the infamy of his disclosures to the strength of his success and to the necessities of his pupil. Thus Trompe-la-Mort did not surrender his last secret until the moment when the weak poet, subdued by the habitual enjoyment of Parisian pleasures, of success and of gratified vanity, had become his slave body and soul. In the very spot where Rastignac had formerly been tempted by this devil and stood fast, Lucien fell. More adroitly handled, more craftily compromised, the poet was vanquished above all by his delight at having won a position of eminence. Evil, which in its outward form is poetically called the devil, brought against this man, half woman as he was, all its most alluring temptations, gave him much and asked little in return. Herrera's main argument was that eternal secret that Tartuffe promised to Elmire. Repeated proofs of perfect devotion, like that of Seid for Mohammed, finished the horrid work of the subjugation of Lucien by a Jacques Collin.

Esther and Lucien had used up all the funds that had been entrusted to the honesty of the prison banker. This exposed them to a terrible day of reckoning; but besides this, the dandy, the forger and the courtesan all had debts. At the moment that Lucien was about to succeed, the tiniest pebble beneath the foot of one of these three beings might bring down the whole chimerical framework of a fortune so daringly built.

At the ball of the Opera Rastignac had recognized Vautrin of the Vauquer establishment, but he knew that indiscretion meant death; besides Madame de Nucingen's lover and Lucien exchanged looks in which fear was hidden on either side beneath the veneer of friendship. In the moment of danger Rastignac would undoubtedly have been delighted to provide the cart that should carry Trompe-la-Mort to the scaffold. Everyone can now understand the sinister joy of Carlos Herrera as he heard of the Baron de Nucingen's love and grasped in a single thought all the advantage that a man of his stamp might derive from the unfortunate Esther.

"Go," he said to Lucien, "the devil protects his almoner."

"You are smoking in a powder mill," said Lucien.

"*Incedo per ignes*," answered Carlos with a smile. "It's my trade."

*

Toward the middle of the last century the Grandlieu family was divided into two branches: first the ducal house, destined to come to an end since all the children of the living duke were daughters; secondly, the Vicomtes de Grandlieu, the direct heirs to the title and arms of the elder branch. The ducal line bears gules with three "doullouères" or golden battle-axes arranged in fesse, with the famous "CAVEO, NON TIMEO!" for a motto, an epitome of the history of the house.

The escutcheon of the viscounts is quartered with that of the Naverreins, which is gules with embattled fesse in gold stamped with a knight's helment and the motto "GRANDS FAITS, GRAND LIEU!" The present viscountess, a widow since 1813, has a son and a daughter. Although she had come back half ruined after the emigration, she had recovered a moderate fortune through the devotion of Derville, her lawyer.

On their return in 1804 the Duc and Duchesse de Grandlieu were assailed by the blandishments of the Emperor; and Napoleon, who saw them at his court, restored all that still remained of the estate, amounting to an income of some forty thousand francs. Of all the nobles of the Faubourg Saint Germain who suffered themselves to be cajoled by

Napoleon, the duke and duchess—who was an Ajuda of the elder branch, connected with the Bragances—were alone in refusing to renounce the Emperor and his benefits. Louis XVIII. commended this fidelity when the Faubourg Saint Germain wished to cast it in the teeth of the Grandlieu family; but possibly Louis XVIII.'s sole desire in this step was to exasperate *"monsieur."* Everybody expected a match between the young Vicomte de Grandlieu and Marie Athénais, the youngest daughter of the duke, at this time aged nine. Sabine, the next elder, had been married to the Baron du Guénic before the revolution of July. Josephine, the third, had become Madame d'Ajuda-Pinto after the death of the marquis' first wife, Mademoiselle de Rochefide— alias Rochegude. The eldest daughter had taken the veil in the year 1822. The second, Mademoiselle Clotilde-Frédérique, at this time twenty-seven years of age, was deeply in love with Lucien de Rubempré. We must not ask whether the mansion of the Duc de Grandlieu, one of the handsomest on the Rue Saint Dominique, exerted a thousand fascinations over Lucien's spirit. Every time that the great gate swung back on its hinges to admit his carriage, he felt that tickled vanity of which Mirabeau used to speak.

"Though my father was a plain apothecary at Houmeau, I have an entrance here."

Such was his thought. Besides he would have committed many another crime beyond that of his league with a forger to preserve the privilege of ascending the short flight of steps before the porch, to hear the lackey announce "Monsieur de Rubempré!" in the great parlor, dating from the time of Louis XIV., that was built after the fashion of the salons of Versailles, filled with the cream of Parisian society, and known at the time as "*le petit château.*"

The noble Portuguese lady who cared little for going abroad, spent the greater part of her time surrounded by her neighbors the Chaulieus, the Naverreins, and the Lenoncourts. The pretty Baronne de Macumer—born a de Chaulieu—, the Duchesse de Maufrigneuse, Madame d'Espard, Madame de Camps, and Mademoiselle des Touches—who was connected with the Brittany branch of the Grandlieus—often came to call there going or coming from the Opera. The Vicomte de Grandlieu, the Duc de Rhetoré, the Marquis de Chaulieu, who some day was to be the Duc de Lenoncourt-Chaulieu; his wife, Madeline de Mortsauf, granddaughter of the Duc de Lenoncourt; the Marquis d'Ajuda-Pinto, the Prince de Blamont-Chauvry, the Marquis de Beauséant, the Vidame de Pamiers, the Vandenesses, the old Prince de Cadignan, and his son, the Duc de Maufrigneuse, were all frequent guests in this splendid salon, where they breathed the atmosphere of the court, and where manners, fashion and wit were all well suited to the nobility of the family whose aristocratic bearing had eventually effaced the recollection of their Napoleonic bondage.

The old Duchesse d'Uxelles, the mother of the

Duchesse de Maufrigneuse, was the oracle of this salon which had been closed to Madame de Sérizy, although she was one of the de Ronquerolles.

Introduced by Madame de Maufrigneuse, who had forced her mother to intrigue in favor of Lucien, with whom she had been madly in love for the past two years, the attractive poet held his position, thanks to the influence of the Grand Almonry of France and to the aid of the Archbishop of Paris. He was not, however, admitted until a royal prescript had restored to him the name and arms of the house of Rubempré. The Duc de Rhétoré, the Chevalier d'Espard and a few others were jealous of Lucien and periodically succeeded in prejudicing the Duc de Grandlieu against him by whispering anecdotes of his antecedents. But the pious duchess, surrounded by the dignitaries of the church, and Clotilde de Grandlieu upheld him. Furthermore, Lucien understood the enmity he met with to be in consequence of his former relations with Madame d'Espard's cousin, Madame de Bargeton, who had since become Comtesse du Châtelet. Feeling the importance of obtaining a foothold in so powerful a family and urged by his secret counselor to seduce the affections of Clotilde, Lucien summoned all the courage of an upstart; he went to the house five days out of the seven, he smiled at the poisoned arrows of envy, he endured with grace the most insolent of glances, and answered wittily to the thrusts of his enemies. His constancy, the charm of his manner and his courtesy hushed every scruple and overcame every obstacle. Always at his best in the parlors of the Duchesse de Maufrigneuse, whose burning letters written at the height of her passion were carefully preserved by Carlos Herrera; the idol of Madame de Sérizy; welcomed to the house of Mademoiselle des Touches, Lucien, well pleased as he was to be received in these three houses, learned from the priest to maintain the utmost reserve in all his relations.

"You must not devote yourself to many households at once," said his secret mentor. "He who goes everywhere has interest with no one. The great protect only those whom they see every day, who rival their furniture and become a necessity like the sofa that they sit upon."

Lucien was accustomed to think of the salon of the Grandlieus as his field of battle, and kept all his clever thoughts and words, his news, his courtly graces in reserve for the evenings which he passed there. Insinuating, fascinating, forewarned by Clotilde of all the dangers he must avoid, he flattered every passing fancy of M. de Grandlieu. At first Clotilde merely envied the happiness of the Duchesse de Maufrigneuse, but soon she learned to love Lucien desperately.

Well aware of all the advantages of such an alliance, Lucien played the lover's part as Armand, the last young "star" of the Comédie-Française, would have played it. He wrote Clotilde letters, which were certainly literary masterpieces of the first rank; and Clotilde answered, trying to rival his genius in expressing her mad love on paper; for she had but this way of loving. Every Sunday Lucien heard mass at Saint Thomas Aquinas'. To all appearances he was a fervent Catholic, and devoted himself to writing monarchial and religious tracts which accomplished wonders. And then he wrote admirable articles for all the newspapers devoted to the congregation. He would not consent to take any pay, and signed his contributions with a simple "L." He brought out political pamphlets at the request of King Charles X., or of the Grand Almonry without demanding the slightest compensation.

"The king," he would say, "has done so much for me already that I owe him my life."

Besides, for some time past Lucien had been considered for the appointment of secretary in the cabinet of the first minister; but Madame d'Espard had stirred up so much opposition that the Maitre Jacques of Charles X. hesitated to take the step. Not only was Lucien's position too vaguely defined, and the words, "What does he live upon?" that were on every lip as Lucien rose into prominence, unanswered, but still more, friendly as well as inimical curiosity went from scrutiny to scrutiny and found more than one weak spot in the cuirass of the ambitious young hero. Clotilde played into the hands of her father and mother as an innocent spy. A few days before, she had drawn Lucien into the embrasure of a window to talk with him and warn him of the objections of the family.

"Find an estate worth a million and you shall

have my hand. That is what my mother said," Clotilde had told him.

"They will ask you later whence your money comes," Carlos remarked when Lucien reported this apparently final alternative.

"My brother-in-law must have made a fortune," Lucien observed. "We shall have a responsible agent in him."

"Then it's only the million that we need," Carlos cried. "I shall not forget it."

To explain fully Lucien's position at the Grandlieu house, we must add that he had never dined there. Not Clotilde, nor the Duchesse d'Uxelles, nor Madame de Maufrigneuse, who was always excellently disposed to Lucien, could wrest this favor from the old duke, so suspicious did that gentleman remain of the poet whom he called "le sire de Rubempré." This shadow, manifest to every one in the room, touched Lucien's pride to the quick as he felt that his presence was scarcely more than tolerated. The world has a right to be particular; it is so often deceived. To shine in Paris without a well-known fortune, without an avowed calling, is a position which no artifice can long render tenable. The higher Lucien climbed the greater force he gave to the objection, "What does he live upon?" He had been forced to admit to Madame de Sérizy, to whom he owed the support of the attorney-general Granville and of a minister of state, the Comte Octave de Bauvan, president at a sovereign court, that he was over head and ears in debt.

As he entered the court-yard of the house where dwelt the realization of his lofty hopes, he said to himself bitterly, thinking of the decision of Trompe-la-Mort:

"I hear everything cracking beneath my feet."

He loved Esther, and he wished Mademoiselle de Grandlieu to be his wife! Strange position! He must sell one to have the other; one man alone could make the bargain without hurt to Lucien's honor, and that man was the counterfeit Spaniard. Each must be equally discreet toward the other. A compact like this in which each is by turn master and slave is rare indeed.

Lucien chased away the clouds that darkened his brow. He entered the salon of the Grandlieu house radiantly gay. The windows chanced to be open, and the sweet smells of the garden perfumed the drawing-room, in the middle of which was a stand covered with a mass of flowers. The duchess, seated on a sofa in one corner, chatted with the Duchesse de Chaulieu. Several ladies made up a group that was noticeable for the different attitudes of its members, each calculated to express some feigned sorrow. In society nobody is interested in grief or suffering; there, words are everything. The men were pacing the salon or walking in the garden. Clotilde and Joséphine were busied about the tea-table. The Vidame de Pamiers, the Duc de Grandlieu, the Marquis d'Ajuda-Pinto, and the Duc de Maufrigneuse were playing whist in a corner. When Lucien was announced, he crossed the drawing-room to pay his respects to the duchess, and asked her the reason of the sadness painted upon her face.

"Madame de Chaulieu has just received some dreadful news: her son-in-law, the Baron de Macumer, the ex-Duc de Soria, is dead. The young Duc de Soria and his wife, who had gone to Chantepleurs to nurse their brother, have written of the sad event. Louise is completely overcome."

"A woman is not loved twice in her life as Louise was loved by her husband," said Madeleine de Mortsauf.

"She will be a rich widow," added the old Duchesse d'Uxelles, casting her eyes upon Lucien, whose face maintained its impassibility.

"Poor Louise," said Madame d'Espard, "I understand her, and I pity her."

The Marquise d'Espard had the dreamy air of a woman full of soul and heart. Although Sabine de Grandlieu was but ten years old she glanced knowingly at her mother, but her almost mocking expression was instantly rebuked by a frown. This is what is called, " bringing up children well."

"If my daughter resists that frown," said Madame de Chaulieu, with her most motherly air, " her future will make me uneasy. Louise is very romantic."

"I cannot imagine," said the old Duchesse d'Uxelles, " from whom our girls have acquired that characteristic."

"It is difficult nowadays," said an old cardinal, " to reconcile the heart with decorous behavior."

Lucien had not a word to say and went toward the tea-table to pay his compliments to the Mesdemoiselles de Grandlieu. When the poet was within a few steps of the group of women, the Marquise d'Espard bent toward the Duchesse de Grandlieu. "You are quite sure that he is really in love with your dear Clotilde?" she whispered.

The perfidy of this question can only be understood after a sketch of Clotilde has been given. That young lady of twenty-seven was standing, and her attitude allowed the malicious glance of the Marquise d'Espard to take in the slight spare figure which looked exactly like a stalk of asparagus. The poor girl's corsage was so flat that it did not even admit of the colonial resource known among dressmakers as "a false fichu." Besides, Clotilde, who knew that her name endowed her with sufficient advantages, far from endeavoring to conceal the defect, took heroic measures to make it prominent. By wearing tight-fitting gowns she gave herself the crude stiff figure that sculptors of the middle ages sought to impart to the statues they placed in relief against the background of cathedral niches. Clotilde was five feet four inches. If it be allowable to make use of a familiar expression which has, at least, the merit of being easily understood, she was all legs. This defect in proportion gave the upper part of her body an appearance of deformity. Her complexion was dark; her hair black and coarse, her eyebrows bushy, and her brilliant eyes were already surrounded with dark circles. Her face that was curved like the moon in its first quarter was dominated by a heavy forehead, and made her the very caricature of her mother, one of the most beautiful women of Portugal. Nature loves to play at such tricks as these. We often notice in families a sister of extraordinary beauty, while the same features in the brother become singularly ugly, although the two faces are not without resemblance. Clotilde's mouth was cut inwards from her face and wore an expression of stereotyped disdain. Her lips more than any other feature of her face betrayed the secret workings of her heart, for love had printed upon them a lovely look all the more strange because her cheeks were too brown to blush and her black eyes too hard to tell her story. In spite of her great disadvantages, in spite of her stiff carriage, she derived from her training and her race an air of grandeur, a lofty countenance and what the French call the "*Je ne sais quoi,*" due, perhaps, to the simplicity of her dress, which marked her as the daughter of a noble house. Her looks were improved by her hair, and she passed for a beauty on account of its luxuriant thickness and length. Her voice, which she had cultivated, was charming; she sang exquisitely. Clotilde was surely a young woman of whom the world says: "Her eyes are lovely;" or, "Her disposition is delightful." To someone who addressed her after the English fashion as "Your Grace," she answered, "Call me 'Your Slenderness.'"

"Why shouldn't a man fall in love with my poor

Clotilde?" the duchess answered the marquise. "Do you know what she said to me yesterday? 'If anyone loves me for the sake of ambition, I shall make him love me for myself.' She is clever and ambitious; there are men who delight in both these qualities. As for him, my dear, he is a dream of beauty. And if he can buy the Rubempré estate the king will give him back his title of marquis as a favor to us. After all, his mother is the last Rubempré."

"Poor man, where can he find the million?" exclaimed the marquise.

"That is no business of ours," answered the duchess; "but, come what may, he is incapable of stealing it. And besides, we should never give Clotilde to a schemer, nor to any dishonest man even if he were handsome, young and poetic as M. de Rubempré."

"You are late," said Clotilde, smiling at Lucien with tender interest.

"Yes, I dined out."

"You have been going into society a great deal of late," said she, hiding her jealousy and uneasiness beneath a smile.

"In society?" replied Lucien. "No, simply by the merest chance, I have been dining all the week with various bankers; to-day with Nucingen, yesterday with du Tillet, and the day before at the Kellers."

Lucien had evidently learned the polished insolence of men of rank.

"You have many enemies," said Clotilde as she handed him (and with what grace!) a cup of tea. "They have been telling my father that you are so fortunate as to have sixty thousand francs of debts and that in time to come you will have Sainte Pélagie for a country house. And if you knew what all these calumnies mean to me—It all comes home to me—It is not of my own sufferings that I speak, though my father's looks cut me to the quick, but of what you must suffer if any of this turn out to be true."

"Do not be troubled by all this absurdity. Love me as I love you and give me credit for a few months," answered Lucien, as he laid his empty cup upon the chased silver tray.

"Don't go near my father. He might make some rude remark and as you would never suffer it to pass, we should be lost. That wicked Marquise d'Espard has told him that your mother was a monthly nurse and that your sister has been a sempstress."

"We have been in the depths of poverty," answered Lucien, whose eyes shone with tears. "This is worse than calumny, it is pure falsehood. To-day my sister has more than a million, and my mother has been dead for two years. They have kept this information for the time when I am on the point of succeeding here."

"But what did you tell Madame d'Espard?"

"I was imprudent enough to tell as a joke in the presence of M. de Bauvan and M. de Granville, in

Madame de Sérizy's parlor, the story of the suit which she brought for separation from her husband the Marquis d'Espard. Bianchon had told me about it. M. de Granville's opinion supported by Bauvan and Sérizy had made the keeper of the seals alter his conclusions. Both of them recoiled before the Gazette des Tribunaux and the scandal, so the grounds for the verdict which put an end to the detestable affair were very unflattering to the marquise. If M. de Sérizy has been indiscreet and has made the marquise my mortal enemy, I have at least won his protection, that of the attorney-general, and especially of Count Octave de Bauvan, whom Madame de Sérizy told of the dangerous position in which they had placed me by leaving me to guess the source of their information. The Marquis d'Espard was dolt enough to make me a visit thinking that I was the cause of the decision of the odious lawsuit."

"I am going to deliver you from Madame d'Espard," said Clotilde.

"How?" cried Lucien.

"My mother shall invite the d'Espard children. They are charming and nearly grown up. The father and his two sons will sing your praises here, and we can be very certain never to see their mother again."

"O Clotilde, you are perfect. If I did not love you for yourself, I should love you for your wit."

"It is not wit," she said, and all her love showed about her lips. "Good-bye. Let several days pass before you come again. When you see me at Saint Thomas Aquinas, with a pink scarf you will know that my father's humor has changed. You have an answer glued to the back of the chair on which you sit; it will console you, perhaps. Put the letter you have brought me into my handkerchief."

This young woman was evidently older than twenty-seven. Lucien took a cab at the Rue de la Planche, left it on the boulevard, took another at the Madeleine and ordered the driver to stop in the Rue Taitbout.

*

As Lucien entered Esther's room, at eleven o'clock, he found her in tears but attired to do him honor. She was awaiting her Lucien, reclining upon a divan of white satin embroidered with golden flowers, dressed in a fascinating dressing-gown of India muslin, caught up here and there with bunches of cherry-colored ribbon. She wore no stays, her hair was loosely coiled about the back of her head, and her feet were encased in pretty velvet slippers trimmed with cherry satin. Every candle was lighted and the hookah ready, but she had not smoked her own, which lay before her unlit as if to mark her state of mind. As she heard the doors open, she dried her tears, and bounding from her couch like a gazelle, clasped Lucien in her arms as a floating bit of gauze, blown by the wind, twines itself about a tree.

"Parted," she cried. "Is it true?"

"Pooh, only for a day or two," answered Lucien.

Esther loosened her hold of Lucien, and fell back half-fainting on the sofa. In situations like this, most women babble like parrots! Ah! how they love you! After five years their feelings are the same as on the first morrow of their happiness. They cannot leave you; they are superb in their indignation, despair, love, anger, remorse, terror, sorrow, foreboding! In a word, they are sublime as a scene from Shakespeare. But, count upon it! Such women do not love. When they are all that they say they are, when they love truly, they do as Esther did, as children do, as true love does. Esther did not say a word; she buried her face in the cushions and wept burning tears. Lucien forced himself to raise her. Then he spoke to her.

"But, child, we are not parted. What! after nearly four years of happiness, is this the way you take a short absence? What is it that I have done to all these women?" he added to himself as he remembered how Coralie, too, had loved him thus.

"Ah, sir, you are very handsome!" said Europe.

The senses have their ideal of what is perfect. When to such alluring beauty the sweetness of disposition and the poetic charm which distinguished Lucien are added, we can imagine the intense passion of beings who are so peculiarly sensitive to natural gifts and so ingenuous in their admiration. Esther sobbed softly, and her attitude betrayed her deep grief.

"But, dear heart," said Lucien, "were you not told that my life was at stake?"

As Lucien spoke these words, Esther sprang up like a wild beast; her hair, uncoiled, clustered about her splendid face like the leaves of a tree. She looked fixedly at Lucien.

"Your life!" she cried, raising her arms and letting them fall with a gesture peculiar to women when they are in danger. "But it is true that brute has written of something serious."

She drew a soiled paper from her belt, but seeing Europe, she said to her:

"Leave us, please."

When Europe had closed the door:

"See, this is what *he* wrote me," she added, handing Lucien a letter that Carlos had sent her. Lucien read it aloud.

"You will leave to-morrow at five in the morning; they will take you to a keeper's lodge deep in the forest of Saint Germain, where you will have a room on the first floor. Do not stir from this room until I permit you. You shall want for nothing. The keeper and his wife are trustworthy. Do not write to Lucien. Do not show yourself at the window during the day; but you may walk at night under the keeper's care if you wish to get the air. Keep the curtains pulled down on the way thither. Lucien's life is at stake.

"Lucien will come to-night to bid you good-bye. Burn this before him."

Lucien burned the note instantly in the flame of a candle.

"Listen, my Lucien," said Esther, when she had listened to the note as a criminal listens to the sentence of death that is pronounced upon him. "I shall not tell you that I love you, that would be silly. It is almost five years since it has seemed as natural to me to love you as to breathe—to live. The first day my happiness began, under the protection of the extraordinary man who has kept me here as men keep a little strange animal in a cage, I learned that you must marry. Marriage is a necessary element in your destiny, and God forbid that I should block the path of your success. Your marriage will be my death. But I shall not trouble you; I shall not act like a grisette and kill myself with a pan of charcoal. I have tried it once, and that is enough. Twice would be nauseating, as Mariette says. I shall go very far away, out of France. Asia knows the secrets of her country. She has promised to teach me how to die easily. You prick yourself; all is over in an instant. I ask but one thing, my angel of heaven, and that is that I may not be deceived. I have lived my life; since the day I saw you, in 1824, until to-day I have had more happiness than falls to the lot of ten happy women. So take me for what I am, a woman strong in her weakness. Tell me that you are going to marry and I shall only ask you to say good-bye very tenderly, and then you shall never hear of me again."

There was a moment's pause after this declaration. Its sincerity could be matched only by the simplicity of the gestures and the accent.

"Is it on account of your marriage?" said she, directing one of her fascinating glances, bright as a dagger blade, into Lucien's blue eyes.

"We have been working for my marriage for eighteen months, and it is not decided yet," answered Lucien. "I know not when it will be decided, but this command has nothing to do with that, my darling girl. It relates to the priest and to me and to you. We are threatened dangerously. Nucingen has seen you."

"Yes," said she. "At Vincennes; then he recognized me?"

"No," answered Lucien, "but he loves you as he loves his bank-book. After dinner, when he had described you and told of your meeting, I smiled involuntarily, like a fool; for in society I am beset by as many pitfalls as a savage in the midst of a hostile tribe. Carlos, who saves me the trouble of thinking, believes the situation dangerous. He has undertaken to checkmate Nucingen if Nucingen attempts to set detectives upon us, and he is capable of doing so, for he spoke to me of the impotence of the police. You have lighted a fire in an old soot-filled chimney."

"And what is your Spaniard going to do?" asked Esther very quietly.

"I know nothing further. He warned me to sleep with one eye open," answered Lucien, without daring to look into Esther's face.

"If this is the truth, I obey with the dog's submission that I profess," said Esther, slipping her arm beneath Lucien's and drawing him into her room. "Did you have a good dinner, dear Lucien, at that wicked Nucingen's?"

"Asia's cookery spoils another dinner, however famous the cook of the house where I dine. But Carême furnished the dinner as he does there every Sunday."

Lucien was involuntarily comparing Esther with Clotilde. His mistress was so beautiful, and her charm so undying, that she had as yet kept away that monster which devours the strongest love, satiety.

"How hard it is," thought he, "that I should find a wife in two volumes. In one poetry, pleasure, love, devotion, beauty, attraction—"

Esther was restless, as women are before they go to bed. She walked up and down, flitted here and there singing. She was like a humming bird.

"In the other, nobility, name, race, honor, rank, knowledge of society! And yet there is no way of uniting them in a single person," said he to himself.

At seven o'clock on the morrow, when he awoke in this charming room of pink and white, the poet found himself alone. He rang the bell and the fantastic Europe appeared.

"What do you wish, sir?"

"Esther."

"She left at a quarter before five. By the father's orders I let in a stranger and asked no questions."

"A woman?"

"No, sir, an English lady—one of those women who do their work at night, and we have orders to treat her as if she were our mistress: what can you want of that scare-crow? Poor lady, how she wept as she got into the carriage! 'There's no other way,' she cried; 'I left him, poor darling, while he slept,' she said to me as she wiped her

IN THE RUE TAITBOUT: ESTHER AND LUCIEN

tears: 'Europe, if he had looked at me or spoken my name I should have staid there, content to die with him.' Do you know, sir, I was so fond of her that I did not point out her successor to her. There's many a waiting-maid who would have broken her heart in such a case."

"Then the stranger is here then?"

"She came in the carriage which took away Madame Esther, sir, and I hid her in my room as I was bid."

"Is she satisfactory?"

"As satisfactory as a second-hand woman could be. But she will find no difficulty in playing her part if you are careful about yours, sir," said Europe, as she went in search of the false Esther.

On the previous evening before going to bed, the all-powerful banker had given his orders to his valet, and by seven o'clock the servants ushered the famous Louchard, the keenest of detectives, into a small parlor where the baron, in dressing-gown and slippers, met him.

"You haf peen making game of me," said he in answer to the officer's salutations.

"I could not do otherwise than I have done, sir. I keep within my own province, and I had the honor of informing you that I could not mix myself up in any affair foreign to my duties. What did I promise you? To put you in communication with the man among my agents who seemed to me best qualified to assist you. But you must be familiar with the barriers that exist between people of different trades. When you build a house you do not make a joiner do a locksmith's work. Just so there are two kinds of police—the political police and the detective police. The agents of the detective police never undertake any work of the political police and vice versa. If you were to address yourself to the chief of the political police you would need a permit from the minister to make use of him for your business, and you would never dare to explain what it is to the director general of the police of the kingdom. Any agent who should turn a penny on his own account would lose his place. And the detective police is just as circumspect as the political police. Thus nobody at the Ministry of the Interior, or at the Prefecture stirs a foot except in the interest of the State or in the interest of justice. If there's a plot or a crime in the case, why, heavens and earth, the chiefs are at your disposal, but you see, baron, that they have other tunes to whistle beside busying themselves with the fifty thousand intrigues that go on in Paris. As for the rest of us, we ought to attend merely to the arrest of debtors; and if we ever go beyond this we run enormous risk in case we disturb anybody's peace. I sent you one of my men, but at the same time I told you that I could not answer for him. You asked him to find you a woman in Paris; Contenson has *done* you out of a note of a thousand without stirring a finger. You might as well look for a needle in a haystack as to hunt through Paris for a woman supposed to have gone to the wood of Vincennes, and whose description corresponds to that of every pretty woman in Paris."

"Gould not Gondanzon" (Contenson), said the baron, "haf dold me ze druth inzteat of ropping me of a note for a tausent francs?"

"Listen, sir," said Louchard, "will you give me a thousand crowns? I am going to give you—sell you a bit of advice."

"Ant does atvice gost ein tausent growns?" demanded Nucingen.

"I am never caught napping, sir," answered Louchard. "You are in love; you wish to discover the object of your passion. You are shrivelling up like a cabbage without water. Your valet told me that two doctors came here yesterday and thought your life in danger. I, alone, can put you in the hands of a clever man. And if your life isn't worth a thousand crowns what the devil is it worth?"

"Dell me ze name of dis glever man, and gount on my chenerosidy."

Louchard took his hat, bowed, and walked away.

"Ze tefil of a man," cried Nucingen, "gome; dake ze money."

"You understand," said Louchard, before taking the money, "that I am selling you purely and simply a suggestion. I shall give you the name and address of the one man who can be of assistance to you; but he is a master."

"Go do ze tefil," cried Nucingen, "dere is no

name but Varschild vich is vort ein tausent growns ant only venn it is zigned at ze foot of a note. I offer ein tausent francs."

Louchard, petty sharper, who had never been able to secure a position as solicitor, notary, bailiff or attorney, leered at the baron significantly.

"For you it is a thousand crowns or nothing. You can get them again in a few seconds at the exchange," he said.

"I offer ein tausent francs," reiterated the baron.

"You would dispute the price of a gold mine!" said Louchard, as he bowed and withdrew.

"I zhall haf ze attress for ein note of five huntret francs," the baron cried out as he bade his valet send in his secretary.

Turcaret exists no longer. To-day the greatest, as well as the most petty, banker employs all his sagacity in the smallest matters: he haggles over art, generosity, love; he would haggle with the pope over an absolution. Thus as he listened to Louchard, Nucingen had rapidly calculated that since Contenson was the right hand of the detective, he must know the address of the master spy he desired. Contenson would let go for five hundred francs what Louchard wished to sell for a thousand crowns. This rapid decision proved conclusively that though the man's heart were a prisoner to love, the old lynx had not lost his head.

"Go yourzelf, zir," said the baron to his secretary, "to ze house of Gondanzon, ze spy of Lichard ze dedectif. Gall a gab, go guickly ant pring him at vonce. I vait for you. You vill go by ze garden toor. Here is ze key, vor it is pest zat no one zould zee ze man at my house. You vill indroduce him into ze leetle garten pafillion. Dry to exegute my gommission mit indelligence."

People came to talk business with Nucingen: still he waited for Contenson, and dreamed of Esther; he said to himself that before many days had passed he should see the woman to whom he owed emotions he had never thought possible; and he dismissed everybody with vague words, and promises of double meaning. Contenson seemed to him the most important being in Paris; every moment he looked out into his garden. At length, after he had given orders for his door to be kept shut, he had his breakfast served in the pavilion which stood in one corner of the garden.

*

In business circles the strange behavior and the hesitation of the keenest, craftiest, most politic of Paris bankers appeared inexplicable.

"What is the matter with the boss?" asked a stockbroker of one of the head clerks.

"Nobody knows. Apparently they are anxious about his health; yesterday his wife had a consultation with Doctors Desplein and Bianchon."

One day that some strangers came to see Newton, he was occupied in physicking one of his dogs named *Beauty*. This Beauty, a female, had destroyed, as everybody knows, an immense work, and Newton had said to her: "Ah, Beauty, you know not what you have ruined." The strangers respected the great man's employment and went away. In every famous life there is a little dog Beauty. When the Maréchal de Richelieu came to pay his respects to Louis XV. after the capture of Mahon, one of the greatest exploits of the eighteenth century, the king said to him: "You know the great news. Poor Lansmatt is dead!" Lansmatt was a door-keeper who happened to be privy to the monarch's intrigues. The bankers of Paris never knew the obligations they owed to Contenson, for the detective was the reason of Nucingen's abandoning to them a vast enterprise, in which he had already embarked. Every day the lynx could aim at a fortune with the artillery of speculation whereas the man was at the orders of pleasure.

The famous banker was sipping his tea and nibbling a few slices of bread and butter with the deliberation of a man whose teeth had been long unwhetted by appetite, when he heard a carriage pull up before the little gate of his garden. In a moment Nucingen's secretary presented Contenson, whom he had found at length in a café near Sainte-Pélagie, where the agent was breakfasting on the fee given him by an imprisoned debtor, who had met with the consideration that expects payment. Contenson, you notice, was a true poem, a Parisian poem. From his appearance, at first sight you would have thought that Beaumarchais' Figaro, Molière's Mascarille, Marivaux's Frontin and Dancourt's Lafleur, those great personifications of daring knavery, of ruse at bay, of stratagem rising ever anew from the ashes of its failure, were commonplace in comparison with this colossus of craft and degradation. In Paris a type is no longer a man, but a spectacle, and represents no longer a single moment of life, but a life-time—many life-times. Bake thrice in an oven a bust of plaster; it will become a sort of base imitation of Florentine bronze. Just so the fires of countless misfortunes, the necessities of awful situations, had bronzed Contenson's head as if the heat of an oven had thrice dried the sweat upon his visage. The deep wrinkles could never again grow smooth; they formed life-long folds with whitened furrows. His yellow face was all wrinkles. The skull, shaped like Voltaire's, was rigid as a death's-head, and had it not been for a few wisps of hair behind, it would scarcely have looked human. Beneath an imperturbable brow his Chinese eyes were set with expressionless gaze, eyes such as those displayed in the window of a tea-shop; unreal eyes simulating life, but the look of which never alters. The nose flat, as that of death's-head, set destiny at defiance, and the mouth, pinched like a miser's, was always open, though it remained discreet as the slit of a letter-box. Calm as a savage, his hands tanned by the sun, Contenson, little, wizened and thin, as he was, still possessed the careless attitude of a Diogenes, who never bends in protestations of respect. And what commentaries on his life and character were written in his dress for those who can read what dress means? First of all, what trousers! Typical bailiff's trousers, black and shiny as the stuff known as "voile," of which they make lawyers' gowns; a waistcoat of embroidered camel's-hair bought at the Temple; a coat of rusty black; the whole costume brushed till it was almost clean, and adorned by a gold-plated watch-chain. Contenson exposed to view a plaited shirt of yellow cambric which formed a background for a false diamond pin. His velvet collar looked as if it were made of iron, and over it protruded folds of deep red flesh. His silk hat shone like satin, but the lining could have furnished enough grease to make two tallow candles, had some grocer bought it and boiled it down. This is but to catalogue the accessories, and it would be more to the purpose to paint the exorbitant pretension that Contenson was able to impart to them. There was a jaunty air about the coat collar and in the fresh polish of the boots with cracked soles to which no French expression can do justice. And to reconcile a mixture of such diverse articles of apparel a clever man would have gathered from Contenson's appearance that had he been a criminal and not an informer, his threadbare clothes would no longer have brought a smile to the lips of a beholder, but would have made him thrill with horror. Judging from his costume an observer would have said, "He is a villain, he drinks, he gambles, he has vices; but he does not get drunk, he does not cheat, he is neither a thief nor a murderer." And certainly Contenson was indefinable until the word "spy" came to mind. This man had worked at as many unknown trades as there are trades which are known. The subtle smile of his pale lips, the restlessness of his pale green eyes, the slightly comic turn of his flat nose showed that he did not want for wit. He had a face of tin and the soul within was like the face. The movements of his features were rather grimaces conceded to civility than the expression of inner feelings. Had he been less ludicrous, he would have been terrifying. Contenson, one of the most curious products of the scum which floats in the seething caldron of Paris, where everything is in ferment, prided himself above all on being a philosopher. He said without bitterness:

"I have great talents; but they count for nothing. I might as well be an idiot."

And he condemned himself, instead of accusing men. Try to find many spies who have not more rancor than Contenson!

"Circumstances are against us," he would say to his superiors; "we might be crystals, but we are grains of sand, nothing more."

His cynicism of dress had a purpose; he cared no more for his city dress than an actor cares for his costume; he excelled in disguises and transformations; he might have given lessons to Frédérick Le Maître for he could turn fop when it served his turn. Long ago in his youth he had been brought up among an ill-conditioned set of small tradespeople.

He displayed a deep antipathy to the detective police, for, under the Empire, he had been in Fouché's employ, and he looked upon his former master as a great man. Since the suppression of the ministry of police, for want of better employment, he enlisted as a detective for business arrests, but his well-known capacity and sharpness made him a valued tool, and the secret chiefs of the political police had kept his name on their lists. Contenson, as well as his mates, was only among the chorus of a drama, while the greater parts were played by their chiefs whenever there was political business afoot.

"Go avay," said Nucingen, dismissing his secretary with a wave of his hand.

"Why is it that this man lives in a fine house and I in a tenement?" said Contenson to himself. "He has tricked his creditors three times; he has stolen; I have never taken a penny that didn't belong to me, and I am cleverer than he."

"Gondanzon, mein frient," said the baron, "you haf tone me out of ein tausent franc note."

"My mistress owed everybody and the devil to boot."

"You haf ein misdress?" cried Nucingen, looking at Contenson with admiration mixed with envy.

"I am only sixty-six," answered Contenson, with the manner of a man whom vice had kept young as a fatal example.

"Ant vat toes she to?"

"She helps me," replied Contenson; "when a thief is loved by an honest woman, either she becomes a thief or he an honest man. For my part, I am still a detective."

"You still haf need of money?"

"Still," returned Contenson, smiling, "my natural condition is to want it as yours is to gain it; we can come to an understanding: you bring it to me and I will look after the spending. You will be the well and I the bucket."

"To you care to earn ein note of fife huntret vrancs?"

"That's a natural question! Do you think I'm

a fool? Do you offer it to help to repair Fortune's injustice toward me?"

"Py no means; I att it to ze fife huntret vrancs zat you haf taken; zat makes veefteen huntret vrancs zat I gif you altogether."

"So you give me the thousand francs I have already and you add five hundred francs more."

"Zat is gorrect!" said Nucingen, nodding his head.

"That only makes five hundred francs," remarked Contenson imperturbably.

"To give!" replied the baron.

"To take; well, what would M. le Baron buy with this?"

"I haf heard zat zere was in Baris ein man capaple of discofering ze vooman I luf ant zat you know his attress. Ein masder of sbying."

"It is true."

"Very vell; gif me ze attress ant you haf ze fife huntret vrancs."

"Where are they?" answered Contenson quickly.

"Here," ejaculated the baron, drawing a banknote from his pocket.

"All right, give them to me," said Contenson, stretching out his hand.

"Vait a pit. Let us go to see ze man ant you shall haf ze money, vor you might zell me blenty of attresses ad zat brice."

Contenson began to laugh.

"I suppose that you have the right to think it of me," he said with an air of self-reproof, "the lower our fortunes sink the greater need for honesty. But, look you, baron; make it six hundred francs and I will give you good advice."

"Gif it, and debend on my chenerosidy."

"I take the risk," said Contenson, "but I am playing high. In my line of business, you know, we move underground. You say: 'Forward, march!' You are rich and you believe that everything yields to money. Money counts for something, it is true. But with money, as the two or three able men of my profession always say, you can do no more than buy men. And there are other things that a man does not think of which cannot be bought. He cannot keep chance in his pay. Besides a clever detective doesn't go to work in that way. Will you get into a cab with me? There is one outside. Luck is as apt to be with you as against you."

"Druly?" said the baron.

"Lord, yes, sir. It was a horseshoe picked up in the street that led the prefect of the police to discover the infernal machine. So then if we should go in a cab, this evening after nightfall, to see M. de Saint Germain he would not care to see you come into his house any more than you would care to be seen going there."

"Zat is drue," said the baron.

"Oh, he's the cleverest of the clever, the famous Corentin's lieutenant, Fouché's right arm; some call him his natural son born at the time that Fouché was a priest; but it's all nonsense I suppose. Fouché made as good a priest as a prefect. But you will never stir that man, mind you, with less than ten bank notes of a thousand francs.—Remember that. —But your business will be done and well done. Nothing seen or heard as they say. I shall see that M. de Saint-Germain is notified and he will assign you some meeting-place where you may be alone with no danger of eavesdroppers, for he runs a risk in bringing the police system to bear upon private affairs. But what can you expect? He's a fearless man, the king of men, and a man who has undergone the most bitter persecution for having saved France, like me and all the others who have saved her."

"Well, zen, you vill write me ze hour zat zhall make me habby," said the baron, smiling at his vulgar jest.

"Aren't you going to grease the wheels, baron?" asked Contenson with an accent at once humble and menacing.

"Chan," called the baron to his gardener, "ged dwendy vrancs vrom Chorches and pring zem do me."

"If you have no other directions than those you have already given, I am doubtful whether even such a master can help you, sir."

"I haf odders," answered the baron superciliously.

"I have the honor of taking my leave, sir," said Contenson as he pocketed the twenty-franc piece; "I shall have the honor of telling Georges where our friend will be this evening, for respectable detectives never write."

"Id's ott how zharp zese fellows are," thought the baron, "zeir drade is like pusiness."

After leaving the baron Contenson walked placidly from the Rue Saint-Lazare to the Rue Saint-Honoré and up this street as far as the Café David. There he glanced through the window and perceived an old man known throughout the district under the name of Père Canquoëlle.

*

The Café David, situated in the Rue de la Monnaie, at the corner of the Rue Saint-Honoré, enjoyed during the first thirty years of this century, a considerable reputation confined to the quarter called "des Bourdonnais." It was the resort of old and retired merchants or of rich contractors still in business, men like Camusot, Lebas, Pillerault, and Popinot; a few landlords like little Père Molineux, and now and then old Père Guillaume came thither from the Rue du Colombier. The company discussed politics, but with discretion, for the spirit of the place was liberal. They chatted over the gossip of the neighborhood, for men must laugh at their fellows.

Like all cafés of the time, the Café David had its original character, and this was Père Canquoëlle, who had been in the habit of going thither ever since 1811, and seemed in such perfect harmony with the honest folk collected about him that nobody hesitated to talk politics in his presence. Occasionally this worthy, whose simplicity was the laughing-stock of his friends, disappeared for a month or two at a time; but his absences that were always attributed to his age or infirmities surprised no one, for he was believed to have passed his sixtieth year as long ago as 1811.

"What has become of Père Canquoëlle?" people asked of the bar-maid.

"I suspect," she would answer, "that some day we shall see his death in the Petites Affiches."

Père Canquoëlle's pronunciation was a perpetual certificate of his origin. He invariably said, "*une estatue, espécialle, le peuble,*" and "*Ture*" for Turk. His name was derived from a small estate called "Les Canquoëlles" (a provincial word for cockchafers), situated in the department of Vaucluse, of which he was a native. People had come to address him as "Canquoëlle," instead of "des Canquoëlles," but he did not take it amiss, as he felt that the nobility had died in 1793. Besides, the property of Les Canquoëlles did not belong to him, for he was the younger son of a younger branch. Nowadays Père Canquoëlle's costume would look odd in the extreme, but from 1811 to 1820 it aroused nobody's surprise. The old man wore shoes with steel buckles cut like crystals, silk stockings with circular stripes alternately blue and white, and silk breeches with oval buckles to match those on his shoes. An embroidered white waistcoat, an old coat of greenish brown with brass buttons, and a shirt with a plaited frill completed his attire. In the middle of the frill glittered a gold medallion, under the glass of which there was a tiny temple made of hair, one of those charming bits of sentiment that assure a man just as a scare-crow frightens a sparrow. Most men are startled and reassured by nothings just as animals are. Père Canquoëlle's breeches were supported by a buckle which, after the fashion of the last century, held them tightly in place above the abdomen. From his girdle hung two parallel chains, composed of several steel strands, each ending in a bunch of watch-charms. His white cravat was fastened behind by means of a small gold buckle. His head, that was powdered snow-white, was capped as late as 1816 by the municipal cocked hat, that was also worn by M. Try, President of the Tribunal. This hat, so dear to the old man, Père Canquoëlle had recently replaced (the worthy gentleman thought that he owed the sacrifice to the time) by that insignificant round hat against which nobody has dared to rebel. A small queue tightly braided and tied with a ribbon, traced on the back of his coat a semi-circular mark, the grease of which was half hidden by a fine sprinkling of powder. In contemplating the distinctive feature of his face, a red nose that was covered with protuberances and fit to figure in a dish of truffles, you would have attributed a pliant, dull and good-natured disposition to this most respectable old man, who was in reality sharp as a steel trap, and, like everybody who frequented the Café David, you would have been duped by him. Nobody there had scrutinized the intelligent forehead, the sardonic mouth and cold eyes of this old man who was glutted with vices and calm as a Vitellius whose imperial belly was, so to speak, palingenetically resuscitated in him. In 1816 a young traveling salesman, Gaudissart by name, a frequenter of the Café David, got drunk between eleven o'clock and midnight in company with an officer on half pay. He was so imprudent as to speak of a serious conspiracy brewing against the Bourbons, that was then ready to burst. The café was empty except for Père Canquoëlle, who was apparently asleep, two sleeping waiters and the bar-maid. Within twenty-four hours Gaudissart was arrested, and the plot discovered. Two men perished on the scaffold. Neither Gaudissart nor anybody else ever suspected worthy Père Canquoëlle of having divulged the secret. The waiters were dismissed, every precaution was adopted for a year, and Père Canquoëlle who appeared to share the general fear inspired by the police, even spoke of deserting the Café David altogether, so great was his detestation of the whole system.

Contenson entered the café, ordered a small glass of brandy and never turned his eyes toward Père Canquoëlle, who was busily reading the newspapers; when he had swallowed the brandy he pulled out the baron's gold piece and summoned the waiter by making three sharp taps on the table. The bar-maid and the waiter examined the gold piece with a solicitude that was scarcely complimentary to Contenson; but their distrust was excused by the universal astonishment caused by the detective's appearance.

"Is the gold the fruit of theft or murder?"

Such was the thought of several intelligent and clear-sighted persons who glanced at Contenson beneath their spectacles while they pretended to be absorbed in their papers. Contenson, who noticed everything and was astonished at nothing, wiped his lips disdainfully with a silk handkerchief in which there were not more than three darns, received his change and placed all his coppers in his fob, the once white lining of which was now black as the material of the trousers, not leaving a single penny for the waiter.

"There's a gallows bird," remarked Père Canquoëlle to M. Pillerault, his neighbor.

"Pooh!" answered M. Camusot, who alone had shown no astonishment, aloud to the whole café. "It's Contenson, the right hand of Louchard, our detective. Perhaps the fools have some one to arrest in this neighborhood."

Fifteen minutes later, the worthy M. Canquoëlle rose, took his umbrella and went quietly out.

It is necessary to explain that a subtle man was hidden beneath the exterior of Père Canquoëlle in the same way that Vautrin was concealed in the priest Carlos. This man was named Peyrade. He was born in the south, at Canquoëlles, the only estate of his family, which had formerly been highly respectable. In fact, he belonged to the younger branch of the house of Peyrade, an old but poor family of Comtat, which was still in possession of the small landed property of Peyrade. The youngest of seven children, he had come on foot to Paris, at the age of seventeen, with two six-franc pieces in his pocket, in 1772, actuated by the vices of a passionate temperament and by that brutal desire for wealth which attracts so many Southerners to the capital when they have learned that the family coffers can never furnish them with money to satisfy their appetites. We shall tell the story of Peyrade's youth by saying that in 1782 he was the secret adviser and even the hero of the general lieutenancy of the police, and was especially esteemed by M. Lenoir and M. d'Albert, the last two of the lieutenant generals. The Revolution had no police; it needed none. Espionage, common enough then, went by the name of citizenship. The Directory, a slightly more regular government than that of the Committee of Public Safety, was obliged to create a police, and the first consul completed the system by establishing the prefecture of police and the ministry of general police. Peyrade, the traditional man, organized the staff in conjunction with an associate named Corentin, a much stronger person than the Peyrade of that time, although younger, and one whose genius was confined to the subterranean pathways of the police system. In 1808 Peyrade's great services were rewarded by his nomination to the high position of commissary general of the police at Antwerp. In Napoleon's scheme this prefecture of police was equivalent to the ministry of police that was deputed to take charge of Holland. After the campaign of 1809 Peyrade was relieved of his command at Antwerp by order of the Emperor's cabinet, conveyed post haste to Paris between two gendarmes and thrown into "La Force." Two months later he emerged from prison, after a warning from his friend Corentin, and after undergoing three general examinations of six hours each before the prefect of the police. Did Peyrade owe his disgrace to the marvellous activity with which he had seconded Fouché in the defence of the coasts of France, when they were attacked by what was called at the time the expedition of Walcheren in which the Duc d'Otrante displayed a capacity that alarmed the Emperor? Fouché suspected it at the time; but nowadays when everybody knows what was passing at that crisis in the council of the ministry convoked by Cambacérès, it is a certainty. Thunderstruck by the news of England's counter-thrust to Napoleon's Boulogne expedition, and surprised in the absence of their master, who was then intrenched in the island of Lobau where all Europe thought him lost, the ministers knew not what measures to adopt. The general opinion was to dispatch a courier to the Emperor; but Fouché alone dared frame the plan which he proceeded to put into execution.

"Do as you wish," Cambacérès said to him, "as I value my head—I am going to dispatch a message to the Emperor."

It is well known what an absurd pretext the Emperor employed, on his return, in the presence of the whole council of state to disgrace and punish his minister for having saved France without him. On that day the Emperor doubled the dislike of the two remaining great statesmen of the Revolution, who might perhaps have saved him in 1813, the Prince de Talleyrand and the Duc d'Otrante. In order to sweep Peyrade out of the way, the common charge of extortion was alleged against him, as he had countenanced contraband trade, by sharing certain profits with rich merchants. This was certainly rough treatment for a man who deserved the baton of a commissariat general for his distinguished services. As he had grown old amidst the cares of business, he was in possession of the secrets of every government since the year 1775, the date of his appointment to the general-lieutenancy of police. The Emperor, who thought himself strong enough to create men of what stamp he pleased, was deaf to the representations which were made to him as time went on, in favor of a man who was considered one of the most trustworthy, shrewd and clever among those nameless guardians of the state's welfare. He thought it possible to replace Peyrade by Contenson; but Contenson was at that time profitably engaged by Corentin. Peyrade was injured all the more deeply because, libertine and glutton as he was, he found himself that women regarded him as they would a pastry cook who delights in dainties.

Vicious habits had become ingrafted into his very nature; he could no longer exist without high living and gambling, in short, he led the life of an unostentatious nobleman; a life which fascinates any man of marked ability who has learned to require extravagant pleasures. Besides, until this time he had spent money freely and had squandered it without ever being called to account; for the government was never rigorously exact with him or with his friend Corentin. His cynical wit led him to love his position for another reason: he was a philosopher. Last of all, a detective, on whatever round of the police ladder he may be, can never, any more than a galley-slave, return to a profession that men call liberal or honest. Once stamped, once registered, detectives and condemned criminals have assumed, like deacons of the church, a character which can never be washed away. The spy is numbered among those beings on whom society brands a fatal destiny. To his misfortune Peyrade had taken a great fancy to a pretty girl, a child he knew to be his own by a celebrated actress, to whom he had done a great service, and who, in return, had shown him gratitude for three months. Peyrade had brought back his daughter with him from Antwerp and was now living in Paris without other resource than an annual allowance of twelve hundred francs accorded by the prefecture of police to the old pupil of Lenoir. He lodged in the Rue des Moineaux, on the fourth story, in a little suite of five rooms leased at two hundred and fifty francs a year.

If there is any man who feels the use and the tenderness of friendship, is it not the moral leper, whom the rabble call a spy, the people a detective, and the administration an agent? Thus Peyrade and Corentin were friends like Orestes and Pylades. Peyrade had moulded Corentin as Vien moulded David; but the pupil soon surpassed his master. They had been associates in more than one enterprise (see *A Dark Affair*). Peyrade, delighted at having discovered Corentin's merit, had launched him on his career, by preparing for him an easy triumph. He compelled his pupil to make use of a mistress who despised him, as a bait to entrap another man (see *The Chouans*). At the time Corentin was scarcely twenty-five! Corentin, long one of those generals of whom the minister of police is the constable, had retained, under the Duc de Rovigo, the prominent position he had held beneath the Duc d'Otrante. But, then, the same system prevailed among the general as among the detective police. In every affair of importance, the three, four, or five cleverest agents were summoned to a conference.

The minister, forewarned of some scheme or conspiracy through any medium, would say to one of his police colonels:

"What do you need to arrive at such a result?"

Corentin or Contenson would answer after ripe examination:

"Twenty, thirty, forty thousand francs."

Then when the order to march was once given the exclusive choice of men and methods was left to the judgment of Corentin or of the appointed agent. The detective police, with the famous Vidocq, followed this same system in the discovery of crimes.

The political as well as the detective police chose its men principally among the recognized, registered, habitual agents, who compose, as it were, the rank and file of this secret force, so necessary to a government, despite the rhetoric of philanthropists or of petty moralists.

The excessive confidence placed in two or three generals of the type of Peyrade and Corentin allowed them the privilege of employing unknown persons, although it was still their duty to consult the minister in cases of importance. The experience and the cunning of Peyrade, however, were indispensable to Corentin, who, during the tempest of 1810, made use of his old friend, consulted him in every matter and contributed largely to his support. Corentin found means to bestow about one thousand francs a month on Peyrade. On his side, Peyrade was of immense service to Corentin. In 1816, on the occasion of the disclosure of the plot in which the Bonapartist Gaudissart was concerned, Corentin tried to have Peyrade readmitted to the general police force of the kingdom; but an unknown influence defeated Peyrade. This was the reason: in their anxiety to become indispensable, Peyrade, Corentin and Contenson, at the instigation of the Duc d'Otrante, had organized, on behalf of Louis XVIII., a counter-police in which the agents of the original force were employed. Louis XVIII. died possessed of secrets which will remain secrets for most carefully informed historians. The struggle between the general police of the kingdom and the counter-police of the king engendered several horrible conflicts, the secret of which has been guarded by more than one scaffold. This is neither the time nor the place to enter into the details of this subject, for the *Scenes of Parisian Life* are not the *Scenes of Political Life;* it is enough to show what were the means of existence of the man whom the whole Café David called Père Canquoëlle, and what the threads were that bound him to the mysterious and terrible power of the police.

From 1817 to 1822, Corentin, Contenson, Peyrade and their agents were often employed to keep watch over the minister himself. This explains the minister's motives in refusing to employ Peyrade and Contenson; for, unknown to them, Corentin had awakened the minister's suspicions about them, in order to use his friend for his own purposes when he thought his reinstatement impossible. The ministry at this time trusted Corentin, and charged him to keep a careful eye on Peyrade; a step which amused Louis XVIII. Corentin and Peyrade were then masters of the situation. Contenson had long been attached to Peyrade and was still faithful to him. He was admitted into the detective service by the orders of Corentin and of Peyrade. Thus with the mad enthusiasm inspired by a profession that is lovingly followed, these two generals delighted to place their cleverest soldiers in the spots where they could pick up most evidence. Besides, Contenson's vices and depraved habits, which had sunk him lower than his two companions, required so much money that he needed extra work. Contenson, without committing any indiscretion, had told Louchard that he knew the only man who could satisfy the Baron de Nucingen; and Peyrade was actually the single agent who could usurp the power of the police for the benefit of an individual, without fear of punishment. At Louis XVIII.'s death, Peyrade lost not only all his importance but even the income of his position as his Majesty's attendant detective. Believing himself indispensable, he had continued to lead his accustomed life. Women, good cheer and the Foreigners' Club had swept away every attempt at economy. Peyrade, like all men that are well fitted for vice, enjoyed an iron constitution. But, from 1826 to 1829, when he was almost seventy-four, to use his own expression, he felt the brake on the wheels. Year by year Peyrade saw his fortunes dwindling. He witnessed the decay of the police, and found to his dismay that the government of Charles X. was abandoning its good traditions. Session after session the chamber clipped the appropriations on which the existence of the police depended, for its members disliked this method of government and were determined to correct the morals of the institution.

"They want to do the cooking in white gloves," remarked Peyrade to Corentin.

Corentin and Peyrade foresaw 1830 in 1822. They knew the secret hatred that Louis XVIII. bore to his successor, a hatred which explained his unceremonious behavior towards the younger branch, and without which his reign and policy would be an insoluble enigma.

Peyrade's love for his natural daughter had increased as he grew older. For her sake he had assumed his civilian's disguise, for he wished to marry his Lydie to an honest man. For the past three years he had desired to install himself either at the prefecture of the police or at the central office of the general police of the kingdom, in some open and avowed position. He had succeeded in inventing such a position, the need of which, he told Corentin, was sure to be felt sooner or later. His plan was to create at the prefecture of the police a so-called bureau of evidence, which should serve as an intermediary between the police of Paris proper, the detective police and the police of the kingdom, in order to improve the general administration of all these scattered forces. Peyrade, alone, in spite of his age, and with fifty-five years of experience, would be the link which should join these three separate systems—would be, in a word, the keeper of records to whom politics and justice should turn for light in obscure cases. By these means Peyrade hoped that, with the aid of Corentin, he might be able to pick up a dowry and a husband for his little Lydie. Corentin had already mentioned this scheme to the Director-General of the police of the kingdom; but the Director-General, a Southerner, without speaking of Peyrade, thought it necessary that the proposition should originate with the prefecture.

At the moment when Contenson had tapped the table thrice with his goldpiece, a signal which meant "I have something to say to you," the senior detective was intent upon this problem, "By what person, through what interest can I stir the Prefect of police?" Yet all the time he looked a very imbecile as he pored over his Courrier Français.

"Our poor Fouché!" thought he as he moved slowly along the Rue Saint Honoré. "That great man is dead! Our go-betweens with Louis XVIII. are in disgrace. Then, as Corentin was saying to me yesterday, nowadays nobody believes in the activity or intelligence of a man who is past seventy. Ah! why did I ever learn to dine at Véry, to drink expensive wine, to sing *la Mère Godichon,* and to gamble when I have the money? To make his way a man must have something more than natural wit, as Corentin said; he must have the wit to behave himself. Dear old M. Lenoir was a wise prophet of my lot when he told me I should never come to anything after the Collier business, when he learned that I had not stayed in my hiding-place in Oliva's room."

*

Since the venerable Père Canquoëlle—he was called Père Canquoëlle at home—had remained in the Rue des Moineaux, fourth floor, you may be sure that he had discovered in the situation of his lodgings peculiarities that were favorable to the exercise of his terrible employment. Built at the corner of the Rue Saint-Roch his house was bounded on one side by an empty lot. As it was divided into halves by means of the staircase, on every story there were two rooms completely isolated. These two rooms faced the Rue Saint Roch. Above the fourth story rose the attics, one of which served for a kitchen while the other was the apartment of Père Canquoëlle's only servant, a Flemish woman named Katt, who had been Lydie's nurse. Père Canquoëlle had chosen as his bed-room the first of the two detached chambers; the second he used as his office. A thick partition formed the back wall of this room. The window which looked out on the Rue des Moineaux faced a blank corner wall. As the whole length of Peyrade's bed-chamber separated the two friends from the stairway, they feared neither eye nor ear when they discussed their business in the office, that was so perfectly adapted to their horrid trade. By way of precaution, Peyrade had laid a straw mattress, a coarse drugget and a very thick carpet in the servant's bed-room, under the pretext of adding to the comfort of his daughter's nurse. More than this, he had blocked up the chimney, and made use of a stove, the pipe of which, laid through the exterior wall, abutted on the Rue Saint-Roch Finally he had stretched several carpets on the floor in order to prevent the slightest noise from penetrating to the lodgers on the lower story. An adept in the art of spying, he sounded partition wall, ceiling and floor once every week, and examined them like a man trying to kill some annoying insect. This absolute security from witnesses or listeners recommended the place to Corentin as a council chamber, whenever he did not conduct his deliberations at home. Corentin's dwelling was known only to the Director-General of the police of the kingdom and to Peyrade; he received there persons despatched as emissaries on occasions of grave importance, by either ministry or court; but no agent, no inferior police officer was admitted. He transacted the business of his trade in Peyrade's quarters. In this commonplace-looking room, schemes were laid and resolutions formed which could tell strange tales and curious dramas if the walls had tongues. There, from 1816 to 1826, vast interests were discussed, and discoveries made of the germs of events destined to weigh heavily upon France, and there, ever since 1819, Peyrade and Corentin, as far-seeing as Bellart the Attorney-General, and far better informed than he, had whispered to each other:

"If Louis XVIII. refuses to strike such and such a

blow to rid himself of some prince or other, it is a sure sign that he detests his brother. Is it his purpose to bequeath him a revolution?"

Peyrade's door was ornamented with a slate, on which at times there appeared cabalistic signs and figures written in chalk. This infernal algebra offered an easy solution to the initiated.

Opposite to the meanly furnished apartment of Peyrade, Lydie's suite was composed of an antechamber, a small parlor, a bed-chamber and a dressing-room. Lydie's door, like that of Peyrade's, was constructed of a plate of sheet-iron, a third of an inch thick, wedged between two strong oaken boards and armed with locks and a system of hinges that rendered it as difficult to force as prison doors. Thus although the house had a narrow entrance, was built over a shop, and was even without the protection of a janitor, Lydie lived there with nothing to fear. The dining-room, the small parlor and the bed-chamber, with boxes of flowers in every window, were dusted with Flemish cleanliness and luxuriously furnished.

The Flemish nurse had never left Lydie, whom she called her daughter. Both of them went to church with a regularity which gave an excellent opinion of Père Canquoëlle to the royalist grocer who was established in the house at the corner of the Rue des Moineaux and the Rue Neuve-Saint-Roch, and whose family, cook and salesmen occupied the ground floor and the first story. The proprietor lived on the second floor, and the third had been leased for the past twenty years by a lapidary. Every lodger was given a key to the back door. The grocer's wife was quite content to receive letters and packages addressed to these three peaceable households, especially as the grocery shop was provided with a letter-box. Without these details neither strangers nor those familiar with Paris would have been able to understand the mystery and calm, the unconstraint and security which made this house exceptional in Paris. From midnight till morning, Père Canquoëlle could spin the web of any plot, and receive spies, ministers, women and girls without arousing anybody's suspicion. Peyrade, of whom the Flemish nurse had said to the grocer's cook, "He would not hurt a fly!" passed for the best of men. He spared no expense for his daughter Lydie, who had had Schmucke for a music-teacher, and was enough of a musician to compose. She had learned to wash in sepia, and to paint in two styles of water-color.

Every Sunday Peyrade dined with his daughter. On that day the worthy man was a father, pure and simple. Although no devotee, Lydie was religious; she received the sacrament at Easter, and confessed every month. Now and then, however, she allowed herself the slight diversion of the theatre, and in fair weather she walked in the gardens of the Tuileries. These were all her pleasures, for she led the most secluded of lives. Lydie adored her father and was completely ignorant of his sinister powers and mysterious business. No ungratified wish had troubled the pure life of this pure girl. Slender, beautiful as her mother, gifted with a heavenly voice and a finely moulded face, set off by the blonde curls of her lovely hair, she looked like one of those angels more mystical than real, which some early painters have sketched on the backgrounds of their "Holy Families." The glance of her blue eyes seemed to cast a ray from heaven upon whomsoever she deigned to look. Her dress, simple, maidenly and unexaggerated in style, carried with it charming suggestions of respectable home life. Imagine an old Satan, the father of an angel, drinking in new life from her holy companionship, and you will have an idea of Peyrade and his daughter. Had anybody stained his diamond, the father would have invented for his destruction one of those horrid pitfalls which under the Restoration entrapped so many poor wretches and brought them to the scaffold. Ten thousand francs a year supplied the wants of Lydie and of Katt, whom she called her nurse.

As he turned down the Rue des Moineaux Peyrade perceived Contenson; he passed him, went up to his apartment, and then, hearing the step of his agent on the stair, let him in before the cook had opened the kitchen door. A bell rung at the opening of a latticed door on the third story, warned the lodgers of the third and fourth floors of the approach of any visitor. It is useless to add that after midnight Peyrade wrapped the bell carefully in cotton.

"Why such haste, Philosopher?"

Philosopher was the nickname that Peyrade gave to Contenson, and it was not undeserved by this Epictetus of detectives. The name of Contenson hid, alas! one of the most ancient names of the feudal nobility of Normandy.

"But there's something like ten thousand to be earned."

"What is it? Something political?"

"No, only tomfoolery! The Baron de Nucingen, you know the old licensed robber I mean, is neighing after a woman he caught sight of in the Bois de Vincennes, and have her he must, or he will die of love. They had a consultation of doctors yesterday, so his valet told me. I have already relieved him of a thousand francs under pretence of finding the girl."

And Contenson described the meeting of Nucingen and Esther, adding that the baron had some fresh intelligence of the matter.

"Good," said Peyrade, "we shall find the Dulcinea. Bid the baron drive in a close carriage to the Champs Élysées, Avenue Gabriel, at the corner of the Allée de Marigny."

Peyrade saw Contenson to the stair, and then rapped upon his daughter's door in the way agreed upon between them. He entered radiant. Chance had thrown in his way a means of gaining the place he had so long desired. He threw himself into a deep arm-chair, and after kissing Lydie's forehead, said to her:

"Play me something."

Lydie played him a piece composed by Beethoven for the piano.

"Prettily played, my darling," said he, taking his daughter in his lap. "Do you know that we are twenty-one years old? We must find a husband, for our father is over seventy."

"I am happy here," she answered.

"You love nobody else but me, and I so ugly and so old?" asked Peyrade.

"Whom would you have me love?"

"I am going to dine with you, my pet, tell Katt. I think of taking a house and finding a place for myself and a husband worthy of you, some excellent young man, full of talent, whom you may be proud of some day."

"I have never seen but one man whom I should like to be my husband."

"You have seen one?"

"Yes; near the Tuileries. He passed me with Madame de Sérizy on his arm."

"What is his name?"

"Lucien de Rubempré. I was sitting beneath a lime tree with Katt, not thinking of anything. On one side of me were two ladies, and one of them said, 'There go Madame de Sérizy and the handsome Lucien de Rubempré.' Then I looked at the couple about whom these ladies spoke. 'Ah, my dear,' answered the other, 'some women are very lucky. There is nothing she cannot have, because she was one of the Ronquerolles, and her husband is powerful.' 'But, my dear,' replied the first,

'Lucien costs her dear.' What does that mean, papa?"

"It is the kind of nonsense they talk in society," replied Peyrade to his daughter, with a kindly air. "Perhaps they were alluding to political events."

"Now you have questioned me and I have answered. If you want me to marry, find me a husband who looks like that young man."

"Child!" answered the father, "among men, beauty is not always the sign of worth. Young people endowed with a pleasing exterior meet with no difficulty at the outset of life; they do not use their talents, they are corrupted by the advances which the world makes toward them, and there comes a time when they must pay interest for their gifts! I long to find for you the man whom rich and stupid citizens leave unaided and unprotected."

"What kind of a man is that, father?"

"A man of unrecognized talent. But, my darling girl, I have the means of searching every garret in Paris, and fulfilling your programme by finding for you a man as handsome as the rake whom you describe, only he shall be a man born to glory and to riches, and sure to make his mark in the world. Oh! I never thought of it before, but I must have an army of nephews, and among them perhaps I may find one worthy of you. I am going to write, or ask somebody to write, to Provence."

Strange to say, at that very moment, a young man, dying of hunger and exhaustion, traveling afoot from the department of Vaucluse, a nephew of Père Canquoëlle, was entering Paris by the Barrière d'Italie in search of his uncle. In the dreams of the family, to whom their uncle's occupation was unknown, Peyrade offered many hopes: they imagined him come back from the Indies with his millions, and it was in consequence of the romances told about him at their fireside that one of his grand-nephews, named Théodose, had undertaken a voyage of circumnavigation in quest of his mythical uncle.

After he had tasted the joys of fatherhood for several hours, Peyrade washed and dyed his hair (for the powder had been a disguise) and, muffled in a heavy greatcoat of blue cloth buttoned up to the chin, a black cape over his shoulders, thick-soled boots on his feet and a special passport in his pocket, walked with slow steps along the Avenue Gabriel, where Contenson, in the dress of an old market-woman, met him in front of the gardens of the Élysée-Bourbon.

"Monsieur de Saint-Germain," said Contenson, giving his former chief his old nickname, "you have helped me to make five hundred francs; but I have been standing there just to tell you that that cursed baron, before giving them to me, went to get some advice at *the house* (the prefecture)."

"I shall need you, no doubt," answered Peyrade. "See our numbers, 7, 10 and 21: we can make use of those men, and no man shall be the wiser, neither they, nor the police, nor the prefecture."

Contenson walked away and took his stand near

the carriage in which M. de Nucingen was awaiting Peyrade.

"I am M. de Saint-Germain," said Peyrade to the baron, as he stepped up to the carriage window.

"Very vell; ged een mit me," replied the baron, who immediately ordered the coachman to drive on toward the Arc de Triomphe de l'Étoile.

"You have been to the prefecture, baron? That was scarcely fair. May I ask what you said to the Prefect and what answers he gave you?" inquired Peyrade.

"Bevore gifing fife hundert vrancs to ein knave like Gondenzon, I vished to know veder he hat earnet zem. I zimply zaid to ze Brevect of ze bolice zat I dezired to embloy an achent of ze name of Beyrate, aproad, on a telicate mission, ant asked eef I could haf an unleemited convidance een him. Ze brevect anzered me zat you vere ein of ze gleverest and mosd honesd men in ze pizness. Zat ees ze whole avvair."

"Will you tell me your story, sir, now that you have been intrusted with my real name?"

When the baron had gabbled through a long and elaborate explanation in his frightful Polish Jew accent and had described his meeting with Esther, the cry of the groom who was stationed behind the carriage, and his own futile efforts, he concluded by telling what had passed on the previous evening in his drawing-room; the smile that had escaped Lucien de Rubempré, the suspicions of Bianchon and some of the dandies present relative to an acquaintance between the lovely stranger and the young men.

"Listen, sir: first of all, you must give me ten thousand francs on account, for expenses; for your very life is at stake in this matter; and since your life is a perfect manufactory for turning out business, we must leave no stone unturned to unearth this woman for you. Ah! you are caught this time."

"Yez, gaught."

"If I need more I shall tell you so, baron; trust to me," answered Peyrade. "I am not, as you think, a detective. In 1807 I was Commissioner-General of the police at Antwerp, and now that Louis XVIII. is dead, I can confide to you that for seven years I directed his counter-police system. I am not to be haggled with. You see, baron, I cannot estimate the selling price of the consciences I must buy, before I have examined a job with care. You need feel no anxiety; I shall succeed. Don't imagine that you can satisfy me with any sum whatever; I wish something quite different for my reward."

"Eef only eet ees not ein kingtom," said the baron.

"It is less than nothing for you."

"Gondent."

"You know the Kellers?"

"Very vell inteet."

"François Keller is the son-in-law of the Count de Gondreville; and the Count de Gondreville dined at your table yesterday with his son-in-law."

"How ze tefil to you know?" cried the baron. "Chorches must haf tolt you, for he ees alvays blapping."

Peyrade laughed. The baron noticed his amusement and conceived strange suspicions of his servant.

"The Count de Gondreville is in a position to obtain an appointment in the prefecture of the police which I desire, and concerning which the prefect must receive a memorandum within forty-eight hours," said Peyrade. "Demand the appointment for me. Stir up the Count de Gondreville's interest, keep it at the boiling point, and thus you can repay the service I shall do you. I ask nothing more than your word, for if you fail it, sooner or later you shall curse the day that you were born."

"I gif you my sacret vort to to my pest."

"If I only did my best for you, it would not be enough."

"Very vell, I vill to eet, honesdly."

"Honestly. That is all I ask for," said Peyrade, "and honesty is the only novel gift that we can make each other."

"Honesdly," reiterated the baron. "Vere to you vish me to led you oud?"

"At the foot of the Bridge of Louis XVI."

"At ze pridge of ze Jamber," said the baron to his footman, who came to the carriage window.

"I zhall haf ze unknown, zen!" thought the baron as he drove away.

"Strange," thought Peyrade as he walked back

to the Palais Royal, where he proposed to attempt to treble the ten thousand francs and make a dowry for Lydie; "it is my duty to scrutinize the private life of the young man whose look alone has bewitched my daughter. He must have the eye to catch a woman," he added to himself, making use of one of those individual expressions which he had invented for his private use. His own observations and those of Corentin were summed up in sentences which, though they violated the rules of language, were not deficient in energy and picturesqueness.

*

The Baron de Nucingen entered his house a changed man. He amazed his household and his wife; his color was good and his expression animated. He was in high spirits.

"Stockholders beware!" said Du Tillet to Rastignac. They were taking tea after the opera in Delphine de Nucingen's little parlor.

"Yez," answered the baron, smiling, for he had overheard his friend's pleasantry, "I lonc to to pizness."

"So you have seen your enchantress?" inquired Madame de Nucingen.

"No," replied he; "I have only hobe of finding her."

"Does a man ever love his wife like this?" exclaimed Madame de Nucingen, feeling a pang of jealousy or pretending that she did.

"When she is yours," said Du Tillet to the baron, "you must ask us to sup with her, for I am most curious to examine the woman who has been able to make you so young again."

"Zhe ees ein masderbiece of greation," answered the old banker.

"He will walk into a trap like a child," whispered Rastignac in Delphine's ear.

"Pooh! he makes money enough to—"

"To lose a little, doesn't he?" suggested Du Tillet, interrupting his hostess.

The baron was pacing up and down the floor as if his legs needed stretching.

"Now's the time to induce him to pay your latest debts," whispered Rastignac to Madame de Nucingen.

At this very moment Carlos, who had been in the Rue Taitbout giving his final directions to Europe, the principal actress in a comedy invented to deceive the Baron de Nucingen, was walking confidently away. He was accompanied as far as the boulevard by Lucien, who felt a secret fear at seeing his demoniacal companion disguised so perfectly that he himself could recognize only his voice.

"Where in the devil did you find a woman more beautiful than Esther?" he demanded of his corrupter.

"She was not to be found in Paris, my boy; complexions like that are not made in France."

"I haven't yet recovered from my amazement. The Callipygian Venus has not such a figure. A man would damn himself for her. But where did you find her?"

"She's the handsomest woman in London. Drunk with gin, she murdered her lover in a fit of jealousy. The lover was a wretch whom the London police is well rid of, and they have sent the woman to Paris for a time in order to let the affair blow over. The wench has been well educated. She's a parson's

daughter, and speaks French as if it were her
mother tongue. She knows not and must never
know the part she is playing here. She has been
told that if she pleased you she could squeeze millions out of you, but that you were jealous as a
tiger, and she has been given the same programme
of life that Esther had."

"What if Nucingen should like her better than
Esther?"

"Ah! you've come to that, have you?" cried
Carlos. "To-day you are in terror because the
very thing that frightened you yesterday has not
come to pass. You have no reason to fear. This
girl is fair and pale, with blue eyes; she's a complete contrast to the lovely Jewess, and nothing less
than Esther's eyes can fire a man as worn out with
dissipation as Nucingen. How the devil could you
hide a scare-crow? When this doll has played her
part I shall send her, under trusty guidance, to
Rome or to Madrid, where she will have many
lovers."

"Since we have her with us for so brief a space,"
said Lucien, "I shall return to her."

"Go, my son; amuse yourself. To-morrow you
will have one day more. I myself am waiting for
someone whom I have charged to find out what is
going on at the Baron de Nucingen's."

"Whom?"

"The mistress of his valet; for we must never be
ignorant of what is passing in the enemy's camp."

At midnight Paccard, Esther's groom, met Carlos

on the Pont des Arts, the spot best suited in all Paris for a secret conference. While they talked the groom kept watch on one side, while his master scanned the opposite direction.

"The baron went to the prefecture of the police this morning between four and five," said the groom, "and to-night he boasted that they had promised to find for him the woman whom he had seen in the Bois de Vincennes."

"We shall be watched," said Carlos, "but by whom?"

"He has employed Louchard, the commercial detective, before."

"That's nonsense," replied Carlos. "We have only the police night-watch and the detective police to fear; the moment that they halt it is our turn to march."

"There's one thing more."

"What?"

"The prison comrades. Yesterday I saw Lapouraille. He has cooled off a family and he has ten thousand five-franc pieces in gold!"

"They will catch him," said Jacques Collin; "that's the murder in the Rue Boucher."

"What are the orders?" asked Paccard, with a deferential air, as if he were a marshal receiving the commands of Louis XVIII.

"You will go out every evening at ten o'clock," answered the counterfeit priest, "and ride at a smart pace in the Bois de Vincennes, in the Bois de Meudon, and in the Bois de Ville d'Avray. If

anybody watches you or follows you, don't disappoint
him. Be obliging, communicative, and don't refuse
a bribe. You must talk about the jealousy of
Rubempré, who is madly in love with *madame*, and
who above all things wants it kept secret that she
is his mistress."

"Enough. Shall I go armed?"

"Never!" answered Carlos sharply. "What good
would a weapon do you? It would only get you into
trouble. Whatever happens don't use your hunt-
ing-knife. As you can break the legs of the strongest
man by the blow I taught you, and can fight against
three sergeants and be certain of stretching two of
them on the ground before they can fire at you,
what are you afraid of? Haven't you your staff?"

"You are right," said the groom.

Paccard, known as *Vielle-Garde, Fameux-Lapin,*
and *Bon-là,* was a man with sinews of whipcord and
arms of steel. He wore Italian whiskers, hair like
an artist's, and a beard like a sapper's. His face
was pale and impassive as that of Contenson; he
succeeded in concealing the fierceness of his character, and was blessed with the appearance of a
drum-major, that disarmed all suspicion. A criminal
escaped from Poissy or from Melun could not have
such serious self-conceit nor such unshaken faith in
his own merit. The Giafar of the Haroun-al-Ras-
chid of the galleys, he displayed toward his master
the same affectionate admiration that Peyrade had
for Corentin. A tall man, he was excessively long-
legged, with a narrow chest and none too much flesh

on his bones; he walked on his two long pike-staves with a sedate step. His right foot never advanced until his right eye had scanned all exterior appearances with the calm rapidity peculiar to the robber and the spy. The left eye imitated the right.

A step, and then a look! Spare, agile, ready for anything at any hour, had it not been for his insidious enemy, drink, Paccard, as Jacques declared, would have been quite perfect, so admirably was he equipped with the talents indispensable to a man at war with society. The master, however, had eventually persuaded the slave to compromise and never touch a drop before evening. On his return home Paccard gulped down the liquid gold that he poured out in a succession of small glasses from a big-bellied stone bottle that had come from Dantzic.

"I shall keep my eyes open," he said, donning his magnificent hat and plume after bowing to the man whom he called *his confessor.*

We have described the train of events by which Jacques Collin, Peyrade, and Corentin, each so strong in his own sphere, came to fight upon the same field and employ their genius in a struggle where every contestant battled for his passions or for his interests. It was a silent but a terrible combat, wherein were lavished talent, hatred, wrath, marches, countermarches, stratagem, and strength enough to build a fortune. Profound mystery enveloped the men and means employed by Peyrade, who was seconded by his friend Corentin in a piece of work that seemed to them child's play. History is silent on this subject as it is silent on the true causes of many revolutions.

The result was as follows:

Five days after the interview between Nucingen and Peyrade in the Champs Élysées, one morning a man of some fifty years, dressed in a blue suit with a somewhat distinguished figure, a face of the leaden whiteness that public life gives to diplomates, and an air that might have marked a minister of state, stepped out of a handsome carriage and tossed the reins to his groom. A lackey who was sitting on a bench in the peristyle rose respectfully to open the splendid plate-glass door, and the stranger asked whether the Baron de Nucingen was visible.

"Your name, sir?" inquired the servant.

"Tell the baron that I come from the Avenue Gabriel," answered Corentin. "If there are any visitors be careful not to say that name aloud, or you would be turned out of doors."

A minute later the servant returned and conducted Corentin through several inner rooms to the baron's private office.

Corentin exchanged an impenetrable look for a look of the same nature from the banker, and both bowed politely.

"Baron," began Corentin, "I come to you in Peyrade's name."

"Gut," ejaculated the baron, clicking the bolts of the two doors.

"M. de Rubempré's mistress lives in the Rue Taitbout in the old apartment of Mademoiselle de

Bellefeuille, the ex-mistress of M. de Granville, the attorney-general."

"Och, zo near me," exclaimed the baron; "how sdrange!"

"I readily understood how you fell in love with such a magnificent woman; she was a delight to look upon. Lucien is so jealous of the girl that he has forbidden her to show herself; and he is dearly loved in return, since, during the four years that she has succeeded to Mademoiselle Bellefeuille's apartment and calling, not even the neighbors, the janitor, nor the lodgers in the house have caught sight of her. The child never goes out except at night; when she goes, the curtains of the carriage windows are drawn, and she herself is veiled. It is not merely for motives of jealousy that Lucien conceals the woman; he must marry Clotilde de Grandlieu, and he is at present the favored lover of Madame de Sérizy. Naturally, he clings to the mistress who advances his fortunes, and to his betrothed. So you are master of the situation, for Lucien will sacrifice his pleasure to his interests and his vanity. You are rich; this will probably be your last love; be generous. You can gain your end through the waiting-maid. Give the soubrette some ten thousand francs; she will hide you in her mistress's room, and for you the game is well worth the candle."

No figure of rhetoric can describe the short, jerky, concise utterance of Corentin. The baron noticed it, and could not help showing astonishment, an expression that he had long since banished from his impassive features.

"I come to ask you for five thousand francs on behalf of my friend Peyrade, who has lost five of your bank notes,—a small mishap," continued Corentin, in his most commanding tone. "Peyrade knows his Paris too well to spend money on advertising, and he has counted upon you. But this is not the most important thing," continued Corentin, in a voice that seemed to deprive his demand for money of all serious import. "If you would avoid sorrow in your old age secure for Peyrade the place he requested; you can secure it for him with ease. The Director-General of the police of the kingdom received a note yesterday on this subject. All that is necessary is that Gondreville address the Prefect of the police. So, simply tell Malin, Count de Gondreville, that it is to help one of those persons who succeeded in ridding him of the De Simeuse gentlemen, and he will take the proper steps at once."

"Here, zir," said the baron, producing five notes of a thousand francs each, and presenting them to Corentin.

"The waiting-maid has an intimate friend, Paccard, a big groom, who lives in the Rue de Provence at a coachmaker's, and lets himself as an outrider to anyone who cares to cut a princely figure. You can reach Madame Van Bogseck's waiting-maid through Paccard. He's a big Piedmontese dunce, overfond of his vermouth."

This confidence so daintily tossed to the baron, in the fashion of a postscriptum, was evidently the compensation for five thousand francs. The baron sought to divine the character of Corentin, who, as he was intelligent enough to perceive, was not a common spy, but rather a director of spies. He no more succeeded, however, in reading Corentin than an archæologist succeeds in reading an inscription, three-fourths of the letters of which are wanting.

"Vat ees ze name of ze vaiting-mait?" he demanded.

"Eugénie," replied Corentin, who bowed to the baron and went out.

Transported with delight the Baron de Nucingen abandoned his desk and his business and went up to his room, happy as a young man of twenty who enjoys in perspective his first rendezvous with his first mistress. The baron took all the thousand-franc notes from his private safe—fifty-five thousand francs, a sum which might have purchased the happiness of a village—and placed them in his coat pocket. The prodigality of millionaires can only be compared to their greed for gain. The instant a Crœsus feels a caprice or a passion, money is no longer anything to him; it is harder for him to acquire a caprice than gold. Enjoyment is a rare blessing in a life of satiety, crammed with the excitement born of vast speculations, that has long ceased to stir his bloodless heart. For example: One of the richest capitalists in Paris, a man of well-known eccentricity, meets one day on the boulevard an excessively pretty little working-girl, accompanied by her mother; this grisette was leaning on the arm of a young man who was dubiously dressed and strode along with a vulgar swagger; at the first glance the millionaire falls in love with the young girl. He follows her to her house; he enters; she tells him of her life—a medley of balls at the Mabille, of days without bread, of play-going and toil; he grows interested and leaves five notes of a thousand francs beneath a five-franc piece. Shameful generosity! Next morning a famous upholsterer, Braschon, comes to take the grisette's orders, furnishes a suite of her choice, and lavishes twenty thousand francs upon it. The working-girl feeds on fantastic hopes. She buys gowns for her mother suited to their altered fortunes; she flatters herself that she will be able to place her former lover in the office of some insurance company. She waits— one, two days; then one, two weeks. She thinks that she is bound to be faithful, and runs into debt. The capitalist, called away to Holland, had forgotten the working-girl; he never once entered the paradise where he had placed her, and she fell thence as low as a woman can fall in Paris. Nucingen did not gamble, Nucingen was no patron of the arts, Nucingen had no imagination; so he was driven headlong into his passion for Esther, with a blind ardor that entered into the calculations of Carlos Herrera.

After breakfast the baron summoned Georges, his valet, and bade him go to the Rue Taitbout to request

Mademoiselle Eugénie, the waiting-maid of Madame Van Bogseck, to come to his office, in order to discuss an affair of importance.

"You vill vait vor her ant gonduct her to mein room, ant keep delling her zat her vortune ees mate."

Georges had endless trouble in persuading Europe-Eugénie to come. Her mistress, she told him, never permitted her to go out; she might lose her position, etc., etc. Nor did Georges fail to sing his own praises in the baron's ear, and received ten louis for his pains.

"If madame goes out to-night without her," said Georges to his master, whose eyes shone like carbuncles, "she will come about ten o'clock."

"Gut! You vill gome at nine o'clock to tress me ant aranche my hair, for I vish to look my very pest. I tink zat I zhall abbear bevore my miss-dress or elze money ees not money."

Between twelve and one o'clock the baron dyed his hair and his whiskers. He took a bath before dinner, and at nine o'clock he perfumed himself and attired himself like a bridegroom in his finest clothes. Apprised of this metamorphosis, Madame de Nucingen could not resist the pleasure of seeing her husband.

"Heavens! how ridiculous you look!" cried she. "At least put on a black satin cravat instead of that white one which makes your whiskers appear still stiffer than they are; and besides, you are the image of an old fogy of the time of the Empire, and give yourself the air of a parliamentary councillor. Take off those diamond studs; they are worth a hundred thousand francs apiece. That monkey would beg them of you and you could never refuse her. It is as well to put them in my ears as to offer them to such a woman as she."

The poor banker, who was struck by the justice of his wife's remarks, reluctantly obeyed her.

"Reteeculous! Reteeculous! I haf nefer zaid zat you vere reteeculous ven you dressed youzelf een you pest vor ze zake of your leetle Mennesir de Rasdignac."

"I trust that you have never found me ridiculous. Am I the woman to make such solecisms in my dress? Look, turn round! Button your coat up within two buttons of the top like the Duc de Maufrigneuse, and, above all, look young."

"Sir," said Georges, "here is Mademoiselle Eugénie."

"Atieu, matame," exclaimed the banker.

He accompanied his wife beyond the limits of their respective apartments to make sure that she could not listen to the conference.

He returned, and taking Europe by the hand with a kind of ironical respect, he ushered her into his room.

"Vell, my tear, you are very lugky, vor you zerve ze luffliest vooman een ze uniferse. Your vordune ees mate eff you vill sbeak een my pehalf ant pe een my eenterests."

"I wouldn't do it for ten thousand francs," cried

Europe. "You know, baron, that before all else I am an honest girl."

"Yez, I exbect to pay vell vor honesdy. Zat ees vat ve gall in pizness guriosidy."

"But that's not all," said Europe; "if you shouldn't please my mistress, and that's possible, she will get angry; I shall be discharged—and my place is worth a thousand francs a year."

"Ze gabidal of ein tausent francs ees dventy tausent francs; ant eef I zhould gif zem to you you vould loose notting."

"Ho, ho! if that's the tune you are playing, old boy," exclaimed Europe, "things are quite changed. Where are they?"

"Here," replied the baron, displaying the bank notes one by one.

Each bank note seemed to strike a flash of fire from Europe's eyes, that revealed the cupidity he had anticipated.

"You pay for the place, but honesty,—conscience?" said Europe, raising her crafty face and darting a serio-comic glance at the baron.

"Gonzience ees gheaper zan ze blace; put led us make eet fife tausent vrancs more," said he, adding five thousand-franc notes.

"No, twenty thousand francs for the conscience, and five thousand for the place if I lose it."

"As you blease," he replied, adding the five bills. "Put, to earn zem you must gonzeal me een your misdress' chamber turing ze night, ven zhe ees alone."

"If you will swear to me never to tell who it was that let you in, I consent. But I warn you of one thing: my mistress is strong as a Turk; she loves M. de Rubempré madly, and if you were to give her a million in bank notes she would not be unfaithful to him. It sounds preposterous, but when she loves she's worse than if she were virtuous. When she goes to walk in the woods with my master he rarely sleeps in the house. She has gone there to-night, so I can hide you in my room. If she comes back alone I shall come and get you. You will stay in the parlor; I shall not close the door of her bed-room, and the rest—Lord! the rest is for you to do."

"I vill gif you ze tventy-five tausent vrancs in ze barlor. Eet iz gif ant take."

"Ah!" said Europe, "you are no more suspicious than that? Excuse a little—"

"You vill haf jances enough to throddle me; ve zhall begome agguainted virst."

"All right. Be in the Rue Taitbout at midnight; but take with you thirty thousand francs at the least. A maid's honesty, like a cab, is much dearer after midnight."

"Eet vould pe more brutent to gif you ein jecque on ze pank."

"No, no," said Europe; "bank notes, or the game's up."

At one o'clock in the morning the Baron de Nucingen, concealed in the garret where Europe slept, was a prey to all the disquietudes of a man in search of adventure. He scarcely breathed, his blood seemed to boil down to his very toes, and his head was bursting like an overheated steam engine.

"I zvear I enchoyed more than ein hundert tausent growns' vorth," said he afterward, when he described his situation to Du Tillet.

He listened for the slightest noises of the street, and at two in the morning caught the sound of his mistress' carriage rolling back from the boulevard. When the front door turned on its hinges his silk waistcoat rose and fell in time with the beating of his heart; he was really to see the heavenly glowing face of Esther! The step on the stairway and the slipping sound of a curtain on its rod pierced his heart. The expectation of this supreme moment excited him more than if his fortune had been at stake.

"Ah!" moaned he to himself. "Zis ees to liff. Ah! eet ees to liff too much; I zhall be capable of notting."

"My mistress is alone; come down," said Europe as she appeared. "Above all, don't make a noise, you fat elephant."

"Vat elephand," repeated he smiling, and treading as if red-hot bars of iron were beneath his feet. Europe led the way, with a candle in her hand.

"Here; gount zem," said the baron, handing the bank notes to Europe as soon as he reached the parlor.

Europe took the thirty notes with a serious air and went out, closing the door upon the banker. Nucingen walked straight to the bed-room. The handsome Englishwoman was standing there, saying, "Is that you, Lucien?"

"No, mein luff—" answered Nucingen, who did not finish his sentence.

He stood stupefied at the sight of a woman who was the perfect opposite of Esther—fair hair instead of the dark tresses which he had seen, weakness instead of the strength he had marveled at, a soft Breton night where the sun of Arabia had glittered!

"Ah, where did you come from? what's your name? what do you want?" cried the Englishwoman, pulling the bell rope, though the bells made no answer.

"I haf sduffed ze pells mit gotton. Put to not pe afraid. I am going avay," said he. "Tirty tausent vrancs gone to ze togs. You are reely ze misdress of Mennesir Licien te Ripembré?"

"Something of the kind, my boy," replied the Englishwoman, who spoke French with ease. "Put who may you pe, bray?" she added, mimicking Nucingen's accent.

"A most delutet man," he answered piteously.

"Delutet in drying to gatch a bretty vooman?" she asked jokingly.

"Bermid me to zend you do-morro ein zet of chewels to remint you of ze Paron te Nichenguenne."

"I ton't know heem," said she, shaking with laughter; "but the set of jewels will be welcome, my fat housebreaker."

"You to know heem. Atieu, montame. You are

feet for a king; put I am only ein poor panker of zixty years ant more, ant you haf zhowed me how bowerful ees ze wooman whom I luff, vor your gott-like peaudy has not mate me to vorget her."

"Put zis luffly greature, as you gall me—" responded the Englishwoman.

"Ees not zo luffly as zhe who virst insbiret me."

"You were speaking of *dirdy* thousand francs—to whom did you give them?"

"To your rasgally vaiting-mait."

The woman called; Europe was not far distant.

"Oh!" shrieked Europe, "a man in your room, and a man who isn't my master. Horrors!"

"Did he give you thirty thousand francs to induce you to let him in?"

"No, madame; both of us together are not worth as much."

And Europe began to scream, "Help, thieves!" so violently that the terrified banker rushed to the door. Europe pushed him down the staircase.

"You fat rascal," she cried, "you would denounce me to my mistress! Thieves, robbers!"

The infatuated but despairing baron succeeded without further molestation in gaining his carriage which was waiting on the boulevard. He no longer knew in what detective to trust.

"Perhaps madame would like to rob me of my profits?" exclaimed Europe, returning toward her mistress like a Fury.

"I don't know French customs," said the Englishwoman.

"I have but a single word to say to my master and out madame goes to-morrow," replied Europe insolently.

"Zat gursed vaiting-mait," said the baron to Georges, who naturally asked whether his master were satisfied, "has ropped me of dirdy tausent vrancs, put it ees all my misdake, my very gread misdake."

"So your get-up counted for nothing. The deuce! I don't advise you to perfume yourself again for nothing."

"Chorches, I tie of tesbair. Mein heart ees gold, gold as ize, Esder, mein frient!"

Georges was always his master's friend in a great crisis.

*

Two days after this scene, which Europe had described far more amusingly than it can be written, for she enlivened it with her mimicry, Carlos was breakfasting alone with Lucien.

"Neither the police nor anybody else must pry into our business," said he in a low tone, as he borrowed Lucien's cigar to light his own. "It is unwholesome. I have discovered a daring but sure method of keeping our baron and his agents quiet. You will go to see Madame de Sérizy and make yourself attractive. You will tell her in conversation that out of kindness to Rastignac, who has long since wearied of Madame de Nucingen, you consent to play the part of a cloak to conceal his mistress. M. de Nucingen, wildly in love with the woman whom Rastignac has secreted—this will amuse her—has taken into his head to set the police on your track; thus though you are perfectly innocent of the sins of your compatriot, your interests at the Grandlieus are in danger of being compromised. You will then implore the countess to lend you the influence of her husband, who is a minister of state, to obtain admission to the prefecture of the police. Once there make your complaint to the prefect, but make it prudently, like a man who is soon to enter the vast machine of government and to become one of its most important adjuncts. You will discuss the police system as a statesman would; you will praise everything, the prefect included. The most perfect machines will sputter and splash their oil. Don't pretend to be more angry than necessary. You are not to appear displeased with the prefect; but make him promise to oversee his people, and ask him not to act harshly toward anyone. The more suave and gentlemanlike you are the more fiercely will the prefect proceed against his agents. We shall then be left in peace and we can bring back Esther, who must be crying like the does in the forest."

At that time the Prefect was an old magistrate. Old magistrates are too young as Prefects of the police. Imbued with law, perfectly at home in all legal questions, their hand is slow to use those arbitrary means that are often enough required by some crisis in which action of the prefecture should resemble that of a fireman ordered to put out a fire. In the presence of the vice-president of the Council of State the Prefect enumerated more defects in the police system than actually existed; he deplored the abuses, and did not forget the visit that the Baron de Nucingen had paid him, and the information he had demanded concerning Peyrade. The Prefect promised to check the individual excesses of his agents and at the same time thanked Lucien for addressing himself directly to him, swore secrecy, and looked as though he understood the whole intrigue. Fine-sounding phrases concerning private liberty and the inviolability of the home were exchanged between the minister of state and the Prefect, to whom M. de Sérizy observed that though the highest interests of the realm occasionally demanded secret acts that were contrary to law, yet crime began when these methods of state were applied to individual interests.

The next day, as Peyrade was on his way to his dear Café David where he was accustomed to watch the bourgeois with the delight of an artist gazing at budding flowers, a gendarme in civilian's dress accosted him in the street.

"I was on my way to your house," he whispered; "I have orders to conduct you to the prefecture."

Peyrade hailed a cab and got in, together with the gendarme, without making the slightest remonstrance.

The Prefect of the police treated Peyrade as if he had been the lowest turnkey of a prison. As he talked he walked up and down the pathway of the small garden of the prefecture of the police, which at that time extended the length of the Quai des Orfévres.

"It is not without reason, sir, that since 1809 you have been outside of the administration. Don't you know to what you expose us and to what you expose yourself?"

The reprimand ended in a thunder-clap. The Prefect announced harshly to poor Peyrade that not only was his annual allowance to be stopped, but that in addition he himself would be the object of special supervision. The old man received this blow with perfect calmness. Nothing is more immovable or impassive than a ruined man. Peyrade had lost all his money at the gambling table. Lydie's father had counted on his appointment and found himself left without other resource than the alms of his friend Corentin.

"I have been Prefect of the police; I admit that you are entirely right," said the old man quietly to the official, who, enveloped in his judicial majesty, shrugged his shoulders significantly. "But permit me, without any attempt to excuse myself, to explain to you that you don't understand me at all," Peyrade went on, casting a searching glance at the Prefect. "Your words are either too severe for the old Commissary-General of the police of Holland or too gentle for a mere detective. Only," added Peyrade, after a pause as he perceived that the prefect kept silence, "remember what I have had the honor to tell you, sir, though I shall not interfere with *your police* nor importune you with my own justification, you will have occasion to see that in this matter somebody is deceived; at this moment it is your servant, later you will say, 'It was I.'"

And he bowed to the Prefect who stood apparently wrapt in thought, trying to conceal his astonishment. He returned to his lodging, his body weak and trembling, mad with rage against the Baron de Nucingen. The fat financier alone could have betrayed a secret concentrated within the brains of

Contenson, Peyrade and Corentin. The old detective accused the banker of trying to avoid payment when once his end was attained. A single interview had sufficed for him to divine the sagacity of the most sagacious of bankers.

"He makes everybody bankrupt, even ourselves; but I shall have my revenge," said Peyrade to himself. "I have never asked a favor of Corentin, but I shall ask him now to help me revenge myself on this fat-witted old money-bags. Damned baron! You shall know the stuff I am made of when you wake up some morning to find your daughter dishonored. But does he love his daughter?"

The evening of this catastrophe, which destroyed the old man's last hopes, he seemed ten years older. Talking with his friend Corentin he mingled his lamentations with tears that fell at the thought of the sad future which he must bequeath to his daughter, who was his idol, his pearl, his thank-offering to God.

"We shall follow up this matter," said Corentin; "but first of all we must know whether it was the baron who betrayed you. Were we wise in relying on Gondreville? That old rascal owes us too great a grudge not to attempt our ruin; besides I must have his son-in-law Keller watched. He's an ass in politics, and quite capable of dipping into some conspiracy to overturn the elder branch for the benefit of the younger. To-morrow I shall know what is going on at Nucingen's house, whether he has seen his mistress, and who it is that has tightened the curb so suddenly. Don't lose heart. The Prefect will not keep his position long. The times are ripe for revolutions, and revolutions are our sunshine."

A singular whistle resounded in the street.

"It's Contenson," said Peyrade, as he placed a light in the window, "and it's some private business of mine."

The next instant the faithful Contenson appeared before these two gnomes of the police whom he revered as genii.

"What brings you?" demanded Corentin.

"Something new. I was coming out of 113 where I had lost everything; whom should I see in the galleries? Georges! He has been discharged by the baron under suspicion of being a spy."

"So this is the effect of a smile that escaped me," said Peyrade.

"Oh, the disasters that I have seen caused by smiles!" exclaimed Corentin.

"Without counting those caused by horse-whipping," added Peyrade, alluding to the Simeuse affair. (See *A Dark Affair.*) "But tell us, Contenson, what happened?"

"This is what happened," replied Contenson: "I loosened Georges' tongue, and paid for liquor of every color under heaven till he was drunk; I myself must be like an alembic. Our baron went to the Rue Taitbout, redolent of perfume. He found there the handsome woman whom you know. But the whole thing was a farce. The Englishwoman was not his *luffly sdranger*, and he had spent thirty thousand francs to bribe the chambermaid; sheer madness! He thinks himself a great man because he accomplishes little things with an enormous capital; invert the phrase and you have the problem that the man of genius solves. The baron came back in a pitiful plight. The following day Georges played the saint and said to his master: 'Why do you employ these gallows-birds? If you would trust to me I should find his unknown love, for the description you have given me is quite enough; I will ransack all Paris.' 'Go,' said the baron, 'I will pay you well!' Georges confided all this to me, mingled with the most ridiculous details. It never rains but it pours, and the next day the baron received an anonymous letter which read somewhat like this: 'M. de Nucingen is dying of love for an unknown woman,—he has already thrown a great deal of money to the dogs; if he consent to stand at midnight at the further end of the Pont de Neuilly, to get into a carriage behind which he will see the mounted groom of the Bois de Vincennes, and to allow his eyes to be bandaged, he will see her whom he loves. Since his wealth may lead him to suspect the purity of the intentions of those who act thus, M. le Baron may be accompanied by his faithful Georges. There will be no one else in the carriage.' The baron goes there with Georges, without telling him anything. Both of them allow their eyes to be blindfolded and their heads to be swathed in veils. The baron recognizes the groom. Two hours later the carriage, which jogged along like a coach of Louis XVIII.—God bless his soul! He was a king who knew what the police ought to be—stopped in the midst of a wood. The baron, whose eyes have been unbandaged, sees his quest in a carriage that has also stopped, then she disappears instantly; and the carriage—at the same pace as Louis XVIII.'s coach—takes him back to the Pont de Neuilly, where he finds his own conveyance. They had put in Georges' hands a small note which read thus: 'How many thousand-franc notes has M. le Baron spent in order to meet his love?' Georges gave the note to his master, and the baron, believing Georgés is in league with me or with you, Monsieur Peyrade, to fleece his master, discharged him promptly. The dolt of a banker! He never should have sent Georges away until he *hat med mit zuczess.*"

"Did Georges see the woman?" inquired Corentin.

"Yes," replied Contenson.

"Well," cried Peyrade, "what does she look like?"

"Oh!" answered Contenson, "he said but a word,—a sun of beauty!"

"We're tricked by rogues cleverer than we!" exclaimed Peyrade. "The scoundrels want to sell the woman to the baron for all that she'll bring."

"Ja, mein herr!" replied Contenson; "when I learned that your ears were boxed at the prefecture, I persuaded Georges to blab."

"I should like to know who bowled me over,"

remarked Peyrade; "we should see whose blade was the longer."

"We must play at eavesdropping," said Contenson.

"He's right," said Peyrade; "we must slip into the crannies to listen and wait—"

"That's the method to study," exclaimed Corentin. "Just at present I've nothing to do. Be very cautious, Peyrade; we must always be obedient to the Prefect."

"M. de Nucingen is a good subject to bleed," observed Contenson. "He has too many thousand-franc bank notes in his veins."

"Lydie's dowry was in it!" whispered Peyrade in Corentin's ear.

"Come, Contenson, we must be going. We'll leave our father to sleep. Fare—well; to—morrow!"

"What an odd bit of business our friend was aiming at," said Contenson to Corentin on the doorstep. "What! to marry his daughter with the price of— Ha! Ha! It might make the theme for a charming play—a moral one, too, called *The Maiden's Dower.*"

"Ah! How you are made, you people, and what ears you have!" said Corentin to Contenson. "Surely mother nature provides all her species with the qualities necessary to the services she expects of them! Society is but a second nature!"

"What you say is very philosophic," replied Contenson; "a professor would develop it into a system!"

"Keep yourself informed of everything that goes

on at M. de Nucingen's in connection with the fair unknown," continued Corentin with a smile, as he walked along the street in company with the detective; "in a general way, I mean; don't use too much finesse about it."

"We can watch and see whether the chimneys smoke," said Contenson.

"A man like the baron can't be a successful lover without having it known," continued Corentin. "Besides, men are our cards; we must never let them trick us."

"The deuce! That would be like the criminal at the scaffold amusing himself by cutting the executioner's throat," exclaimed Contenson.

"Your little joke is always ready," answered Corentin, with a faint smile that scarcely wrinkled his plaster masque.

The affair was of immense importance apart from its results. If the baron had not betrayed Peyrade, who could have taken the trouble to interview the Prefect of the police? For Corentin it involved the possible discovery of traitors among his men. He went to bed musing upon the same question which agitated Peyrade.

"Who made the complaint to the Prefect? To whom can this woman belong?"

Thus each side in perfect ignorance of the other, Jacques Collin, Peyrade and Corentin, drew nearer and nearer together; while poor Esther, Nucingen and Lucien were fated to be swept into a struggle that was already begun, and was destined to assume terrible proportions in consequence of the vanity peculiar to police officials.

Thanks to Europe's ability the most menacing portion of the sixty thousand francs of debt weighing upon Lucien and Esther was cancelled. The confidence of the creditors was not even shaken. For a moment Lucien and his corrupter could pause for breath, like hunted beasts lapping a little water on the border of some marsh; they could continue to skirt the edge of the precipice along which the strong man led his weak disciple to the gallows or to success.

"To-day," said Carlos to his slave, "we stake all for all; but luckily the cards are marked and the gamesters children."

For some time in obedience to his terrible mentor Lucien devoted himself to Madame de Sérizy. He was never to be suspected of having a kept mistress; and besides, from the delight of being loved, from the allurements of a worldly life he borrowed strength to shake off his besetting cares. He followed Mademoiselle Clotilde de Grandlieu's directions and never saw her except in the Bois or in the Champs Elysées.

On the day following Esther's imprisonment in the keeper's lodge, the enigmatical and terrible being of whom she stood so much in awe came to ask her to sign three blank papers that were stamped, and moreover bore the hazardous words: "Accepted for sixty thousand francs," on the first; "accepted for one hundred and twenty thousand francs," on the second; "accepted for one hundred and twenty thousand francs," on the third. In all, three hundred thousand francs of acceptances. By writing "good for," you make an ordinary note. The word "accepted" constitutes a bill of exchange and subjects you to arrest, and renders the imprudent signer liable to five years' imprisonment, a penalty almost never inflicted by the police court, but which is applied to old offenders by the court of assizes. The law concerning imprisonment is a remnant of the dark ages, which is not only stupid but has also the rare merit of being useless, for it is never able to reach criminals. (See *Lost Illusions.*)

"It is to save Lucien from embarrassment," said the Spaniard to Esther.

"We are sixty thousand francs in debt, and with these three hundred thousand francs perhaps we may clear ourselves."

Having antedated these bills of exchange by six months, Carlos had them drawn on Esther by a man who was still unfathomed by the police, and whose adventures, in spite of the excitement they had at first aroused, had been quickly forgotten, drowned as they were by the uproar of the mighty symphony of July, 1830.

This young man, one of the most bare-faced of swindlers, son of a bailiff of Boulogne, near Paris, was named Georges-Marie Destourny. The father, forced to sell his office on account of business reverses, left his son, in 1824, without resources of any kind, except for the brilliant education that small tradesmen take a foolish delight in bestowing upon their children. At twenty-three, the young and gifted law student had already abjured his father by writing his name thus on his cards:

GEORGES D'ESTOURNY.

This card lent him a flavor of aristocracy. The young dandy had the audacity to keep a tilbury and groom, and to haunt the clubs. His story needs but a word: he had become the confidant of several women of doubtful character, and did business at the Stock Exchange with their money. At length he came to grief with the police, and was indicted for using cards that were suspiciously lucky. He had accomplices, young men whom he had led astray, devoted slaves, the sharers of his fashion and his credit. Compelled to flee, he neglected to pay his balance at the Exchange. All Paris, the Paris of robbers and clubs, of boulevards and manufactures, was shaken by his double misdemeanor.

In the days of his glory Georges d'Estourny, handsome, kindhearted and generous as a highwayman, had maintained la Torpille for several months. The counterfeit Spaniard based his calculations on Esther's acquaintance with the famous blackleg—an accident peculiar to women of her class.

Georges d'Estourny, whose ambition grew bolder with success, had taken under his protection a man who had come from a remote corner of some department to do business at Paris, and whom the

Liberal party wished to indemnify for the fines he had courageously incurred during the struggle of the press against the government of Charles X., the persecution of which had slackened under the Martignac ministry. It was then that they had pardoned Sieur Cérizet, the responsible newspaper editor, who was surnamed Cérizet the fearless.

But Cérizet, outwardly patronized by the chief Radicals on the Left, engaged in an occupation which combined the qualities of business agency, bank and commission house alike. His position in the business world recalled the servants who advertised in *Petites Affiches*, representing themselves perfectly qualified for everything. Cérizet was delighted to ally himself with Georges d'Estourny, who thenceforth became the director of his steps.

By virtue of the anecdote concerning Ninon, Esther must pass for the faithful guardian of a portion of Georges d'Estourny's fortune. An endorsement in blank, signed "Georges d'Estourny," rendered Carlos Herrera master of the sums he had created. The danger of this forgery ceased the instant that either Mademoiselle Esther, or somebody else on her account, could or should pay.

After he had made careful inquiries in regard to the business house of Cérizet, Carlos understood the man to be an obscure personage determined to make his fortune—but lawfully. Cérizet, who was d'Estourny's real backer, held as security certain important sums then involved in speculations at the Exchange, which gave him what title he had to call himself a "banker." All this takes place at Paris; for though people may despise a man, nobody can despise his money.

Carlos went to see Cérizet with the intention of making use of him for his own purposes; for by good fortune he had come into possession of all the secrets of this worthy associate of d'Estourny.

The courageous Cérizet dwelt on the *entresol* of a house in the rue du Gros-Chenet, and Carlos, who had himself mysteriously announced as an envoy on behalf of Georges d'Estourny, surprised the so-called banker, still pale with alarm at the message. The priest found in the modest office a small man with thin, fair hair, and recognized from Lucien's description the Judas of David Séchard.

"Can we talk here with no danger of being overheard?" said the Spaniard, who had been suddenly metamorphosed into an Englishman with red hair and blue spectacles, neat and proper as a Puritan on his way to meeting.

"And why, sir?" inquired Cérizet. "Who are you?"

"M. William Barker, creditor of M. d'Estourny; but since you desire it I will show you the need of closing your doors. We are well aware, sir, what your relations are with the Petit-Clauds, the Cointets, and the Séchards of Angoulême."

At these words Cérizet sprang to the door, shut it, and dashing to another door which opened into a bed-room, bolted that too; then he said to the stranger, "Not so loud, sir!"

He gazed at the sham Englishman intently as he said, "What do you want of me?"

"Lord bless you, sir!" answered William Barker, "every man for himself in this world. You have in your possession the funds of that fool d'Estourny. Don't be alarmed; I haven't come to demand them of you; but, upon my pressing him, that rascal, who richly deserves the gallows—this is between you and me—has given me these bills, telling me that there was a chance of raising money upon them; and as I don't wish to pursue the business in my own name, he told me that you would not refuse me yours."

Cérizet examined the bills of exchange; then he said, "But he's no longer at Frankfort."

"I know it," answered Barker; "but he might have been there at the date of these drafts.'

"But I don't care to be responsible," said Cérizet.

"I don't ask such a sacrifice of you," replied Barker; "but you can accept them. If you receipt them and the drafts, I'll see to their being cashed."

"I am amazed to see d'Estourny so suspicious of me," observed Cérizet.

"In his position," answered Barker, "you can't blame him for placing his eggs in more than one basket."

"Do you think so?" inquired the petty man of business, handing to the sham Englishman the bills of exchange properly endorsed.

"I know that you keep his funds carefully," said

Barker; "I am sure of it! They are at this moment lying on the gaming-table of the Exchange."

"My fortune depends upon—"

"Upon losing them — ostensibly," interrupted Barker.

"Sir!" cried Cérizet.

"Stop, my dear Monsieur Cérizet," said Barker coldly, interrupting Cérizet, "you have done me a service in expediting this payment. Be so kind as to write me a letter in which you say that you return me these receipted bills on behalf of d'Estourny, and that the prosecuting sheriff is to consider the bearer of the letter as the possessor of these three drafts."

"Will you tell me your names?"

"No name!" replied the English capitalist. "Write: 'The bearer of this letter and of the bills.' You shall be well paid for your services."

"How?" demanded Cérizet.

"To be brief, you remain in France, don't you?"

"Yes, sir."

"Well, Georges d'Estourny will never enter France again."

"Why?"

"To my certain knowledge there are more than five persons who are ready to murder him, and he knows it."

"I am no longer surprised that he writes me for money to embark on a venture in the Indies!" exclaimed Cérizet. "And unfortunately he has obliged me to invest everything in government bonds. We are already in debt to the house of Du Tillet for the balance of sundry accounts. I live from hand to mouth."

"Try to get out of your scrape."

"Ah, if I had only known this sooner!" cried Cérizet. "I have missed my fortune."

"One last word!" said Barker. "Discretion! You are capable of that; but there is another quality less certain—fidelity. We shall meet again, and I shall make your fortune."

After having cast this wretch a hope well calculated to insure his discretion for a long time to come, Carlos, still disguised as Barker, called upon a sheriff, on whom he could count, and charged him to procure a definitive judgment against Esther. "They are sure to pay," said he to the sheriff; "it's an affair of honor; we simply wish to proceed according to rule."

Barker made arrangements that Mademoiselle Esther should be represented before the Tribunal of Commerce by an attorney, in order that judgment might be made after the hearing of both parties. The sheriff, who had orders to act courteously, made a copy of all the acts of procedure, and went in person to attach the furniture in the Rue Taitbout, where he was received by Europe. The sentence of arrest for debt once promulgated, Esther was apparently at the mercy of three hundred and odd thousand francs of indisputable debts.

This step did not call upon Carlos for great inventive power. This vaudeville of false debts is very often played in Paris. There live subordinates to Gobseck and to Gigonnet, who, in consideration of a percentage, lend themselves to this *quibble*, for they make a joke of this scandalous trick. In Paris all things are done in jest, even crimes. Thus they fleece recalcitrant relations or niggardly passions which yield to flagrant necessity or pretended dishonor. Maxime de Trailles had many times made use of this method derived from comedies of the old school. Only Carlos Herrera, who wished to save the honor of his cloth and keep Lucien's reputation untarnished, had recourse to a forgery in which there is no danger, and the practice of which is still rousing the indignation of the law.

In the neighborhood of the Palais Royal there is, I am told, an exchange for these forged bills, where any man may purchase a signature for three francs.

Before entering upon the problem of the three hundred thousand francs destined to stand guard before the bed-chamber, Carlos determined that M. de Nucingen should pay him an extra hundred thousand francs at the start. This was his plan:

By his orders Asia posed before the infatuated baron as an old woman in the confidence of the fair unknown. Even down to the present day painters of manners have brought upon the scene many men in the guise of usurers; but they have forgotten the woman usurer, the Madame la *Resource* of to-day, a singularly curious personage, called by the polite world *the dealer in cast-off finery*. This part was well suited to the fierce Asia, who owned two establishments, one at the Temple, and the other in the Rue Neuve Saint Marc; both managed by women of her own choice.

"You must assume the character of Madame *de Saint Estève*," he said to her.

Herrera wished to see Asia in her disguise. The sham procuress was attired in a gown of flowered damask, remade from the old curtains of some boudoir attached for debt. Over her shoulders was spread one of those old-fashioned cashmere shawls, too threadbare to have a market price, that end their lives on the back of women such as she. She wore a collar of handsome lace, frayed at the edges, and a hideous hat; her feet were encased in Irish-leather shoes, above which protruded her fat legs, clad in black silk open-work stockings.

"See the buckle of my belt!" she exclaimed, pointing to the doubtful jeweled clasp of a girdle which stood out in front of her large vulgar person. "What style! And the whole effect—how charmingly ugly it makes me! Oh! Mame Nourisson has given just the right swagger to my dress."

"Be sweet as honey," said Carlos; "be almost timid, and suspicious as a cat; above all make the baron blush for having made use of the police, without seeming to be in the least afraid of its agents. Finally give him practically to understand in terms more or less clear that you defy all the police in the world to discover the prize. Cover your traces well. When the baron becomes so familiar that you can slap him on the stomach and call him 'fat rascal,' grow insolent and make him step about like a lackey."

After a warning from the procuress that any appeal to the police would destroy his chances of ever seeing her again, Nucingen caught sight of Asia as he made his way afoot to the Bourse. She was sitting mysteriously in a wretched shop in the Rue Nueve Saint Marc. How many times have amorous millionaires trod these muddy byways, and with what delight, the Paris pavements know! Madame de Saint Estève aroused despair, then hope, and played each against the other. The baron desired to learn every particular in regard to his beloved at any price.

During all this time the sheriff was not idle, and advanced all the faster because, in the absence of all opposition on Esther's part, he acted within the time prescribed by law, without a delay of even twenty-four hours.

Lucien, under the escort of his mentor, paid five or six visits to the recluse at Saint Germain. The brutal contriver of these machinations had considered these interviews necessary to prevent Esther's beauty from fading; for her beauty was his capital. No sooner had they emerged from the keeper's lodge than the priest led Lucien and the poor courtesan to a spot beside an untraveled road, where there was a view of Paris, and where they could not be overheard. As the sun rose, all three sat down upon the trunk of a fallen poplar and looked at the landscape, one of the most splendid in the world, embracing the course of the Seine, Montmartre, Paris and Saint Denis.

"My children," said Carlos, "your dream is dreamed. You, my sweet, will never again see Lucien; or, if you should see him, it can only be as if you had known him five years ago for a very few days."

"So death has come to me!" she said, without shedding a single tear.

"It's five years since you were taken ill," replied Herrera. "Call yourself a consumptive and die without bothering us with your lamentations. But you will see that you can live yet, and happily too! Leave us, Lucien; go and cull a few *sonnets*," said he, pointing to a field a few steps away.

Lucien cast upon Esther an imploring glance, a glance peculiar to men at once feeble and covetous, of tender heart and cowardly character. Esther answered by a nod which meant: "I am about to listen to the headsman and learn how I must place my head beneath the axe. I shall have the courage to die well." Her gesture was so lovely, yet so full of horror that the poet wept; Esther sprang to him, clasped him in her arms, drank the tear upon his cheek, and whispered, "Don't be afraid." One of those sentences spoken with the gesture, the glance and the tone of delirium.

Carlos made his explanation concise and without ambiguity. He painted with fiercely characteristic words Lucien's critical situation, his footing in the Grandlieu household, his splendid fortune in case of success, and lastly, the necessity for Esther to sacrifice herself for his glorious future.

"What must I do?" she cried frantically.

"Obey me blindly," replied Carlos, "and of what have you a right to complain? It only rests with you to ensure yourself a happy lot. Like your old friends, Tullia, Florine, Mariette, la Val-Noble, you must become the mistress of a rich man whom you do not love. Our plans once fulfilled, your lover is rich enough to make you happy."

"Happy!" said she, raising her eyes toward heaven.

"You have had four years of paradise. Can you not live on such memories?"

"I shall obey you," she answered, drying the tears in the corners of her eyes. "You needn't feel disturbed for my fate. As you have said, my love is a mortal illness."

"That is not all," continued Carlos; "you must still be beautiful. At twenty-two years and a half, thanks to your good fortune, you are at the highest point of your beauty. Lastly, above all else, become la Torpille once more. Be light-hearted, prodigal, crafty, with no pity for the millionaire whom I shall give to you. Listen to me: the man is a robber of well-lined purses; he has been without compassion for multitudes of people; he has grown fat on the fortunes of the widow and the orphan; you shall be their revenge. Asia will come for you in a cab, and to-night you will be in Paris. To allow the slightest suspicion of your four years' love for

Lucien to escape would be to discharge a pistol into his brain. You will be asked what became of you. You will answer that you have been traveling with an excessively jealous Englishman. You used to have wit enough to carry off a hoax, and you must try to get it back again."

Have you ever seen a dazzling kite, the giant butterfly of childhood, all sparkling with gold, hovering in mid-air? For an instant the children forget the string, a passer-by cuts it, and, in college phrase, gives the meteor its head; the kite falls with terrific rapidity. Such was Esther after listening to Carlos.

HOW MUCH LOVE COSTS OLD MEN

PART SECOND

HOW MUCH LOVE COSTS OLD MEN

*

Almost every day for a week Nucingen made his way to the shop in the Rue Neuve Saint Marc to bargain for the delivery of the woman he loved. There, at one time under the title of Saint Estève, at another under the name of her creature, Madame Nourisson, Asia sat enthroned among a medley of splendid garments, worn to that unpleasing stage in which gowns are no longer gowns, and yet have not become rags. The frame was in harmony with the picture which this woman presented, for shops of this kind are one of the most sinister peculiarities of Paris. Here the stranger sees heaps of old clothes which death has tossed down with his fleshless hand; he hears the death-rattle of a consumptive echoing from the folds of a shawl, and pictures the anguish of poverty hidden under a gown stitched with gold. Fearful struggles between luxury and hunger have left their mark upon the fluttering laces. It is easy to imagine the face of a queen beneath a plumed turban, which from its position vividly recalls the features of its former owner. It is the hideous in the beautiful! The scourge of

Juvenal, wielded by the official hand of the appraiser, scatters the moth-eaten muff and the scarred furs of poor girls who parted with them in their last extremity. It is a heap of faded flowers where, here and there, are still to be seen the roses of yesterday that were worn but for an hour; on its top always crouches the hag Opportunity, the cousin-german of Usury, bald, toothless and eager to sell the shell, so often has she sold the kernel; the gown without the woman, or the woman without the gown! Asia sat there like the turnkey of a prison, like a vulture with bloody beak in a field of dead bodies, exulting in her element; more frightful than the gross horrors about her, which make the passer in the street shudder, as he recognizes with amazement one of his earliest and purest keepsakes hung in a filthy window, behind which is grimacing a true specimen of the retired Saint Estève order. Growing more and more exasperated, and advancing from one ten thousand francs to another, the baron had eventually offered sixty thousand francs to Madame de Saint Estève, who only answered with a grinning refusal that would have made a baboon despair. After a restless night, in which he had recognized the great disorder into which thoughts of Esther had thrown his mind and after realizing unexpected profits at the Stock Exchange, he arrived, one morning, fully decided to pay the hundred thousand francs demanded by Asia; but he was determined to extract a vast quantity of information from her.

"So you've made up your mind, my fat friend?" said Asia, tapping him on the shoulder.

The most ignominious familiarity that exists is the first tax that women of this kind extort from the unchecked passions or the woes that have been confided to them; they never rise to the height of their client, they drag him down to sit side by side with them on their mud-heap. Asia surely was a pattern of obedience to her master.

"I musdt," replied Nucingen.

"And you are not robbed," added Asia. "Women have been sold much dearer than the one you have to pay for now—relatively. There are women *and* women. De Marsay gave sixty thousand francs for the sake of Coralie, who is dead now. The woman you desire cost a hundred thousand francs originally; but for you, you old rascal, it's a mere trifle."

"Put vere ees zhe?"

"Ah! you shall see her. I am like you: give and take. Ah! my friend, your passion has led you into folly. These girls! it's hardly fair. At this moment the princess is what we call a 'beauty of the night.'"

"Eine peaudy!"

"Come, don't be a ninny. She has Louchard on her track; I have lent her fifty thousand francs myself."

"Dventy-vife, you mean!" exclaimed the banker.

"Great heaven! Twenty-five for fifty, of course," replied Asia. "That woman, to do her justice, is honesty itself; she had nothing but herself. She said to me, 'Dear Madame Saint Estève, I am hunted down, you alone can help me; give me twenty thousand francs and I will mortgage my heart to you.' Oh! what a lovely heart she has! None but I know where she is. The slightest indiscretion would cost me my twenty thousand francs. Formerly she used to live in the Rue Taitbout. Before she left, her furniture was attached for the expenses. Those thieves of bailiffs! You know what they are, you, who are a power in the Exchange. But as I was saying, she wasn't stupid; she rented her apartment for two months to an Englishwoman, a beauty, who had that little numskull, Rubempré, for a lover, and he was so jealous that he never allowed her out of the house except at night. But since the furniture is to be sold, the Englishwoman has packed up and left—for, besides, she was much too expensive a luxury for a little tomtit like Lucien."

"You to ein panking pizness," remarked Nucingen.

"Naturally," said Asia, "I lend money to pretty women. It pays me, for I get a double percentage."

Asia was delighted to caricature the part of those women who, however acrid they might be, were yet more insinuating and more gentle than she, and seek to justify their trade by excuses overflowing with the most charitable motives. Asia posed as a woman bereft of her illusions, her five lovers and her children, who, in spite of her experience, allowed

IN THE RUE TAITBOUT: ESTHER'S ARREST

herself to be "robbed" by everybody. From time to time she paraded certificates issued by the Mont de Piété in order to display the luckless chances to which her business was subject. She represented herself as bent beneath a load of debt, and to complete her sorrows she was so unaffectedly hideous that the baron ended by believing her the person she claimed to be.

"Very vell, eef I bay ze hundert tausent vrancs, vere zhall I zee her?" said he with the gesture of a man whose mind is resolved for every sacrifice.

"In that case, my fat friend, you will come this very night in your carriage and stop opposite the Gymnase; that's the way," said Asia. "You will stop at the corner of the Rue Sainte Barbe. I shall be there on the watch; we shall go on together and find my black-haired mortgage. Ah! what lovely hair my mortgage has! Esther has but to take out her comb and she is covered from head to foot. Even if you do know figures, you look stupid enough about everything else. I advise you to stow the girl away, for they will shut her up at Sainte Pélagie without delay the day after they find her, and they are searching now."

"Vould eet pe bossible to puy pack ze trafts?" inquired the incorrigible lynx.

"The sheriff has them, but they can't be secured now. The child was carried away by a foolish infatuation, and ran through a sum which had been entrusted to her charge and which she is now asked to return. She is only twenty-two, and a little foolish still."

"Gut! gut! I vill zee to eet," said Nucingen, assuming his shrewdest air. "Eet ees vell unterzdood zat I zhall pe her brodecdor."

"Ah, you fat rascal! To make her love you is your own affair, and you have means enough to buy a make-believe love that is almost as good as if it were real. I put the princess in your hands; she must follow you, and I shan't worry about the rest. But she is accustomed to luxury and the utmost attention. Ah, my boy, she's everything that a woman should be. Had she not been, do you suppose that I should have lent her twenty thousand francs?"

"Zo zen, eet ees a pargain. Zis efening!"

The baron arrayed himself once more in the bridal attire which he had donned on a former occasion. This time the certainty of success made him double his powders and his perfumes. At nine o'clock he met the detestable woman at the appointed place and took her into his carriage.

"Vere?" demanded the baron.

"Where?" replied Asia. "In the Rue de la Perle at the *Marais*, an address to fit the circumstances. For your pearl is in the mire, but you'll wash her, won't you?"

When they had arrived at the place indicated by this direction, the counterfeit Madame de Saint Estève said to Nucingen with an ugly grin:

"We must go a few steps further afoot. I was not fool enough to give you the right address."

"You rememper eferyting," replied Nucingen.

"It's my trade," she answered.

Asia guided Nucingen to the Rue Barbette, whence he was conducted to the fourth story of a furnished house occupied by an upholsterer of the district. When he beheld, in the midst of a poverty-stricken room, Esther in the dress of a working-woman, toiling over a piece of embroidery, the millionaire grew pale. At the end of a quarter of an hour, during which Asia appeared to be engaged in a whispered conversation with Esther, the young-old man could scarcely speak.

"Montemisselle," he stammered finally to the poor girl, "vill you haf ze gutness to aczept me vor your brotecdor?"

"I must perforce, sir," said Esther, while two big tears slipped from her eyes.

"Ton't gry. I vish to renter you ze habbiest of voomankint. Only luff me ant you vill fint dis ees zo."

"But, my pet, the gentleman is reasonable," said Asia; "he is well aware that he is past sixty, and he will be very indulgent. Look up, my sweet angel, it is a father I have brought you."

"I must tell her so," whispered Asia in the ear of the ill-contented banker. "You can't catch swallows by firing pistols. Come this way," added Asia, as she led Nucingen into the next room. "You remember our little agreement, my cherub?"

Nucingen drew a pocket-book from his coat and counted out the hundred thousand francs, while Carlos, who was hidden in a closet, waited with lively impatience until Asia placed them in his hands.

"Here are a hundred thousand francs that our man has invested in Asia; now we are going to induce him to invest as many in Europe," said Carlos to his accomplice, as they stood on the stairway.

He disappeared after having given his instructions to Asia, who returned to the room where Esther sat, weeping hot tears. Like a criminal condemned to death, the child had spun for herself a romance of hope, and now the fatal hour had struck.

"My dear children," said Asia, "where are you going? For the Baron de Nucingen—"

Esther gazed at the famous banker with a gesture of astonishment, admirably counterfeited.

"Yes, mein chilt, I am ze Paron te Nichinguenne."

"The Baron de Nucingen must not, cannot remain in a pig-sty like this. Listen to me. Your old waiting-maid, Eugénie—"

"Ichénie! of ze Rie Daidpoud?" exclaimed the baron.

"Yes, yes; the legitimate guardian of the furniture," continued Asia, "the person who leased the suite to the English beauty."

"Ach, I unterstant!" said the baron.

"Your old waiting-maid," continued Asia, with a respectful gesture toward Esther, "will be glad to receive you to-night; and the detectives will never dream of searching the old apartment which you left three months ago."

"Atmiraple! atmiraple!" cried the baron. "Bezides, I know ze dedectifes ant I know ze vorts to make zem fanish."

"You will find Eugénie a sly one," said Asia. "It was I who gave her to this lady."

"I know her vell," the baron exclaimed with a laugh. "Ichénie haz zdolen vrom me dirdy tausent vrancs."

Esther made a gesture so full of horror that an honest man would have staked his fortune on its sincerity.

"Oh! py mein own vault," added the baron; "I vas in bursuit of you," and he went on to tell the blunder to which the lease of the apartment to an Englishwoman had given rise.

"So you see, madame," said Asia, "Eugénie never told you a word about that. Ah, she's a sly fox! But this lady has grown accustomed to the girl," she added to the baron, "so after all you had better keep her."

Asia took Nucingen aside and said to him:

"Five hundred francs a month to Eugénie, who is busy feathering her nest, and you will know everything her mistress does. Let her be her maid. Eugénie will be all the more kindly disposed toward you now that she has fleeced you a bit. No chain binds women to a man more strongly than the recollection of having fleeced him. But keep a tight rein on Eugénie; she'll do anything in the world for money; it's horrible!"

"Ant you?"

"I," rejoined Asia, "I repay myself."

Nucingen, profound calculator as he was, had a bandage over his eyes; he acted like a child. The sight of this pure-minded and adorable Esther, drying her eyes and passing her needle through the border of her embroidery with all the modesty of a guileless maiden, gave once more to this infatuated old man the sensations which he had felt in the Bois de Vincennes; he would have given away the key of his safe; his youth had come again; his heart was overflowing with adoration, and he was only waiting for Asia's departure to throw himself on his knees before this Raphaël Madonna. This sudden birth of childhood in the heart of a sly old man is one of the social phenomena that physiology can most easily explain. The hidden cause of the effect was youth with all its sublime illusions that still lay hidden, crushed under the weight of business, stifled by ceaseless calculation and the perpetual pressure of money-getting cares, ready to burst into bloom like a forgotten seed, the splendid blossoms of which are called into being by a few late gleams of transitory sunlight. At twelve years of age, a clerk in the old house of Aldrigger, in Strasbourg, the baron had never set foot in the world of sentiment. Thus he stood motionless before his idol, a million confused speeches in his brain and not one upon his lips. Then the man of sixty-six returned and the baron obeyed a brutal impulse.

"Vill you gome to ze Rie Daidboud?" said he.

"Where you will, sir," answered Esther rising.

"Vere you vill!" repeated he rapturously. "You are ein anchel gome town vrom heafen, ant I luff you as eef I vere ein fery young man, aldough I haff gray hair."

"Ah! you might as well call it white. For it's much too black to be called gray," said Asia.

"Pe off, you file zeller of human vlesh. You haff your money. To not zlopper ofer zis vlower of luff," cried the banker, balancing his account for all the indignities he had swallowed by this savage apostrophe.

"You old blackguard, you shall pay for your words!" exclaimed Asia, menacing the banker with a gesture worthy of the fish-market, that made him shrug his shoulders. "Between the cup and the lip there's room for a viper and there you shall find me," she added, frenzied by Nucingen's disdain.

A millionaire, whose money is guarded by the Bank of France, whose house is protected by a regiment of servants, and who himself drives abroad safely ensconced in a carriage drawn by swift English horses, fears no misfortune; so the baron surveyed Asia calmly with the conscious superiority of a man who had just given her one hundred thousand francs.

This majesty produced its effect. Asia beat her retreat down the stairway, grumbling and muttering some excessively revolutionary phrases about a scaffold.

"What did you say to her?" asked the *Virgin of the needlework*. "She's a good woman."

"Zhe has zolt you, zhe has sdolen vrom you."

"When a girl is as wretched as I," answered she, with an accent that would have melted the heart of a diplomat, "who succors or cares for her?"

"Boor tarling!" said Nucingen, "to not zday here einoder minute."

Nucingen gave his arm to Esther, led her away just as she was, and assisted her into his carriage with more respect, perhaps, than he would have felt for the handsome Duchesse de Maufrigneuse.

"You zhall haf ein splentit garriage, ze brittiest in Baris," said Nucingen, as they drove along. "All ze telights of luxury zhall pe pestowed on you. Eine queen zhall not pe more rige zan you. You zhall pe resbected like a Cherman girl avder her pedrotal; you shall pe vree. To not gry. Listen! I luff you druly mit ein bure luff. Efery dear of yours bierces mein heard."

"Can a man love, with real love, the woman he buys?" asked the poor girl in an entrancing voice.

"Choseff was solt py his prothers pecause of his firdue; eet zays zo in ze Piple. Pesides, in ze East ein man puys his lechitimade wife."

Once again in the Rue Taitbout Esther could not look upon the scene of her past happiness without the most painful emotions. She lay upon a divan, motionless, and dried her tears one by one without hearing a word of the passionate phrases of love which the banker poured forth. He knelt at her feet; she gave no heed; she let him keep her hands when he took them, yet she was ignorant, as it were, even of the sex of the creature who was warming her feet, which he had discovered to be very cold. She continued to weep burning tears over the baron's head, and he to rub her ice-cold feet from midnight until two o'clock in the morning.

"Ichénie," said the baron at length, summoning Europe, "dry to eentuce your misdress to go to bett."

"No," cried Esther, springing to her feet like a frightened deer, "never here."

"Wait, sir; I know my mistress; she is meek and gentle as a lamb," said Europe to the banker. "Only don't oppose her too abruptly; you must influence her gradually. She has been so unhappy here! See how worn the furniture is! Let her have her own way. Have some charming little house furnished for her as prettily as can be. Perhaps, when she sees everything about her quite changed she will be changed too. Perhaps she will think you better than you are and will be heavenly sweet. Oh! she has not her peer! And you can boast of having made a most admirable purchase: a kind heart, pretty manners, a delicate instep, such a complexion, and such a color! Ah! and wit to make a man laugh at the gallows' foot. She is capable of attachment, too—and how well she knows what becomes her! Then, if she is expensive, a man, as they say, gets something for his money. Here, all her gowns are attached, so her clothes are three months behind the style. But she is so good that I love her myself, though she is my mistress.

But try to be reasonable, and think what it is for such a woman as she to see herself in the midst of furniture that has been attached—and for whom? For a miserable wretch who has tossed her aside. Poor little woman! she's no longer herself."

"Esder, Esder," murmured the baron. "Go to bett, my anchel. Ah! eef eet ees I zat you vear, I zhall not zdir vrom zis zova," he cried, burning with the purest love as he looked at Esther, who was always weeping.

"Then," answered Esther, as she took the baron's hand and kissed it with a tender expression of gratitude that made something very like a tear gather in the lynx's eye, "I am very grateful."

And, running into her bed-room, she closed the door behind her.

"Zere ees zometing inexblicable in dis," thought Nucingen in his excitement. "Vat vill zey zay at home?"

He got up and looked out of the window:

"Mein garriage ees zdill zere. Ze tay vill preak zoon."

He walked up and down the room.

"How Montame te Nichinguenne vould make vun of me, eef zhe zhould efer know how I haf bassed zis night."

He felt as if he had acted foolishly, and pressed his ear against the bed-room door.

"Esder!"

No answer.

"Mein Gott! zhe ees sdill grying," said he, as he walked across the room and lay down on the sofa.

*

Some ten minutes after sunrise the Baron de Nucingen, who had been lying stretched upon a sofa in a restless and unnatural sleep, was startled by Europe from a dream such as comes to a man under such circumstances, full of those swift combinations that are one of the inexplicable phenomena of medical physiology.

"Ah, heavens!" cried she. "Madame! Soldiers! Gendarmes! The law! They are going to arrest us—"

At the moment that Esther opened her door and appeared, ill-covered by her dressing-gown, her bare feet in slippers, her hair floating loose, so beautiful that the angel Raphaël would have lost heaven for her sake, five unclean wretches burst in through the parlor door and advanced toward the heavenly creature as she stood like an angel in some religious picture of the Flemish school. A man stepped forward—Contenson; the horrid Contenson laid his hand on Esther's moist shoulder.

"You are Mademoiselle Esther van—" he said.

With a single blow upon Contenson's cheek Europe sent him sprawling his whole length on the floor, making use at the same time of the well-known boxing trick to administer to him a sharp kick in the legs, known to those who practice boxing in France.

"Back!" she shrieked. "Hands off my mistress!"

"She has broken my leg," groaned Contenson, rising with difficulty; "she shall pay for it."

From out of the mass of five bailiffs, in bailiff's uniform, with hideous hats cocked upon their yet more hideous heads of streaked mahogany, with leering eyes, mutilated noses and grinning mouths, stepped Louchard dressed more decently than his men, but with his hat still on his head and an expression at once derisive and conciliating.

"Mademoiselle, I arrest you," said he to Esther; "and as for you, woman," he added, turning toward Europe, "if you are refractory you will be punished, and all resistance is useless."

The rattle of guns as their butts fell upon the marble tiles of the dining-room and hall, announced that there was another force outside, and lent emphasis to this speech.

"And why arrest me?" asked Esther innocently.

"Our little debt," answered Louchard.

"Ah! it's true!" exclaimed Esther. "Let me dress."

"I am sorry, mademoiselle, but I must first make sure that you have no means of escape in your bedroom," said Louchard.

Everything had passed so rapidly that the baron had not yet had time to interfere.

"Vell, I am now eine zeller of human vlesh, Paron te Nichiguenne!" cried the terrible Asia, as she glided past the bailiffs to the divan, pretending to be surprised at discovering the banker there.

"File wredch," exclaimed Nucingen, drawing himself up in all his financial majesty. The next instant he threw himself between Esther and Louchard, who took off his hat at an exclamation from Contenson.

"Baron de Nucingen!"

At a gesture from Louchard, the bailiffs withdrew from the room, uncovering their heads respectfully as they went. Contenson alone remained.

"Will you pay, baron?" inquired the detective, his hat in his hand.

"I bay," answered he, "put I muss know vat eet ees all apout."

"Three hundred and twelve thousand francs and some centimes, expenses paid; but this does not include the arrest."

"Dree huntert tausent vrancs!" cried the baron. "Zat ees doo tear ein avakening vor ein man who has bassed ze night on a zofa," he added in a whisper to Europe.

"Is this really the Baron de Nucingen?" asked Europe of Louchard, accentuating her doubt with a gesture that Mademoiselle du Pont, the latest soubrette of the Theâtre Français, might have envied.

"Yes, mademoiselle," said Louchard.

"Yes," replied Contenson.

"I anzer vor her," said the baron, for Europe's doubt touched him in a sensitive spot; "allow me to sbeak ein vort to her."

Esther and her elderly lover went into the bedroom. Louchard thought it necessary to press his ear against the lock.

"I luff you petter zan my life, Esder; put vy gif to your greditors money zat vould petter fit your burse? Go to brison, I vill go ant puy up zese huntert tausent growns mit ein huntert tausent vrancs ant you zhall haf dwo huntert tausent vrancs for yourzelf."

"The scheme is useless," cried Louchard. "The creditor is not in love with mademoiselle!—not he. You understand? He wants more than ever since he has learned that you were at her feet."

"You vool!" exclaimed Nucingen to Louchard, opening the door to let him come into the room. "You don't know vat you zay; I vill gif you dventy ber zent eef you vill arranche ze avvair."

"Impossible, baron."

"What, sir, have you the heart to allow my mistress to go to prison?" broke in Europe. "Do you need my wages, my savings? Take them, madame; I have forty thousand francs."

"Ah! my poor girl, I have never known you before!" cried Esther, clasping Europe in her arms.

Europe burst into tears.

"I bay," said the baron, piteously drawing out a memorandum book whence he took one of those little squares of printed paper which the bank gives to bankers, and upon which they have but to fill in the desired sum clearly in figures to create drafts payable to bearer.

"It's no use, baron," said Louchard; "I have orders not to receive payment except in gold and silver specie; but since it is you, I will be satisfied with bank notes."

"Der tefil!" cried the baron. "Zhow me your varrants."

Contenson displayed three packages covered with blue paper, which the baron took, still looking at Contenson, in whose ear he whispered:

"You vould haf tone ein petter tay's vork py varning me."

"Eh! did I know you were here?" answered the detective, indifferent whether Louchard overheard him or not. "You are unfortunate in not keeping me in your confidence. They are fleecing you," added the profound philosopher, shrugging his shoulders.

"Drue," thought the baron. "Ah! mein tar ling," he added aloud, his eyes fastened on the drafts, although he was speaking to Esther, "you are ze fictim of ein invernal sgountrel, of ein zvintler!"

"Oh, God! yes," said poor Esther, "yet he loved me well!"

"Eef I hat known, I zhould haf but a varning, indo your hants, not do bay."

"You are crazy, baron," said Louchard; "there is a second endorsee."

"Yes," he answered, "zere ees a zegont entorzee —Cérissed, a man to pe varnt against."

"He has a mental disorder, and is trying to make a pun," said Contenson, smiling.

"Will you write a line to your cashier, sir?" said Louchard. "I'll despatch Contenson to him and go myself to look after my people. It's growing late, and everybody will know."

"Go, Gondenson!" cried Nucingen. "Mein cazhier lifes on ze gorner of ze Rie tes Madhirins and ze Argate. Here ees an order zo zat he shall go to Ti Dilet or to ze Kellers', in gase ve haf not dree huntret tausent vrancs, vor our money ees all at ze pank. Tress yourzelf, mein anchel," added he to Esther, "you are vree. Olt vomen," he exclaimed, turning to Asia, "are more tancherous zan young ones."

"I am going to put the creditor in a good humor and he will give me something to amuse myself with to-day," said Madame de Saint Estève to Asia; then, with a mocking bow, added *"I pear no maleece, paron!"*

Louchard took his vouchers from the baron's hands, and remained alone with him in the parlor, where, half an hour afterward, the cashier returned, followed by Contenson. A moment later Esther appeared in a dress that was charming, although it had been so hastily assumed. When the money had been counted out by Louchard, the baron desired to examine the vouchers once more; but Esther seized them with the quickness of a cat and laid them away in her secretary.

"What are you going to give to the rabble, baron?" asked Contenson of Nucingen.

"You haf nod peen ofer bolide," said the baron.

"And what do you say to my leg?" cried Contenson.

"Luchart, you vill gif Gondenson huntret vrancs on ze palance of ze pill."

"Zhe ees eine peautiful voman!" said the cashier to the Baron de Nucingen as they left the Rue Taitbout; "put she gosts Mennesir le Paron ferry tear."

"Geep my zecret," said the baron, who had also enjoined secrecy on Contenson and on Louchard.

Louchard went away, followed by Contenson; but Asia, who was on the watch, stopped him on the street.

"The bailiff and creditor are there in a cab; they are thirsty," she said, "and there's grease to be had."

While Louchard counted the bills, Contenson was at liberty to examine the client. He caught sight of Carlos' eyes and distinguished the shape of his forehead beneath the wig, which he judged rightly to be a disguise; he took the number of the cab while seeming in perfect ignorance of everything that went on about him. Asia and Europe puzzled him to the last degree. He thought the baron a victim of extraordinarily clever persons, and with the more reason because Louchard had been strangely reserved when he had demanded his services; besides, Europe's blow had not struck Contenson on the tibia alone.

"That shows she has been at Saint-Lazare," said he, rising.

Carlos dismissed the bailiff, paid him generously,

and said to the cabman as he handed him his fare:

"Drive to the steps of the Palais Royal."

"Ah! in the morning?" thought Contenson, who overheard the order. "Something's in the wind."

Carlos reached the Palais Royal at a pace which gave him little to fear from followers. Then he traversed the galleries, after his fashion, and taking a second cab on the Place du Château-d'Eau, gave his order to the coachman:

"Passage de l'Opera, on the side towards the Rue Pinon."

Fifteen minutes later he entered the Rue Taitbout. The moment that she saw him, Esther cried out:

"Here are the fatal notes!"

Carlos took the drafts, examined them, and then went to burn them in the kitchen fire.

"The game is played!" he cried, displaying the three hundred and ten thousand francs rolled up in a package which he produced from the pocket of his greatcoat. "These and the hundred thousand francs that Asia got out of him enable us to act."

"My God! my God!" moaned poor Esther.

"Fool," said the savage calculator; "be but ostensibly the mistress of Nucingen, and you will be able to see Lucien; he is Nucingen's friend, and I don't forbid you to love him."

Esther saw a faint glimmer of light through the darkness of her life; she breathed again.

"Europe, my girl," said Carlos, drawing her into

a corner of the boudoir where no one could overhear a word of their conversation, "Europe, I am pleased with you."

Europe raised her head and looked at him with an expression which altered her faded countenance to such a degree that Asia, who was watching the scene from the doorway, wondered whether the interests by which Carlos held Europe might not be still deeper than those which riveted her to the Spaniard.

"This is not all, my girl. Four hundred thousand francs are nothing for me. Paccard will give you a bill for the silver-plate amounting to thirty thousand francs, on which there are certain receipts for partial payments; but our jeweler, Biddin, has incurred expenses. Our furniture which was seized by him will doubtless be advertised to-morrow. Go and see Biddin; he lives in the Rue de l'Arbre-Sec; he will give you certificates from the Mont de Piété for ten thousand francs. You understand: Esther has ordered a quantity of silver-plate and has put it in pawn, although she has not paid for it; she will be threatened with a trifling indictment for fraud. Thus the jeweler must be given thirty thousand francs and the Mont de Piété ten thousand more in order to get back the plate. Total, forty-three thousand francs, including expenses. The plate is full of alloy, the baron will have it renewed, and in this way we may be able to pick up a few thousand-franc notes extra. You owe—what to the dressmaker for two years?"

"Possibly six thousand francs," replied Europe.

"Very well; if Madame Auguste wishes to be paid and to preserve her custom she must make a memorandum of thirty thousand francs dating from four years ago. The milliner must do the same. The jeweler, Samuel Frisch, the Jew in the Rue Sainte-Avoie, will lend you promissory notes; we must *owe* him twenty-five thousand francs, and we shall have had six thousand francs advanced on our jewels at the Mont de Piété. We shall return the jewels to the jeweler; the stones will be half imitation, but the baron will never look at them. Thus you will make our *punter* disgorge a hundred and fifty thousand francs within a week."

"Madame ought to help me somewhat," answered Europe; "speak to her, for she sits there as though she were struck dumb, and makes me exert more wit than three authors do in a play."

"If Esther plays the prude, tell me," said Carlos. "Nucingen owes her a carriage and pair; she will prefer to choose and buy them herself. You must select the horsedealer and carriagemaker with whom Paccard lodges. We can buy handsome horses of him at a high price; they will go lame within the month and then we can change them."

"We might make six thousand francs on a perfumer's bill," said Europe.

"No!" he answered, shaking his head, "go gently on from one concession to another. Nucingen has only put his arm in the machine; we must have his head. Besides all this I need five hundred thousand francs."

"You can have them," replied Europe; "madame could get about six hundred thousand out of the fat imbecile by melting a little towards him, and then ask four hundred for loving him."

"Listen to this, child," said Carlos; "the day when I am in possession of the last hundred thousand francs, there will be twenty thousand francs for you."

"What good can they bring me?" said Europe, letting her arms drop like a woman for whom life is no longer possible.

"You can go back to Valenciennes, set yourself up handsomely in business and become an honest woman if you like; there are all sorts of tastes in the world. Paccard thinks of it sometimes; there is no brand on his shoulders and almost none on his conscience. You might suit each other," replied Carlos.

"Back to Valenciennes! Do you think of it, sir?" cried Europe, startled.

Born at Valenciennes, the daughter of two poor weavers, Europe was sent, at the age of seven, to a cotton manufactory, where modern industry abused her physical strength, and vice degraded her before her time. Seduced at twelve and a mother at thirteen, she became bound to persons living in the depths of degradation. In a trial for murder, she was summoned as a witness before the court of assizes, and at sixteen she was induced, by a remnant of right feeling and by the terror that surrounds the law, to secure, by her testimony, the condemnation of the accused to twenty years at hard labor. The criminal, one of those men whose very natures are fed by a passion for revenge when they are beneath the hand of justice, had said to the child in the presence of the entire court:

" In ten years, as now, Prudence—Europe's name was Prudence Servien—I shall return to kill you were I to be guillotined for it."

The president of the court endeavored to comfort Prudence Servien by promising her the support and influence of the law; but the poor girl was struck with such terror that she fell ill and remained for nearly a year in the hospital. Justice is a creation of the brain, represented by a collection of individuals, uninterruptedly renewed, whose memories and good intentions are like themselves, excessively changeable. Bars and tribunals can do nothing to prevent crime. They are invented to accept it when it is already in existence. On this account a preventive police would be a benefit to the country; but the word "police" alarms the legislator of to-day, who is no longer able to distinguish between the words, "to govern," "to administrate," and "to make laws." The legislator strives to concentrate all power in the State, as though the State were able to act! Then the galley-slave is free to meditate upon his victim and to wreak his revenge, since justice thinks of neither. Prudence, who had a general instinctive idea of her danger, left Valenciennes, and at seventeen went to Paris to hide herself. There she practiced four trades of which the most respectable was that of chorus girl in a small theatre. She met Paccard and told him the story of her misfortunes. Paccard, the right arm, the zealot of Jacques Collin, spoke of Prudence to his master, and when the master had need of a slave, he said to Prudence:

"If you will serve me as men serve the devil, I will rid you of Durut."

Durut was the galley-slave, the sword of Damocles suspended above the head of Prudence Servien. Without these details many critics would have found Europe's attachment to her master somewhat fantastical, and no reader could have understood the extraordinary effect which Carlos was about to produce upon her.

"Yes, child, you can return to Valenciennes. Take this and read it."

And he handed her the journal of the evening before, pointing with his finger to the following paragraph:

"Toulon.—Yesterday took place the execution of Jean François Durut. In the morning the garrison," etc.

Prudence let the paper fall. Her legs gave way beneath the weight of her body. Life was once more before her; for, as she said, she had not cared for bread since the menace of Durut.

"You see, I have kept my word. I needed four years to secure Durut's execution— by drawing him into a trap. Finish my work well here, and you will find yourself at the head of a small business in your own country, with twenty thousand francs in your pocket and Paccard for a husband; for I shall allow him to retreat into respectability."

Europe picked up the paper and read unweariedly with glistening eyes every one of those details which the newspapers have never wearied of giving concerning the execution of galley-slaves during the past twenty years—the impressive spectacle, the priest who has always absolved the sufferer, the old criminal exhorting his ex-colleagues, the leveled guns, the kneeling criminals; then the commonplace reflections that never do anything toward changing the system of the galleys swarming with eighteen thousand crimes.

"Asia must be reinstated in the house," said Carlos.

Asia stepped forward, still mystified by Europe's pantomime.

"In order to have her installed as cook here, you will begin by serving the baron a dinner such as he has never eaten before," he continued. "Then you will tell him that Asia has lost her money at play, and has been obliged to take a situation again. We shall need no groom. Paccard will be coachman; coachmen are rarely obliged to leave their seats and once in them they are scarcely accessible, so detectives will find him difficult to reach. Your mistress must make him wear a powdered wig and a cocked felt hat with lace trimmings. That will alter him; besides I'll make him up."

"Are we to have other servants with us?" demanded Asia, glancing askance at the priest.

"We shall have several honest people," replied Carlos.

"All numskulls!" added the mulatto.

"If the baron rents a house, Paccard has a friend who is suitable for janitor; we shall not need more than one valet and a kitchen-maid. It will be easy for you to watch two strangers."

As Carlos was about to go, Paccard appeared.

"Stay here, there are people in the street," said the groom. This speech, simple as it was, startled everybody. Carlos went upstairs to Europe's room and remained there until Paccard came for him in a hired carriage, which drove into the courtyard. Carlos lowered the curtains and was carried away at a pace well calculated to disconcert pursuit.

When he reached the Faubourg Saint-Antoine he ordered the carriage to stop in the neighborhood of a cab-stand, whither he walked on foot and soon after entered the Quais Malaquais, secure from all curious observation.

"Look here, child," said he to Lucien, showing him four hundred bills of one thousand francs each; "this, I hope, goes on account for the price of the Rubempré estate. We'll speculate with a hundred thousand of it. Omnibuses have just been started in Paris. The Parisians are sure to take to them, as they are a novelty; in three months we shall triple our funds. I know all about the business; they will pay splendid dividends out of the capital in order to advertise the stock—a trick they learned from Nucingen. When we repair the Rubempré estate we shall not pay for everything immediately. You must go and see des Lupeaulx and you beg him to recommend you himself to an attorney named Desroches, a shrewd devil whom you will visit at his office. You will speak to him about going to Rubempré and examining the estate and will promise him twenty thousand francs for himself, provided that he can buy land about the ruins of the château to the amount of eight hundred thousand francs, and arrange matters so that it will bring you in an income of thirty thousand francs."

"How you go on! on! on!"

"I never stop. It's no time for joking. You will invest three hundred thousand francs of it in Treasury bonds so as not to lose any interest. You may leave them with Desroches. He's as honest as he is cunning. This done, you must hurry away to Angoulême, and induce your sister and brother-in-law to lay a friendly little lie upon their consciences. Your relations can declare that they have presented you with six hundred thousand francs in order to facilitate your marriage with Clotilde de Grandlieu. There's nothing dishonorable in that."

"We're saved!" cried Lucien, dazzled at the thought.

"You, yes!" answered Carlos; "but you will never be perfectly secure until you come forth from

Saint Thomas Aquinas' with Clotilde as your wife."

"What do you fear?" inquired Lucien, apparently full of solicitude for his counsellor.

"There are busy-bodies on my trail. I am forced to maintain the appearance of a real priest and it's very troublesome. The devil even won't protect me any more when he sees me with a breviary under my arm."

At this same moment the Baron de Nucingen, who had walked away arm in arm with his cashier, reached the door of his mansion.

"I vear much," said he as he entered, "zat I haf mate put a zorry gampaign. Pah! ve vill mague ub vor eet."

"Ze meesvortune ees zat ze paron vill pe dalked apout," answered the honest German, anxious only for decorum's sake.

"Yes, meine misdress, py rights, zhould pe in a bozission vorthy of me," answered this Louis XIV. of the counting-house.

*

Confident of possessing Esther sooner or later, the baron became once more the great financier which he had been. He returned to the management of his business with such alacrity that his cashier, on discovering him the next morning at six o'clock in his office, looking over papers, rubbed his hands together in delight.

"Tecitetly, paron, lasd efening vas egonomigal vor you," said he, with a German smile, half shrewd, half foolish.

If rich people like the Baron de Nucingen have more chances than others of losing money they have also more chances of winning it, even when they surrender themselves to their passions. Although explanation of the financial policy of the celebrated house of Nucingen will be found elsewhere, it may be observed here that such vast fortunes are not acquired or made, and do not increase or endure, in the midst of the commercial, political and industrial revolutions of our time, without immense losses of capital, or, if you like, without levying assessments upon private property. Very little new wealth is poured into the common treasury of the world. Every fresh monopoly represents a new injustice in the general redistribution. The State gives back what it demands, but what a house of Nucingen takes, it keeps. This terrible blow at the nation eludes the law for the same reason that Frederick II. would have turned into a Jacques Collin or a Mandrin, if, instead of battling for provinces he had speculated in the smuggling trade or on floating capital. To compel the states of Europe to borrow at ten or twenty per cent, to gain this ten or twenty per cent from the public funds, to exact wholesale contributions from the industries of the country by securing complete control of raw materials, to toss to the originator of an undertaking a rope holding him above water until he has resuscitated his half-drowned enterprise, in short all those struggles for financial success, constitute the vital policy of money. There are surely risks for the banker as well as for the conqueror; but there are so few people in a position to engage in these contests that the lambs have no place in them. The shepherds play the great parts. Besides, as the *exécutés* (to use the slang word current in the Exchange) are guilty of having wished to gain too much, but little interest is taken in the misfortunes caused by the schemes of men like Nucingen. A speculator blows out his brains, a broker absconds, a notary runs away with the money of a hundred households—a worse crime than murder—a banker becomes insolvent: and all these catastrophes are forgotten in a few months at Paris, soon covered by the oceanic turmoil of the mighty city. The colossal fortunes of Jacques Cœur, of the Medici, of Ango of Dieppe, of Aufredi of La Rochelle, of Fugger, of Tiepolo, and of Corner were honestly made in former times, through privileges due to ignorance in regard to the origin of all precious commodities; while to-day clearness of vision has penetrated so far among the masses, and competition has reduced the profits to such a degree that every fortune, rapidly built, is the effect of a chance discovery, or the result of a legal theft. Perverted by scandalous examples, petty trade has responded, especially during the past decade, to the dishonesty of the schemes of larger firms by tampering with raw materials. Wherever chemistry is practiced wine is no longer drunk; and the culture of vines is falling into disuse. People sell adulterated salt in order to escape a tax. The law is appalled by this universal fraudulence, French commerce is suspected by the entire world, and England is equally demoralized. In France, the evil comes from political legislation. The charter proclaimed the reign of money, and thus success becomes the highest criterion of an atheistic age. In addition to this, corruption in the higher spheres, in spite of results that are outwardly brilliant and specious reasoning, is infinitely more hideous than the ignoble, almost personal, corruption in the lower spheres, a few details of which add a grotesque, or I might say a terrible element to this "Scene of Parisian Life." The government that takes fright at every new idea, has banished from the theatre all comic representations of what actually exists to-day. The townspeople, less liberal than Louis XIV., tremble at the approach of the *Mariage de*

Figaro, forbid the performance of the political *Tartuffe*, and surely would never permit *Turcaret* on the stage. For Turcaret now reigns supreme. From this time comedy is told, not played; and the book becomes the less rapid but surer arm of a poet.

During this morning, in the midst of the going and coming of audiences, directions and rapid conferences, which made Nucingen's office a kind of financial Salle des pas Perdus, one of his brokers announced to him the disappearance of one of the cleverest and richest members of the firm, Jacques Falleix, brother of Martin Falleix, and successor of Jules Desmarets. Jacques Falleix was nominally a broker employed by the firm of Nucingen, but, in concert with Du Tillet and the Kellers, the baron had plotted his destruction as deliberately as if he were discussing the slaughter of a Paschal lamb.

"He coult holt oud no longer," answered the baron complacently.

Jacques Falleix had rendered vast services in stock jobbing. In a crisis, a few months before, he had helped the firm out of serious difficulty by an audacious manœuvre; but to expect gratitude from men of Nucingen's class is it not like looking in midwinter for tenderness among Ukrainian wolves?

"Poor man!" returned the broker. "He expected this catastrophe so little that he had furnished a small house in the Rue Saint Georges for his mistress and spent a hundred and fifty thousand francs in paintings and furniture for it. He was so fond

HOW MUCH LOVE COSTS OLD MEN

of Madame du Val Noble! There's a woman forced to leave it all. Everything there is owed for."

"Gut! gut!" said the baron to himself. "Zis ees chust ze chance to rebair my loszes of lasd night.—He has baid vor nodding?" demanded he of the broker.

"Not he," replied the latter; "what upholsterer would have been idiot enough to refuse credit to Jacques Falleix? It seems that there is an admirable cellar too. By the bye, the house is for sale; he counted upon buying it. The lease is in his name. What stupidity! Silver, furniture, wines, carriage, horses, will all be sold wholesale, and what will the creditors realize?"

"Gome do-morrow," said Nucingen; "I zhall haf zeen to all zat, ant eef zey ton't teclare pankrubtzy, but gonzent to arranche madders amigably, I autorize you to ovver ein reasonaple brice vor ze vurnidure, ant you may dake ze leaze."

"That's easily done," said the broker. "Go there this morning and you will find one of Falleix's partners there with the upholsterers, who are anxious to secure the proceeds of the sale; but Madame Val Noble holds their invoices in Falleix's name."

The Baron de Nucingen despatched a clerk forthwith to his notary. Jacques Falleix had spoken to him about this house which was worth, at the most, sixty thousand francs; and he wished to take immediate possession for the sake of enjoying a landlord's privileges in regard to the rents.

The cashier—honest man that he was!—came to ask whether his master had lost anything in Falleix's failure.

"On ze gondrairy, mein gut vriend Volfgang, I am going to make ein huntert tausand vrancs."

"How?"

"I zhall haf ze leetle house zat ze boor tefil Valleix has peen brebaring vor his misdress vor ze bast year. I zhall haf ze whole py ovvering ze greditors feefty tausand vrancs ant Masder Gartod, mein nodary, vill haf mein orters apoud ze house, vor ze brobrietor is een neet of money. I neu eet pivore put mein prain hat gone. Een a leetle vhile meine tifine Esder vill haf ein leetle balace. Valleix has daken me zere, eet ees ein miragle and gloze py. Zis veets me like ein glov."

Falleix's failure obliged the baron to go to the Stock Exchange; but it was impossible for him to leave the Rue Saint Lazare without passing through the Rue Taitbout. He was already suffering because he had been for a few hours absent from Esther, and longed to have her always at his side. The gains which he counted upon making from the spoils of his broker made him think very lightly of the loss of four hundred thousand francs that he had encountered. Enchanted with the thought of announcing to his *anchel* the news of her approaching translation from the Rue Taitbout to the Rue Saint Georges, where she should have *ein leetle balace*, in which memories could no longer obscure their happiness, the very paving stones felt soft beneath his feet, and he walked like a young man in a young man's dream. At the corner of the Rue des Trois-Frères, in the middle of his dream, the baron saw himself confronted by Europe, who was approaching with a very forlorn countenance.

"Vere are you coing?" he asked.

"Ah! I was on my way to your house, sir. You were quite right, yesterday! Now, I believe it would have been better if my poor mistress had gone to prison for a few days. What do women know about money matters? The moment her creditors learned that she had returned to her house they all swooped down on us like birds of prey. Yesterday evening at seven they came and pasted up hideous placards saying that her furniture was to be sold next Saturday. But this is nothing. My mistress, who is all kindness, once wished to assist that monster—you know whom I mean?"

"Vat monsder?"

"Oh, the one she loved, that d'Estourny; ah! he was fascinating, but he gambled, and that tells the story."

"He gampled mit markt gards—"

"Well, and what do you do at the Stock Exchange? But let me go on. One day, to prevent Georges from blowing out his brains, as he said he should do, she put all her silver and jewels in pawn at the Mont de Piété though they had never been paid for. The creditors learned that she had paid something on a debt, and they all flocked to the house and made a dreadful scene. They threatened her with the police court—your angel sitting in the dock! Isn't that enough to make a wig stand on end? She bursts into tears; talks of throwing herself into the river. Oh! she'll do it."

"Eef I am to zee you, gut-pye to ze Exchange!" cried Nucingen. "Ant eet ees imbossiple vor me not to go zere, vor I zhall make zometing vor her. Go ant galm her; I vill bay her tets; I zhall zee her ad vour o'glock. Put, Ichénie, dell me zat zhe luffs me ein leetle."

"What! a little? A great deal. Why, sir, nothing but generosity can win a woman's heart. Certainly you might have economized—perhaps a hundred thousand francs—by letting her go to prison. But then you never could have gained her heart. She said to me, 'Eugénie, he is very generous, very kind. He has a noble soul!'"

"Zhe sait zat, Ichénie?" cried the baron.

"Yes, sir, to me."

"Here are den louis, dake zem."

"Thank you. But she is crying at this moment. Since yesterday she has wept as many tears as Mary Magdalene wept in a month. The woman you love is in despair, and, worse than all, for debts which are not her own. Oh! what creatures men are! They are as content to live on a woman's bounty as a woman is to live upon an old man's!"

"Vimen are all alike! Bromising to bay. Eef she vill zign nodding more I bay, put eef zhe write anodder signature, I—"

"What would you do?" said Europe, striking an attitude.

"Mein Gott, I haf no bower ofer her. I vill look avder her leetle pizness. Co ant gonzole her and dell her zat in ein month zhe zhall haf ein leetle balace."

"You have invested at a high rate of interest in a woman's heart, baron. Even I can see that you have grown younger, though I am but a lady's maid; I have often witnessed this phenomenon. It is happiness! Happiness is reflected in a man's face. If you have made several disbursements don't regret them, you will see what they bring you in return. Then, as I told my mistress, she would be the lowest of the low—a monster, if she did not love you, for you are saving her from a hell. Once that she is free from care, you will know her as she is. Between you and me, I can promise you, the night when she wept so much—but what can you expect? A woman clings to the esteem of a man who is going to support her. She dared not tell you all. She wished to run away."

"Run avay!" exclaimed the baron, startled at the thought. "Put ze Exchange, ze Exchange. Go, go, I zhall not go een; put eef I vere to zee her at her vindow ze zight vould gif me new heart."

Esther smiled at Monsieur de Nucingen as he passed before the house and he walked clumsily along, saying to himself:

"Zhe ees eine anchel."

This was the measure Europe had taken to procure

an impossible result. Toward half past two Esther had finished attiring herself as she used to do when she expected Lucien. She was fascinating. Seeing her thus Prudence exclaimed with a glance toward the window:

"Here he comes!"

The poor girl thinking that it was Lucien, sprang forward and saw Nucingen.

"Ah, how you hurt me!" she said.

"It was the only way to make you appear attentive to a poor old man who is going to pay all your debts," answered Europe; "for, at length, they are really to be paid."

"What debts?" cried the girl, who had no thought but to hold fast the love which cruel hands sought to tear from her.

"Those which M. Carlos has made for you."

"What! They amount to more than four hundred and fifty thousand francs already!" exclaimed Esther.

"They still amount to a hundred and fifty thousand francs. But the baron has borne it all very well. He is going to take you away from here and place you *een ein leetle balace.* Heavens! you are not unlucky! If I were in your place, and had him so firmly in hand, after satisfying Carlos, I should have myself presented with a house and an income. You are certainly the most beautiful woman I have ever seen and the most attractive, but ugliness comes so quickly; I have been fresh and pretty myself, and look at me now! I am twenty-three, almost as young as you, and I seem ten years older. An illness is enough. But when a woman has a house in Paris and an income, she is in no danger of ending her life on the street."

Esther no longer heard Europe-Eugénie-Prudence Servien. The will of a man gifted with the genius of corruption had plunged her once again into the mire, with the same force which he had used to draw her thence. They who know love in its infinitude know no one can enjoy its pleasures without learning some of its virtues. Since the scene in her squalid room in the Rue de Langlade, Esther had forgotten her old life completely. Until now she had loved very virtuously, cloistered within her passion. In order to avoid every obstacle the wise corrupter had had the craft to lay his toils in such a way that the poor girl, spurred on by her devotion, was forced into giving her consent to roguery that was already consummated or on the point of consummation. This nicety of cunning reveals the genius of the corrupter, and indicates the method by which he had overcome Lucien. He had created terrible necessities, had dug the mine, filled it with powder, and at the critical moment said to the accomplice: "Give the sign and everything will be blown into the air!" Esther had been formerly imbued with the morality of a courtesan, and had found all these pleasing modes so natural that she estimated her rivals solely by the sums they could induce a man to spend upon them. Ruined fortunes are the chevrons of creatures such as she had been. Carlos, in counting upon Esther's remembrances, was not deceived. These stratagems and artifices of war, a thousand times employed by spendthrifts as well as by the women of her class, did not disturb Esther's mind. The poor girl felt nothing but her degradation. She adored Lucien, and had become the ostensible mistress of the Baron de Nucingen; that was her sorrow. That the counterfeit Spaniard had taken the earnest money; that Lucien was building the castle of his fortune with the stones of Esther's tomb; that a single night of pleasure should cost the old banker a few thousand-franc notes more or less, or that Europe should trick him out of some hundred thousand francs by methods more or less ingenious: no thoughts such as these entered the mind of the loving girl. This was the canker eating at her heart; for five years she had thought herself spotless as an angel. She loved, she was happy. She had not been guilty of the slightest infidelity. This pure exquisite love was to be soiled. Her mind did not draw a contrast between the fair secluded life she had led and the impure life which lay before her. Her feeling was distinct from calculation or poetical feeling. She was conscious of an indefinable and overwhelming sense that from white she had become black; from pure, impure; from noble, ignoble. She longed to be white as snow, and moral stain seemed insupportable. Thus, when the baron had spoken to her of his love, the thought of throwing herself out of the window had come into her mind. She had loved Lucien absolutely as a woman is rarely capable of loving a man. Women who say, and often think they love more than anybody else in the world, dance, waltz, flirt, with other men, dress for society, and go thither to reap their harvest of admiring glances; but Esther had accomplished the miracles of true love without self-sacrifice. For six years she had loved Lucien with the love of actresses and courtesans, who, after having been immersed in filth and impurity, thirst after the nobleness and the devotion of true love, and observe it in its exclusiveness, if I may use this word to express an idea that is so seldom put into practice; nations of the past, Greece, Rome and the East have always secluded their women; the woman who loves should seclude herself. Thus the reader can imagine that, on leaving the fairy palace which had been the scene of her happy romance, to enter the *leetle balace* of a cold old man, Esther was seized by a kind of moral illness. Pressed down by an iron hand she was half sunk in infamy before she had had time to reflect; now for two days she had been reflecting and her heart felt cold as death.

At the words, "ending on the street," she rose quickly and said:

"In the street? No, better end in the Seine."

"In the Seine? And how about M. Lucien?" said Europe.

At this single word Esther fell backward into her chair where she sat with her eyes fixed upon a flower in the carpet, her tears drying up in her burning brain. At four o'clock, Nucingen found his angel plunged in that ocean of reflections and of resolutions on which a woman's spirit floats, and from which her only escape lies in words that are incomprehensible to those who have not sailed upon the same seas.

"Glear your prow, meine bet," said the baron as he took his seat by her side; "you zhall haf no more tets. I zhall make ein arranchement mit Ichénie ant in ein month you vill leaf zis abardmend do ender ein leetle balace. Oh, vat eine luffly hant! gif eet to me zat I may kees eet.—Esther let him take her hand as a dog gives its paw.—Ah! you gif ze hant ant not ze heard, ant eet's ze heard zat I luff."

These words were spoken with so sincere an accent that poor Esther turned her eyes toward the old man with an expression of pity that almost crazed him. Like martyrs, lovers are conscious of a kinship with all who suffer. One sorrow understands another better than any other two feelings in the world.

"Poor man!" said she. "He loves."

The baron heard this word and misunderstood it. He grew pale; the blood boiled in his veins; he breathed the air of heaven. At his age, millionaires pay as much gold as a woman asks for a sensation such as this.

"I luff you as I luff my taughder!" he exclaimed. "Ant I veel zere," he added, laying his hand on his heart, "zat I gannot pear to zee you oddervise zan habby."

"If you only wished to be my father, I would love you dearly; I would never leave you and you would find that I am not wicked, venal nor selfish as I seem to be now."

"You haf peen voolish, like all breddy vomen," answered the baron; "zat ees all. Led's dalk no more apout eet; our own pizness ees to mague money vor you. Pe habby; I reely vish to pe your vader for a vew tays, vor you must haf dime to aggusdom yourselve to mein boor gargase."

"Honestly?" cried Esther, rising and springing upon Nucingen's knees and slipping her arm around his neck in a close embrace.

"Honesdly," he answered, trying to contract his features into a smile.

She kissed his forehead, believing in an impossibility: to stay pure and to see Lucien. She caressed the baron so tenderly that La Torpille revived.

She bewitched the old man and he promised to remain her father for forty days. These forty days were required for the purchase and the furnishing of the house in the Rue Saint Georges. Once in the street, on his homeward way, the baron said to himself, "I am ein ass."

It was true that although he acted as a child in Esther's presence, the moment he had left her he wrapped his lynx's skin about him just as Le Joueur falls once more in love with Angélique when he has lost his last penny.

"Ein half million, ant to pe vere I am; zis ees

doo sdoobid. Put luckily nopody vill know anyding apout eet," said he, three weeks later.

He made excellent resolutions to break loose from a woman whom he had bought so dear; and then, when Esther stood before him, he spent every moment he could spare her in making amends for the brutality of his intention.

"I to not vish," he said at the end of a month, "to pecome ze edernal vater."

In the latter part of the month of December, 1829, on the day before Esther's installation in the small house in the Rue Saint Georges, the baron invited Du Tillet to conduct Florine thither in order to see whether everything were in harmony with Nucingen's fortune, whether the words *ein leetle balace* had been realized by the artists commissioned to make this cage worthy of its bird. Every luxurious invention dating from before the revolution of 1830, contributed to make this house the model of good taste. Grindot, the architect, acknowledged it as the masterpiece of his decorative talent. The staircase had been rebuilt in marble, the stucco and draperies and gilding applied with sober judgment, and the slightest details, as well as the general effect, surpassed everything of the kind that the century of Louis XV. has left in Paris.

"This is my dream; this and virtue!" said Florine smiling. "And for whose sake are you spending this money?" she asked of Nucingen. "Is it a virgin who has suffered herself to fall from heaven?"

"Eet ees eine voman who ees rising zizzer," replied the baron.

"One way of posing yourself as Jupiter," answered the actress; "and when shall we see her?"

"Oh, the day of the housewarming," exclaimed Du Tillet.

"Not pefore,"—said the baron.

"We must all prink, and powder, and adorn ourselves," continued Florine. "Oh, how the women will burden the lives of their dressmakers and hairdressers for that evening! When is it?"

"I am not ze masder."

"Ah! what a woman!" exclaimed Florine. "How I should like to see her."

"I zhould doo," replied the baron ingenuously.

"What! Are the house, woman, and furniture all new?"

"Even the banker," added Du Tillet; "for my friend seems to me very young indeed."

"He must return to his twentieth year, if only for a moment," said Florine.

*

During the early days of 1830, all Paris was talking about Nucingen's mad love and the boundless luxury of his house. The poor baron, lampooned, ridiculed, and bursting with rage that may easily be imagined, like the financier he was, determined to act upon a plan in accordance with the passion in his heart. He wished to kindle the first fire on his new hearth with the cloak of his magnanimous fatherhood and to secure the reward of his long self-sacrifice. Constantly rebuffed by La Torpille, he resolved to continue his negotiations by letter in order to obtain from her a written agreement. Bankers have no faith except in promissory notes. Thus the lynx arose early on one of the first days of this year, locked himself in his study, and began to compose the following letter, written in excellent French, for, although he pronounced badly, he wrote with great accuracy:

"DEAR ESTHER:

"Blossom of my thoughts and sole happiness of my life, when I told you that I loved you as my daughter I deceived you and deceived myself. I simply wished to express to you in this way the sanctity of my feelings, which are unlike all that men have felt before; first, because I am an elderly man, and secondly, because I have never loved till now. I love you so well that if you were to cost me my fortune I could not love you less. Do not be unjust. Most men could not see in you the angel which I have discerned; I have never even glanced at your past. I love you both as I love my daughter Augusta, who is my only child, and as I should love my wife had she ever loved me. If happiness be the sole absolution possible for an old man, ask yourself whether I am not playing a ridiculous part. I have made you the consolation and the joy of my declining years. You know very well that until my death you will be as happy as a woman can be, and you may be sure that after I die you will be rich enough to be envied by many another woman. In every transaction that I have carried on since I have had the happiness of knowing you, a share of the gain is allotted to you and you have an interest in the house of Nucingen. In a few days you will enter a house, which, if it please you, shall be yours sooner or later. Will you receive me there still as your father or shall I, at length, be rewarded? Pardon me for writing you so plainly; but when I am by your side my courage deserts me, and I feel but too strongly that you are my mistress. I do not mean to offend you; I only wish to tell you all that I suffer, and how cruel waiting is, when at my age every day deprives me of some hope and some enjoyment. The delicacy of my conduct is an additional proof of the sincerity of my intentions. Have I ever acted the part of a creditor? You are like a citadel, and I am no longer young. To my complaints you answer that your life is at stake, and you force me to believe it when I listen to you; but now I fall back among dark griefs and doubts, which are dishonoring to us both. You have seemed to me as candid and as good as you are lovely, but you are pleased to destroy my convictions. Judge for yourself. You tell me that your heart is filled with a great and pitiless passion, yet you refuse to confide to me the name of him you love. Is this natural? You have changed a man of some strength into a man of inconceivable weakness. See to what straits I am come. After five months I am driven to ask of you what future you hold in reserve for my love. Besides, I must know what part I am to play at your approaching housewarming. Money means nothing to me when it is spent for you; I shall not be so silly as to attempt to make this disdain a merit in your eyes; but, though my love knows no bounds, there are limits to my fortune, and I keep it only for your sake. Thus, if by endowing you with all that I possess I could in my poverty secure your affection, I should rather be poor and loved by you than rich and despised by you. You have changed me so completely, my dear Esther, that nobody recognizes me; I paid ten thousand francs for a picture by Joseph Bridau, because you told me that he was a man of talent, although but little known. Besides all this I give five francs in your name to every beggar whom I meet. What, I ask, does this old man demand, who counts himself your debtor, when you do him the honor of accepting any gift at his hands? He wishes only for hope. And, great heavens! what hope it is! Is it not rather the certainty of never receiving from you what I passionately long for? Yet the very flame in my heart will aid your cruel deceit. You will find me ready to submit to every condition that you may care to impose upon my happiness and my rare pleasures, but at least tell me that on the day when you take possession of your house, you will accept the heart and the thralldom of him who signs himself for the rest of his days

"Your slave,
"FRÉDÉRIC DE NUCINGEN."

"How this old money-bags wearies me!" exclaimed Esther, once more a courtesan.

She took a sheet of scented paper and wrote, in as large a hand as the sheet allowed, the celebrated phrase which, to the glory of Scribe, has passed into a proverb, "Prenez mon ours."

Fifteen minutes later, Esther was seized with remorse and wrote the following letter:

"MONSIEUR LE BARON:

"Do not pay the least attention to the letter you received from me; I had fallen back into the folly of my youth; so pardon this fault, sir, in a poor girl who ought to be a slave. I have never felt the degradation of my position so keenly

HOW MUCH LOVE COSTS OLD MEN

as since the day that I was given up to you. You have paid; I owe myself. There is nothing more sacred than the debts of dishonor. I have no right to *liquidate* them by throwing myself into the Seine. A debt can always be paid in that horrid coin which is good only on one side: thus I am ready to obey your commands. I wish to pay in one night all the sums for which, up to this fatal moment, obligations have been given, for I am more than certain that one night with me is worth millions, especially as it will be the only one and my last night. When I have ceased to be a debtor, I can leave this life. An honest woman has chances to rise from a fall, but the rest of us have fallen too low. Thus my resolution is so firmly taken that I beg you to keep this letter in testimony of the cause of the death of her who signs herself for a day,

"Your servant,

" ESTHER."

The letter once despatched, Esther regretted it. Ten minutes later she wrote the following letter:

"Pardon, dear baron, it is I once more. I have had no wish to mock you or to wound you; I simply ask you to reflect upon this simple reasoning: if we remain together in the relations of father and daughter, you will have a pleasure slight, but lasting. If you demand the fulfilment of the contract, you will mourn for me. I do not wish to trouble you longer; the day that you choose pleasure instead of content shall be without a morrow for me.

"Your daughter,

"ESTHER."

At the first letter the baron was the victim of one of those fits of cold anger that may bring death to millionaires; he glanced at himself in the looking-glass, and then rang the bell.

"Ein voot path," he cried to his new valet.

As he was taking his foot bath, the second letter arrived. He read it and fell back senseless. The millionaire was carried to his bed, and when the financier revived, Madame de Nucingen was seated on the foot of the bed.

"The girl is right," said she. "Why do you wish to buy love? Is it sold in the market? Let me see your letter."

The baron handed her the various rough copies which he had made.

Madame de Nucingen read them with a smile. The third letter arrived.

"She is a most extraordinary woman!" exclaimed the baroness after reading the last letter.

"Vat zhall I to, montame?" demanded the baron of his wife.

"Wait."

"Vait!" he repeated, "nadure ees bityless."

"Now, my dear," said the baroness, "you have ended by being very kind to me, and I am going to give you good advice."

"You are eine gut vooman!" said he. "Gondract your tebts, I vill bay vor zem."

"What happened to you at the receipt of the girl's letter touches a woman more than millions spent upon her, or than any letters, no matter how tender they may be. Let her hear about it indirectly, and perhaps you may win her. And don't be too scrupulous; she won't die of it," added the baroness, looking fixedly at her husband.

Madame de Nucingen was completely ignorant of the *child of nature*.

"How glever Montame de Nichengueene ees!" thought the baron, when his wife left him to himself.

But the more the baron admired the policy of the advice which the baroness had given him, the less he could formulate a plan for making use of it. He not only thought himself stupid, but actually admitted it to himself.

The stupidity of a moneyed man, although it has become almost proverbial, is, nevertheless, merely relative. The faculties of our minds are like the aptitudes of our bodies. The dancer's strength is in his legs; the blacksmith's muscle is in his arms; the strong porter in the market practices carrying heavy loads; the singer cultivates his larynx, and the pianist trains his wrists. A banker grows accustomed to combining business operations, to studying his affairs and setting various interests in motion, as the playwright strives to combine situations, to study subjects and to give life to his characters. It is as unfair to expect witty conversation from the Baron de Nucingen as it would be to demand poetic imagery in the demonstration of a mathematician. How many poets are there in an epoch who, in the common intercourse of life, talked as wittily or elegantly as Madame Cornuel? Buffon was heavy; Newton never loved; Lord Byron loved nobody except himself; Rousseau was gloomy and half mad, and La Fontaine was heedless of others. If it be equally distributed, intellect produces fools or mediocrity everywhere; if it be divided unequally it engenders those differences to which we give the name of *genius*, and which, if they could take visible shape, would appear deformities. The same law rules the body; perfect beauty is almost invariably accompanied by want of animation, or stupidity. That Pascal should be at once a great geometrician and a great writer; that Beaumarchais should be an admirable man of business, and that Zamet should be a skillful courtier, are rare exceptions that confirm the principle of the differentiation of intelligence. In the sphere of speculative calculations the banker employs as much wit, address and shrewdness as an astute diplomatist does in that of national interests. Were the banker still remarkable outside of his office he would be a great man. Nucingen multiplied by the Prince de Ligne, by Mazarin, or by Diderot is a human formula that is almost impossible; and yet it exists under the names of Pericles, Aristotle, Voltaire, and Napoleon. The glory of the imperial

sun ought not to hamper a man in his private life;
the Emperor was well-informed, witty and fascinating. M. de Nucingen, purely banker, and like
most bankers, without the inventive faculty, apart
from his calculations, believed solely in absolute
values. In matters of art, he had the good sense to
apply, with his purse in his hand, to experts, and
always secured the best architect, the best surgeon,
the finest connoisseur of pictures or statues, the
most able lawyer, whenever he was interested in
building a house, in watching over his health, in
the purchase of a curiosity, or of an estate. But
since there does not exist an avowed expert in
intrigues, nor a connoisseur in passions, a banker is
at a disadvantage when he loves, and in a sorry
plight when he attempts the management of a
woman. Nucingen could contrive nothing better
than to follow his old path and give money to some
male or female Frontin to act or think for him.
Madame de Sainte Estève alone could put the
baroness' suggestion into practice, and the banker
regretted bitterly that he had ever quarreled with
the odious procuress. Nevertheless, confident of
the magnetism of his cheque book, and of the
sedative effect of drafts signed Garat, he rang for
his valet and bade him find the horrible widow in
the rue Neuve-Saint-Marc, and ask her to come to
his house. In Paris extremes meet on the common ground of passion. There vice welds together
rich and poor, small and great; the Empress
consults with Mademoiselle Lenormand, and the

noble lord can always find a Ramponneau in every century.

The new valet returned two hours later.

"Madame de Saint Estève is ruined, sir," he announced.

"Ach, zo much ze petter!" exclaimed the baron joyously. "Zen I haf her."

"The good woman is apparently rather fond of gambling," replied the valet. "Furthermore, she is under the thumb of a low comedian of one of the theatres in the suburbs, whom, for decency's sake, she tries to pass off as her god-son. It seems she is an excellent cook, and is looking for a situation."

"Zese tefilish beddy cheniuses haf den vays of making money ant ein tossen vays of sbenting it," said the baron to himself, quite ignorant that he was uttering the sentiments of Panurge.

He despatched his servant again in quest of Madame de Saint Estève, who did not make her appearance until the next day. Interrogated by Asia the new valet disclosed to the she-detective the terrible results of the letters written by the baron's mistress.

"He must dote upon that woman," said the valet in conclusion, "for he very nearly died. I myself advised him never to return to her, for she would twist him about her finger in no time. The woman has cost the baron five hundred thousand francs already, people say, without counting the sums he has spent on the little house in the Rue Saint Georges! But she wants money, and nothing but money. When the baroness left my master's room she exclaimed laughingly, 'If this goes on, that woman will make me a widow.'"

"The devil!" answered Asia. "It will never do to kill the hen that lays the golden eggs."

"The baron rests all his hopes upon you," said the valet.

"Ah, that's because I know the way to come round a woman."

"Go in, then," said the valet, bowing low before this occult power.

"So, you are meeting with some trifling annoyance, sir," said the pseudo Madame de Saint Estève, as she entered the sick-room with an humble air. "What can you expect? Everybody is attacked in their weak spot. I, too, have seen misfortune. In two months fortune's wheel has played me an odd turn, for here I am looking for a situation. Neither of us has been reasonable. If you were willing to give me the position of cook in Madame Esther's household, you would find in me the truest of the true, and I would be very useful in watching Eugénie and madame."

"Eet has nodding to to mit zat," said the baron. "I gannot sugzeed in begoming ze masder ant I am dvirled apout like—"

"A top," interrupted Asia. "You have managed everybody else, papa, but the little girl has you in her power, and is amusing herself at your expense. Heaven is just!"

"Chust!" ejaculated the baron. "I tit not

zent for you een orter to hear you dalk apout moralidy."

"Bah, my boy, a little morality hurts nobody. It's the salt of life for such as we, just as vice is for devotees. Tell me: Did you act generously? Did you pay her debts?"

"Yes," whined the baron.

"That was right. You have redeemed her property, that was still better. But be very sure, this is not enough. You have not as yet given her anything to do, and these women do love to *cut a figure.*"

"I am breparing ein leetle surbrize for her in Rue Saint Chorches. Zhe knows eet, put I ton't vish to pe ein ass."

"Very well then, leave her."

"I am avraid zat zhe vould led me go," exclaimed the baron.

"And we wish her in return for our money, my boy," replied Asia. "Listen! We have squeezed millions out of the public. People say that you have twenty-five."

The baron could not repress a smile.

"Well then, you must let one go."

"I vould glatly led eet go," answered the baron, "put no zooner zhall I have led ze virst go zan zey vill temant ein segond."

"Yes, I understand," replied Asia. "You do not wish to say B, for fear of going all the way to Z. Yet Esther is an honest woman."

"Mosd vunterfully honesd!" cried the banker.

"She ees villing to sguare aggounts, put az eef zhe vere baying ein tebd."

"In short, she doesn't wish to be your mistress; she feels some repugnance. I can imagine it; the child has always obeyed her whims. When a woman knows only charming young men, an old gentleman doesn't look attractive. You are not handsome. You are fat as Louis XVIII. and a trifle dull, as every man is who wheedles fortune and lets women alone. Now then, if you have six hundred thousand francs to spare," added Asia, "I will guarantee that she shall become everything you could wish her to be."

"Zix huntert tausent vrancs," cried the baron making a slight start, "Esder has gost me ein million alreaty."

"Happiness is well worth sixteen hundred thousand francs, my fat rascal. You know men to-day who have run through more than two millions with their mistresses. I know women who have even cost lives; women for whom men have been guillotined. You remember that doctor who poisoned his friend? He wished for money in order to secure a woman's happiness."

"Yez, I rememper; put eef I am een luff, I am not an itiot, ad leasd here; vor ven I zee her I vould glatly gif her mein bockedpook."

"Listen, sir," said Asia, striking the pose of a Semiramis. "You have been cleaned out enough. As truly as my business name is Saint Estève, I am on your side."

"Gut, I vill revart you."

"I believe it, for I have shown you that I know how to revenge myself. Besides, remember this, papa," she added, with a terrible look at the baron. "I have the means of putting an end to Esther, as easily as I could extinguish a candle. I know my woman! When the little wretch has made you happy, she will be still more necessary to you than she is at this moment. You have paid me well, you had to be dunned enough, but you did pay the piper. For my part, I fulfilled my engagements, didn't I? And now I am going to propose a bargain."

"What ees eet?"

"You give me a situation as cook in Madame Esther's house; you engage me for ten years. I have a thousand francs a year; you pay the last five years in advance, as earnest money; what does that amount to? Once settled in madame's house I shall find means of inducing her to grant the following concessions: for instance, you order an entrancing gown of Madame Auguste, who knows madame's taste and style, and you give directions for the new carriage to be at the door at four o'clock. After the Stock Exchange you go and see her, and then take a short drive in the Bois de Boulogne. In this way the girl confesses that she is your mistress, and pledges herself to you in the sight of all Paris. One hundred thousand francs. You dine with her—I know how to make a dinner such as you want—; you take her to a stage box at the theatre, the Variétés, for instance; and all Paris says, 'There's that old rogue Nucingen with his mistress.' And it's rather complimentary that you should be thought so. All these advantages, as I am an honest woman, are comprised in the first hundred thousand francs. In this way you will have made great progress before a week is over."

"I zhall haf sbent ein huntert tausent vrancs."

"The second week," continued Asia, who did not seem to hear this piteous exclamation, "madame will be persuaded by these preliminaries to leave her little apartment and to take up her abode in the house you offer her. By this time your Esther has tasted the world again, and has met her old companions; she will be eager to shine, and will do the honors of her palace. This is in the law of nature. Another hundred thousand francs! Lord, sir! you have got what you wanted; Esther is compromised, she is yours. The rest is simple, for you play the principal part, you old elephant—that makes the fat monster open his eyes—. Very well, then, I'll undertake it myself. Four hundred thousand. But you won't have to give them until the day after, old fellow. Isn't that honest? I have more confidence in you than you have in me. If I persuade madame to appear in public as your mistress, to compromise herself, to accept all that you give her, and all this to-day, perhaps you will believe me capable of inducing her to surrender her last redoubt. It's difficult, for it is as much work for you to drag your artillery there as it was for the First Consul to draw his over the Alps."

"Vy?"

"Her heart is overflowing with love, *rasibus*, as you people who know Latin say," replied Asia. "She thinks herself a Queen of Sheba, because she has bathed herself in the sacrifices which she has made for her lover. It's an idea that women take into their heads! Ah, my boy, we must be fair; it's only right that we should. The little goose might die of sorrow because she belonged to you, and I should not be very much surprised; but one thing reassures me, and to raise your spirits I'll tell you that she's a courtesan at heart."

"You haf a chenius vor gorrubtion," said the baron, who had listened to Asia in silent admiration. "Chust as I haf a chenius vor panking."

"Is it a bargain, my duck?" said Asia.

"Done vor feefdy tausent vrancs eenztead of ein huntert tausent, ant ze morning afder mein driumph I vill gif you fife huntert tausent."

"Well then, I'll go about my work," answered Asia. "Ah, you can come," continued she respectfully. "You will find madame already as sweet as honey, and perhaps disposed to be kind."

"Go, go, meine gut vooman," said the baron rubbing his hands.

Then, after a smile toward the hideous mulatto woman, he said to himself:

"How fery nezzessary eet ees to haf blenty of money."

He jumped out of bed, went to his desk and took up the threads of his vast business with a light heart.

*

Nothing could be more fatal for Esther than the plan which Nucingen had adopted. When she fought against infidelity the poor courtesan was fighting for her life. Natural as this defense was, Carlos called it *silly prudery*. Without disregarding the precautions employed in such cases, Asia lost no time in informing Carlos of the interview she had had with the baron, and how she had turned it to account. Carlos' anger was terrible as himself; he took a carriage on the spot and, with the curtains drawn, drove into Esther's courtyard. This double forger was still pale with rage as he went up stairs and appeared before the poor girl. She was standing as she looked at him, then her legs gave way beneath her, and she fell back into an armchair. "What do you want, sir?" she asked, trembling in every limb.

"Leave us, Europe," said he. Esther looked at the maid as a child looks at the mother from whose side he is torn by a blood-thirsty assassin.

"Do you know where you are driving Lucien?" said Carlos, when he was left alone with Esther.

"Where?" she asked in a faint voice as she glanced fearfully at her executioner.

"To the place I have come from, my jewel."

The room swam before Esther's eyes as she looked at the man.

"To the galleys!" he added in a low voice.

Esther's eyes closed, her legs grew limp, her arms fell to her side; she grew very white. The man rang and Prudence appeared.

"Bring her back to consciousness," said he coolly, "I have not finished."

He paced up and down the room while he waited. Prudence Europe was obliged to beg him to place Esther on the bed; he lifted her with a facility that betokened the strength of an athlete. The most violent remedies of the apothecary were needed to restore Esther to the remembrance of her sorrows. An hour later the poor girl recovered strength enough to listen to the living nightmare, who sat on the foot of the bed, his eyes fixed and glistening like two drops of molten lead.

"Sweetheart," he said, "Lucien stands between a life that is brilliant, honored, fitting, happy, and the muddy ditch filled with slime and gravel, on the verge of which he stood when I rescued him. The Grandlieu family demand that your darling possess an estate worth a million before they secure for him the title of marquis and present him with that great catch, called Clotilde, by whose aid he will climb to power. Thanks to us both, Lucien has just bought his maternal manor, the old Château de Rubempré. It didn't cost much,—thirty thousand francs—but his attorney by fortunate negotiations has succeeded in adding to it about a million's worth of real estate, on which three hundred thousand francs have been paid. The château, the costs and the premiums forget the being who is recalled to their remembrance by the happiness which they enjoy anew every morning when they awake to find themselves rich. Lucien is worth more than you. He began by loving Coralie; she died well and good; he did not have a penny with which to bury her, but poet as he was, he didn't do as you did a moment ago, he didn't swoon; he wrote six drinking songs and earned three hundred francs to pay for Coralie's burial. I have those songs, I know them by heart. Go and do likewise; compose your songs; be gay! be wild! be irresistible! and be insatiable. You have understood me? Don't ask me to say more. Kiss papa. Adieu."

Half an hour later, when Europe entered her mistress' room, she found her kneeling before a crucifix in the pose that the most religious of painters gave to Moses before the bush of Horeb, when he sought to depict his deep and perfect adoration before Jehovah. When she had uttered her last prayer, Esther renounced her fair life, the honor which she had won, her glory, her virtue, and her love. She rose.

"Oh, madame, you will never be like this again!" exclaimed Prudence Servien, motionless before the sublime beauty of her mistress.

She turned the mirror quickly so that the poor girl could see herself. Her eyes still retained a portion of the soul that was leaving her for heaven. The complexion of the Jewess was brilliant. Steeped in tears and dried by the fire of prayer, her eyelashes looked like foliage after a summer's rain; the sun of pure love was lighting them for the last time. The expression of her lips was as if she had uttered her last invocation to the angels, from whom, no doubt, she had borrowed the martyr's palm and to whose keeping she had entrusted her life without spot. In a word, she possessed the majesty which must have transfigured Mary Stuart, when she bade good-bye to her crown, to earth and to love.

"I wish that Lucien could have seen me thus," said she, with a stifled sob. "But now," she added in a rasping voice, "to *humbug*."

As Europe heard this word she stood stupefied as if she had heard an angel blaspheme.

"Why do you look at me as though my teeth had become cloves? I am nothing now but a vile and infamous creature, a woman of the streets, a thief, and I am waiting for milord. Heat me a bath and bring me my gown. It's twelve o'clock; the baron will certainly come on his way from the Stock Exchange. I will tell him that I have been expecting him. I want Asia to serve him a dainty dinner, and I mean to drive him to distraction. Come, Europe, make haste; we are going to be merry, and that means that we are going to set to work."

She sat down at her table and wrote the following letter:

"My Friend:

"Had the cook you sent me yesterday never been in my service, I should have thought it was your intention to inform me of the number of fainting fits that you experienced the day before yesterday upon the receipt of my three notes. You must excuse me, I was dreadfully nervous on that day, for I was brooding over reminiscences of my deplorable existence. But I know Asia's sincerity. I do not repent of having caused you some sorrow, since it has served to prove how dearly you hold me. We poor despised creatures are ever thus: true affection touches us far more than to see ourselves the object of wild extravagance. I myself have always been afraid of becoming the peg on which you hang your vanity. I was sad that I could be nothing else for you. Yes, in spite of your loud protestations I thought that you took me for a bought woman, and now you will find me disposed to be kind, but on condition that you will never be wholly disobedient. If this letter can replace your doctor's prescriptions, you will prove it to me by coming to see me immediately after leaving the Stock Exchange. You will find, dressed in her best and loaded with your gifts, her, who signs herself for life,

"Your pleasure machine,
"ESTHER."

At the Exchange the Baron de Nucingen was so gay, happy and pleasant, and allowed himself to be the butt of so many jokes that Du Tillet and Keller, who were present, could not refrain from asking him the reason of his hilarity.

"I am luffed. Zat house-varming vill gome zoon," said he to Du Tillet.

"How much does it cost you?" demanded François Keller brusquely. People said that Madame Colleville had cost François twenty-five thousand francs a year.

"Zis vooman ees eine anchel; zhe has nefer asked me vor ein single benny."

"They never do," replied Du Tillet. "They provide themselves with aunts and mothers so that they need ask for nothing for themselves."

On the way from the Exchange to the Rue Taitbout, the baron said seven times to his coachman:

"You are nod moofing. Vip ze horse."

He climbed the stairs hurriedly, and for the first time he saw his mistress beautiful as are those women whose only occupation is the care of their garments and of their beauty. Fresh from the bath, the flower was sweet and so perfumed that Robert d'Arbrissel would have been conquered. Esther was dressed with fascinating unconventionality. A jacket of black reps adorned with trimmings of rose-colored silk was left open to disclose a skirt of gray satin, the costume that was worn later by the fair Amigo, in *I Puritani*. A scarf of English point lace fell loosely from her shoulders. The sleeves of her gown were caught in with cording, so as to divide the puffs, which for some time past had replaced the overgrown leg-of-mutton sleeves, discarded by fashionable women. Esther had pinned upon her splendid hair a cap of Mechlin lace, of the

HOW MUCH LOVE COSTS OLD MEN

style known as *à la folle*, always ready to fall, yet never falling, which gave her an appearance of uncombed disorder, although the straight white part was distinctly visible on her little head between the heavy locks of hair.

"Is it not dreadful to see madame so beautiful and sitting in a shabby room like this?" said Europe to the baron as she opened the parlor door.

"Zen gome to ze Rie Saint Chorches," replied the baron as he stood motionless in the doorway, like a dog before a partridge. "Ze weader ees magneeficent; ve vill dake ein valk een ze Jamps Elusées, ant Montame Saind Esdèfe mit Ichénie vill dransbort all your glothes ant leenen ant our tinner to ze Rie Saint Chorches."

"I will do everything that you wish," said Esther, "if you will be so kind as to call my cook, Asia, and Éugénie, Europe. I have given these names to all the women who have served me since the first two I ever had. I do not like change."

"Acia, Irobe," repeated the baron, laughing. "How ott you are! You are vull of imachination; I zhould haf eaden numperless tinners pefore galling eine cook Acia."

"Oddity is our nature," said Esther. "Can't a poor girl be fed by Asia and dressed by Europe when you live on the whole world? It is a myth! There are women who would devour the earth, while I do not ask for more than half.—There!"

"Vat eine vooman Montame Saind Esdèfe ees!"

thought the baron as he admired Esther's change of costume.

"Europe, my girl," said Esther, "I need a hat. I ought to have a black satin cape trimmed with rose-color and lace."

"Madame Thomas hasn't sent it. Come, baron, quickly; away with you. Begin your duties of hard labor, that is, of happiness; for pleasure is a heavy burden! You have your carriage; go to Madame Thomas," said Europe to the baron. "Tell your groom to ask for Madame Van Bogseck's cape, and, above all," she added in the baron's ear, "bring her back the prettiest bouquet in Paris. It is winter, so try to get tropical flowers."

The baron descended the stairs and said to his groom:

"Montame Dhomas."

The coachman drew up before the door of a famous pastry-cook.

"Id ees eine milliner, you pig plockhead, nod ein basdry-zhob," exclaimed the baron as he hurried away to the Palais Royal to Madame Prévôt's, where he had a bouquet made up for ten louis, while his groom went to find the fashionable milliner.

As he walks about Paris, the superficial observer wonders what fools buy the fabulous flowers that decorate the windows of the famous florist, and the hot-house fruits of the European Chevet, at whose shop alone, if we except the Rocher de Cancale, there is to be seen a genuine and attractive *review of two worlds.* Every day in Paris more than a hundred infatuations such as Nucingen's spring into being, and prove their reality by offering upon bended knee rarities that queens dare not afford, to women who, in Asia's words, love to cut a figure. Without this little detail an honest bourgeoise could not understand how a fortune melts in the hands of these creatures whose social function, according to the system of Fourier, is perhaps to repair the disasters of avarice and cupidity. These dissipations serve, doubtless, the same purpose in the social body that the incision of a lancet does in a too plethoric body. In two months Nucingen had sprinkled trade with more than two hundred thousand francs.

When the elderly lover returned, night was falling, and the bouquet was useless. In winter the time for going to the Champs Elysées is from two o'clock until four; nevertheless the carriage proved of service in transporting Esther from the Rue Taitbout to the Rue Saint Georges, where she took possession of the *leetle balace.* Never before, let us say it, had Esther been the object of such worship, nor of such profusion; she was amazed at it, but after the pattern of ungrateful royalty she was careful not to display the slightest mark of surprise. When you enter Saint Peter's at Rome, in order to make you appreciate the length and height of the queen of cathedrals, the guide points out the little finger of a statue which, though it is of vast dimensions, appears to be the natural size of a little finger.

Descriptions, however necessary they may be to the history of our customs, have so often been criticised that in this place we must imitate the Roman cicerone. Thus when he entered the dining-room, the baron could not refrain from asking Esther to feel the material of the window curtains, draped with regal abundance, lined with white watered silk, and trimmed with embroidery worthy of the gown of a Portuguese princess. The stuff was made of silk from Canton, and on it the patient Chinese had painted the birds of Asia with a perfection of which the prototype only exists upon the vellum parchments of the Middle Ages, or in the missal of Charles the Fifth, the pride of the imperial library at Vienna.

"Eet gost dwo tausent vrancs ze yart. I paught eet of ein Milord who hat prought eet vrom ze Inties."

"Very pretty! Charming! How pleasant it will be to drink champagne here," said Esther; "the foam will not stain the tiles."

"Oh, madame," said Europe, "only look at the carpet!"

"Zince zey hat tesigned ze garbed vor mein frient ze Tuke Dorlonia, who vound eet too tear, I dook it vrom him vor you, vor you are eine gueen!" exclaimed Nucingen.

By some chance this carpet, the work of one of our most ingenious designers, harmonized with the most fanciful Chinese drapery. The walls painted by Schinner and Léon de Lora, represented voluptuous scenes thrown into relief by carved ebony, bought for a goodly sum from Dusommerard, and forming panels, the simple gold lines of which reflected the light soberly. Now you can judge of the rest.

"You have done well to bring me here," said Esther; "I shall need a full week before I can grow perfectly accustomed to my house, and lay aside the air of an upstart."

"Mein house!" repeated the baron gleefully. "Zen you agzebt eet?"

"Yes, a thousand times yes, you stupid animal," she answered, smiling.

"Ze animal vas—"

"Stupid enough to be caressed," said she, glancing at him.

The poor lynx took Esther's hand and pressed it to his heart; he was animal enough to feel, but too stupid to find a word.

"Zee how eet peats at ein leetle vort of denterness!" said he.

Nucingen led his goddess (*cottess*) to her bedroom.

"Oh! madame," exclaimed Eugénie, "I can't stay here. That bed looks too inviting."

"And so," said Esther, "I wish to make the magician who works these wonders happy. Come, my fat elephant, after dinner we'll go to the theatre. I am famished for a play."

*

It was exactly five years since Esther had been to the theatre. At this time all Paris was flocking to the Porte Saint Martin to see a play that borrowed a terrible reality from the power of the actors, *Richard Darlington*. Like all ingenuous natures, Esther enjoyed shuddering with terror as well as melting into tears of tenderness.

"Let's go to see Frédérick Lemaître," said she; "he is an actor I adore."

"Eet ees ein zafage trama," said Nucingen, who saw that he was suddenly obliged to make himself notorious.

The baron despatched his servant to secure one of the two lower stage boxes. Another Parisian peculiarity! When success, always so transitory in its nature, fills the house there is invariably a stage box to let ten minutes before the curtain rises. When it is not destined to receive a Nucingen and his mistress, the directors reserve it for themselves. Like the hot-house fruits of Chevet, this box is a tax levied upon the whims of the Parisian Olympia.

It is needless to speak of the table service. Nucingen had amassed three several services: a small set, a medium set, and a large set. All the dessert plates and dishes of the large set were of embossed silver gilt. In order to avoid the appearance of overloading the table with too great a mass of gold and silver, the baron had added to each service, dishes of Dresden china of the most charming fragility, and more expensive than a complete silver service. On the table, the linen of Saxony, of England, of Flanders and of France rivaled one another in the perfection of their damasked flowers.

At dinner it was the baron's turn to be surprised as he tasted Asia's cooking.

"I unterstant," said he, "vy you name her Acia; zis ees Aciatic gookery."

"Ah, I begin to believe that he loves me," said Esther to Europe; "he has made something like a joke."

"I haf mate odders, doo," remarked he.

"He's more like Turcaret than any one imagines," exclaimed the courtesan, laughing at this answer that was worthy of a place among the celebrated ingenuous speeches of which the banker had been guilty.

The dishes were highly seasoned and gave the baron such a fit of indigestion that he was obliged to go home at an early hour; and this was all the pleasure he gathered from his first interview with Esther. At the play he was obliged to leave her between the acts and swallow an infinite number of glasses of *eau sucrée.* By a coincidence, so evidently the result of forethought that it could not be called chance, Tullia, Mariette and Madame du Val Noble were at the play that evening. *Richard Darlington* was one of those extreme, yet deserved successes that never occur except in Paris. It was a drama that made all the men imagine they could throw their lawful wives out of the window, and all the women were delighted to see themselves unjustly oppressed. The women said: "This is intolerable! We are too much plagued—but we are used to that sort of thing!"

A creature of Esther's beauty, dressed in Esther's gown, could not cut a figure with impunity in a front box of the Porte Saint Martin. The second act had scarcely begun, when great excitement arose in the box occupied by the two opera dancers, owing to the sudden identification of the beautiful stranger with La Torpille.

"Where can she have come from?" asked Mariette of Madame du Val Noble. "I supposed that she had been drowned."

"Is it she? She seems to me a hundred times younger and lovelier than she was six years ago."

"Perhaps she has been preserved in ice, like Madame d'Espard and Madame Zayonchek," remarked the Count de Brambourg, who had escorted the three women to the play, and had engaged one of the lower tier of boxes. "Isn't she the girl you wished to send me to wheedle my uncle?" added he, turning to Tullia.

"Exactly," answered the singer. "Du Bruel, go to the orchestra and see whether it's really she."

"How she tosses her head!" exclaimed Madame du Val Noble, making use of an admirable expression from the vocabulary of women of her class.

"Oh!" cried the Count de Brambourg, "she has the right to do so, for she's with my friend, the Baron de Nucingen. I'm going to them."

"Can that be the pretended Jeanne d'Arc, who has overthrown Nucingen and with whose praises we have been deafened for the past three months?" said Mariette.

"Good evening, baron," said Philippe Bridau, as he entered Nucingen's box. "So you and Mademoiselle Esther are married? Mademoiselle, I am a poor officer, whom you once helped out of a scrape at Issoudun—Philippe Bridau."

"Don't know you," said Esther, looking about the house with her opera glass.

"Montemoiselle's name," observed the baron, "ees no longer simply Esther; her name ees Matame te Jamby (Champy), ein leetle esdate zat I pought vor her."

"If you give her so many things," said the count, "the ladies who are with me say that Madame de Champy gives herself airs. If you do not care to remember me, deign to recollect Mariette, Tullia and Madame du Val Noble," added this upstart, who had ingratiated himself with the Dauphin through the support of the Duke de Maufrigneuse.

"If your ladies are so good to me, I am inclined to be very polite to them," answered Madame de Champy dryly.

"Good!" exclaimed Philippe. "They are very friendly; they have even surnamed you Jeanne d'Arc."

"Vell, eef zese laties vish your gombany," said Nucingen, "I vill leaf you alone, vor I haf ofereaden. Your garriage ant your zerfants vill gome vor you. Ze tefil take Acia."

"For the first time you would leave me alone!" said Esther. "Do your duty; you must learn to die at your post. I shall need an escort going out. If I were insulted I might look for help in vain."

The egotism of the old millionaire was compelled to yield to the obligations of the lover. The baron suffered and remained. Esther had reasons for detaining *her escort.* If she were to receive her old acquaintances she could not be questioned as seriously in company as she might be alone. Philippe Bridau returned hastily to his box, and described the state of things to the three ballet dancers.

"Ah! It is she who has inherited *my* house in the Rue Saint Georges!" remarked Madame du Val Noble bitterly, for in the language of her class she was *afoot*.

"Probably," answered the colonel; "Du Tillet told me that the baron has spent thrice as much on the house as your poor Falleix."

"Let's go and see her," said Tullia.

"No indeed," replied Mariette; "she's too handsome. I shall call upon her at her house."

"I am self-satisfied enough to venture," said Tullia.

Between the acts the leading opera dancer was bold enough to traverse the theatre and try to renew her acquaintance with Esther, who confined herself to generalities.

"And where do you come from, my dear child?" inquired the dancer, overcome with curiosity.

"Oh! I have spent the past five years in a château among the Alps with an English speculator who was jealous as a tiger. I called him *speck*, for short, because he was smaller than the bailiff of Ferrette. Then I fell into the hands of a banker,—*from Charylla to Sybdis*, as Florine says; and now that I have come back to Paris I am so eager for amusement that I shall become a perfect carnival. I shall keep open house. Ah! I must make up for five years of solitude, and I am beginning to make myself amends. Five years of an Englishman is too much. According to the programme six weeks is enough."

"Did the baron give you this lace?"

"No, that is a vestige of the nabob. Wasn't I unlucky, my dear? He was yellow as a woman laughing at a friend's success. I supposed that he would die before ten months were up. Bah, he was strong as an Alp. Distrust every man who says he has trouble with his liver. I don't want to hear them talk about their livers. Lord de*liver* me! The nabob robbed me; he died without making a will and the family pushed me out of doors as though I had had the plague. So I said to this fat man, 'Pay for two.' You are right to call me Jeanne d'Arc, I have lost England! And perhaps I shall be burned—"

"With love?" asked Tullia.

"Burned alive," replied Esther, who grew dreamy at this.

The baron laughed uproariously at these broad jests, but as he did not comprehend them instantly, his laugh sounded like a forgotten fuse exploding after a show of fireworks is over.

We all live in some sphere of life, and the inhabitants of every sphere are endowed with an equal share of curiosity. The following evening, at the Opera, Esther's return was the talk of the green-room. During the morning hours from two to four, all the Paris of the Champs Élysées had recognized La Torpille and knew that she was the object of Nucingen's adoration.

"Do you know," said Blondet to De Marsay in the lobby of the Opera, "that La Torpille disappeared the very day after we had recognized her here as the mistress of that little Rubempré?"

At Paris, as in the provinces, nothing is secret. The police of the Rue de Jerusalem is not so well organized as that of the world, where every one is a detective, though he knows it not. Carlos had surmised correctly the danger of Lucien's position during the episode in the Rue Taitbout and in the days following its conclusion.

There does not exist a more horrible situation than that in which Madame du Val Noble was placed, and the word *afoot* describes it perfectly. The carelessness and prodigality of these women prevent them from thinking of the future. In the exceptional world to which they belong, and which is far more amusing and witty than people think, the women who are not beautiful with that absolute and almost unalterable beauty, so easy to recognize, in short the women who can be loved only through some caprice, alone think of their old age, and lay by a fortune: the more beautiful they are, the more improvident. "So you are saving your income for fear of growing ugly," Florine once said to Mariette, and this throws light on one of the reasons of their prodigality. When a speculator commits suicide, when a spendthrift comes to the end of his tether, these women fall with frightful rapidity from boundless wealth to absolute penury. Then they fall into the power of the pawnbroker; they sell their exquisite jewels for a song; they contract debts; they do anything to maintain themselves in an apparent luxury, which allows them to recover what they have lost, a coffer from which they can draw. These heights and depths of their life explain very clearly the vast cost of an intrigue, almost always managed in real life by the same method that Asia had employed when she *hooked* —another word in the same vocabulary—Nucingen to Esther. Besides, those who know their Paris well are at no loss to guess the reason, when they meet in that moving and tumultuous bazaar, the Champs Élysées, some woman in a hackney cab, whom six months or a year before they had noticed in a carriage, gorgeous in its luxury and fashion. "When you fall into Sainte-Pélagie, you must know how to bounce back to the Bois de Boulogne," Florine had said as she was joking with Blondet about the little Vicount de Portenduère. A few wise women never risk this contrast. They remain immured in cheap lodging houses or else expiate their profusion by privations such as travelers suffer, lost in some Sahara, but even they do not comprehend the slightest notion of economy. They venture to masque balls; they make a trip into the country; they dress in fine clothes, and walk on the boulevards on bright days. To one another they display that devotion which is the distinctive mark of prescribed classes. Almsgiving costs little to the woman on the crest of the wave who says to herself, "To-morrow I shall be like this." The most efficacious protection, however, is that furnished by women who deal in old clothes. When a usurer of this description becomes a creditor, she stirs up the hearts of old men to pay off the mortgage she holds on hats and slippers. Unable to foresee the ruin of a very rich and shrewd broker, Madame du Val Noble was taken unawares. She had been accustomed to spend Falleix's money for the gratification of her caprices and relied upon him for her future. "How could I have expected this," said she to Mariette, "from a man who has always been such a *good fellow?*" In almost every class of society the *good fellow* is a generous man who lends a few louis here and there without asking for repayment, and rules his conduct in accordance with the dictates of a certain refinement beyond the current, enforced, commonplace morality. Some men called, like Nucingen, virtuous and upright, have ruined their benefactors, while others who are not ignorant of the police court are extraordinarily honest toward women. Perfect virtue as embodied in Alceste, the dream of Molière, is excessively rare. Yet it does exist everywhere, even in Paris. The *good fellow* is the product of a certain grace of character which proves nothing. A man is thus, just as a cat is sleek, or a slipper comfortable. So, according to the general acceptance of the expression "good fellow" among women of this class, Falleix should have warned his mistress of his failure and left her something to live upon. D'Estourny, the genteel swindler, was a good fellow; he cheated at play, but he had put aside thirty thousand francs for his mistress. Thus at gay suppers women answered his accusers: "It makes no difference, you may say what you will; Georges was a good fellow; he had charming manners, he deserved a better fate." In this society women mock at laws, and adore a certain kind of refinement; they can sell themselves, as Esther did, for some secret ideal that is their religion. After saving, with great difficulty, a few jewels from the wreck of her fortunes, Madame du Val Noble sank beneath the weight of the terrible accusation that she had ruined Falleix. She had reached the age of thirty, and, although she was in all the fulness of her beauty, yet she might easily pass for a woman past her prime. For in a crisis such as this a woman has all her rivals against her. Mariette, Florine and Tullia received their friend kindly at dinner, and gave her some assistance; but not knowing the amount of her debts they did not dare to sound the depth of the gulf. An interval of six years amidst the fluctuations of the Parisian sea separated La Torpille from Madame du Val Noble too widely to allow the *woman afoot* to turn for help to the woman in a carriage; but Madame du Val Noble, knowing Esther's generosity well, and feeling sometimes that Esther had inherited her fortune from her, determined to contrive a meeting which should appear the result of chance, although in reality premeditated.

In order to arrive at this end, Madame du Val Noble, fashionably dressed, walked up and down the Champs Élysées on the arm of Théodore Gaillard, who finally married her, and who in this trouble had behaved with great kindness toward his former mistress, giving her boxes at the theatre and securing invitations for her to every *entertainment.* She hoped that on some fine day Esther might be driving there, and that they might meet face to face. Esther had Paccard for a coachman, for within five days her household had been so organized by Asia, Europe and Paccard, acting under Carlos' orders, that the house in the Rue Saint Georges had become an impregnable fortress.

On his part, Peyrade, moved by his profound hatred, by his desire for vengeance, and above all, by his purpose of providing a dowry for his dear Lydie, had chosen the Champs Élysées as the end of his daily walk from the time that Contenson had told him that M. de Nucingen's mistress was to be seen there. Peyrade could get himself up so perfectly as an Englishman, and could speak French so admirably with the chirping accent which the English introduce into our language; he knew English so completely and was so intimately versed in the affairs of that country, whither he had been three times sent by the Parisian police in 1779 and 1786, that he played the part of an Englishman both at the English embassy and in London without awakening suspicion. He had acquired much of the skill of Musson, the famous conjurer, and could disguise himself with so much art that one day Contenson failed to recognize him. Accompanied by Contenson disguised as a mulatto, Peyrade scrutinized Esther and her servants with that seemingly inattentive glance that does not lose the least detail. So it consequently happened that he was in the side alley in which people walk in fine, dry weather after leaving their carriages, the very day that Esther met there with Madame du Val Noble. Peyrade, followed by his mulatto in livery, walked naturally along, like a true nabob, thinking only of himself, behind the two women at such a distance that he could overhear some snatches of their conversation.

"Do come to see me, my dear child," Esther was saying to Madame du Val Noble; "Nucingen owes it to himself not to leave the mistress of his broker without a penny."

"All the more because people say that it was he

who ruined him," said Théodore Gaillard, "and that we can make him squeal by threatening to expose him."

"He dines with me to-morrow. Come," said Esther.

Then she added in a low tone:

"I make him do everything that I wish, and he hasn't had that of me yet."

With this she placed one of her gloved fingers beneath the prettiest of her teeth and made that familiar gesture which means emphatically, "Nothing at all."

-"You have him tight?"

"My dear, as yet he has only paid my debts."

"Is he close-fisted?" exclaimed Suzanne du Val Noble.

"Oh!" replied Esther, "my debts were enough to frighten a minister of finance. Now I wish to get an income of thirty thousand francs before the clock strikes midnight! Oh, he's complaisance itself; I have nothing to complain of. Everything's going well. We shall have a house-warming within the week and you shall be of the party. To-morrow he must offer me the deed of the house in the Rue Saint Georges. A woman can't live decently in such a house as that without an income of thirty thousand francs to turn to in case of mishap. I have known poverty, and I want no more of it. There are certain experiences which you can't see too little of."

"To think of your saying: 'fortune and I are one!' How you have changed!" exclaimed Suzanne.

"It is the air of Switzerland. One becomes economical there. It's the place for you, my dear! Get hold of a Swiss and perhaps he will turn out a husband! For they haven't yet learned to understand women like you and me. In any case you will return with a desire for an income on the public ledger—a most honest and refined desire! Adieu."

Esther stepped into her handsome carriage drawn by the most magnificent pair of dapple-gray mares to be found in Paris.

"The woman getting into her carriage is not to be despised, but I like the one who walks still better," said Peyrade to Contenson, in English; "follow her and find out who she is."

"Hear what that Englishman has just been saying in English," said Théodore Gaillard, repeating Peyrade's words to Madame du Val Noble.

Before venturing to speak in English, Peyrade had uttered a single exclamation in that tongue which caused an expression in Théodore Gaillard's face that made the journalist's acquaintance with English very evident. Madame du Val Noble walked leisurely homeward to a very respectable boarding house in the Rue Louis le Grand, looking to one side to see whether the mulatto were still following her. This establishment belonged to a Madame Gérard, who had received assistance from Madame du Val Noble in the days of her splendor, and was now showing her gratitude by lodging the unlucky woman in a suitable fashion. This good woman, middle class, honest, virtuous, even pious, received the courtesan as a being of a higher order; she had always seen her surrounded by luxury; she took her for a fallen queen; she confided her daughters to her care; and, what was more natural perhaps than we may think, the courtesan was as scrupulous when she took them to the theatre as a mother would have been. The two Mademoiselle Gérards loved her in return. The good and worthy hostess was like those sublime priests who see a creature to save and to love in a woman without the pale of law. Madame du Val Noble respected this goodness, and often as they talked together in the evenings deploring her misfortunes, she envied her. "You are still handsome; you can still come to a good end," Madame Gérard would say to her. Moreover Madame du Val Noble had only fallen relatively. The wardrobe of this lavish and extravagant woman was yet in sufficiently good repair to allow her to appear on occasions like the evening of *Richard Darlington*, at the Porte Saint Martin, in all her glory. Madame Gérard besides paid with a good grace for the carriages that were required to drive this woman who had lost her means of subsistence to some restaurant for her dinner, or to take her to the theatre and to bring her home.

"Well, my dear Madame Gérard," said she to that excellent woman, "my lot is going to change, I think—"

"Then, madame, so much the better; but don't be led astray; think of the future. Don't run into debt. I have so much trouble in getting rid of your creditors!"

"Oh! don't waste a thought on those *dogs:* they have all stolen enormous sums from me. Here are tickets to the Variétés for your daughters—a good box on the balcony. If anybody asks for me before I return let him be shown upstairs. Adèle, my old waiting-maid, will be there; I am going to send her to you."

Madame du Val Noble, who had neither aunt nor mother, was obliged to have recourse to her maid (*afoot,* too) in order to make her play the part of a Saint Estève with the stranger whose conquest would permit her to regain her rank. She was going to dine with Théodore Gaillard, who on that day had a pleasure party on hand; that is to say, a dinner given by Nathan in payment of a wager; one of those orgies to which the host invites his guest with the words, "There will be women there."

*

It was not without weighty reasons that Peyrade had decided to enter the lists in person. Moreover his curiosity, as well as that of Corentin, was so violently aroused that even without reasons he would have willingly mingled in the drama. At this moment the policy of Charles X. had completed its last evolution. When he had intrusted the helm of state to ministers of his own choice, the king prepared to conquer Algiers in order to use the ensuing glory as a passport to what has been called his coup d'état. Within the kingdom conspiracy had died out; Charles X. thought himself without an enemy. In politics, as on the ocean, there are treacherous calms. Thus Corentin had fallen into absolute inaction. In this situation a true hunter, in order to keep his hand in practice, kills crows when partridges have flown. Domitian, himself, killed flies when there were no more Christians. A witness of Esther's arrest, Contenson had, with the exquisite perception of a detective, passed an accurate judgment on that operation. As we have seen, the fellow had not even taken pains to conceal his opinion from the Baron de Nucingen. "For whose profit are they levying contributions on the baron's passions?" was the first question that the two friends asked of each other. When he had recognized Asia as an actress in the comedy, Contenson had hoped to reach the author of the conspiracy through her. She had eluded him, however, hiding for some time like an eel in the mud of Paris, and when he discovered her in the capacity of Esther's cook, the co-operation of the mulatto woman seemed inexplicable. For the first time these two artists in espionage had met with an indecipherable text, although they suspected that it concealed a dark story. After three successive and bold attacks upon the house in the Rue Taitbout, Contenson had encountered nothing but the most obstinate silence. As long as Esther lived in the house the porter seemed under the influence of the most profound terror. Perhaps Asia had promised the entire household that poisonous dishes should revenge the slightest indiscretion. The day following that on which Esther had left her apartment, Contenson had found the porter somewhat more reasonable: he regretted the departure of the lady who, he said, had fed him with fragments from her table. Contenson, disguised as a broker, bargained for the apartment and lent his ear to the porter's sorrows, made fun of him, and cast a slur of suspicion over everything he said by continually repeating "Is it possible?" "Yes, sir, the little lady lived here for five years without leaving the house, while her lover, who was jealous, although she was without reproach, used the greatest precaution in coming and going. He was a very handsome young man, too."

Lucien was still at Marsac, staying with his sister, Madame Séchard; but after his return Contenson despatched the porter to the Quai Malaquais to ask M. de Rubempré whether he would consent to sell the furniture of the apartment lately left vacant by Madame Van Bogseck. The porter then recognized in Lucien the mysterious lover of the young widow, and Contenson cared not to know more. It is easy to imagine the profound though concealed amazement with which Lucien and Carlos were seized. They seemed to think the porter mad and tried to persuade him of his insanity.

Within twenty-four hours a counter-police was organized by Carlos, which surprised the detective in the very act of spying. Contenson, disguised as a butcher's boy, had twice already delivered the provisions purchased by Asia in the morning, and twice he had succeeded in entering the little house in the Rue Saint Georges. Corentin, on his part, was not idle; but the appearance of Carlos Herrera on the scene stopped him short, for he knew at once that this priest, the secret envoy of Ferdinand VII., had come to Paris toward the end of the year 1823. Nevertheless, Corentin felt it necessary to study the reasons which had led the Spaniard to protect Lucien de Rubempré, and it was soon clear to him that Esther had been Lucien's mistress for full five years. Thus the substitution of the Englishwoman for Esther had taken place in the dandy's interests. Lucien had no means of subsistence. The hand of Mademoiselle de Grandlieu had been refused him, and yet he had lately paid a million of francs for the Rubempré estate. Corentin adroitly excited the interest of the Director-General of the police of the kingdom, who was informed by the Prefect of police that the complainants in the case of Peyrade had been none other than the Count de Sérizy and Lucien de Rubempré.

"Now we have it!" exclaimed Corentin and Peyrade.

The plan of the two friends was drawn in an instant.

"This girl has had intrigues," said Corentin; "she has friends among the women of her class, and among these friends one at least must have been unlucky. One of us shall play the part of a rich foreigner and make her his mistress; we will keep her on the best of terms with Madame Van Bogseck. They always need one another's help in the game of love, and so we shall be within their inmost walls."

It was quite natural for Peyrade to think of assuming the disguise of an Englishman. The life of debauchery which must precede the discovery of the plot of which he had been the victim, pleased his fancy, while Corentin, who had grown old in the harness and whose health was none too vigorous, cared little for such excesses. By his disguise as a mulatto Contenson escaped at once from all danger of Carlos' counter-police. Three days before Peyrade's encounter with Madame du Val Noble in the Champs Élysées, the last of the agents of MM. de Sartine and Lenoir, furnished with a formally correct passport, registered at the Hotel Mirabeau in the Rue de la Paix. He had arrived from the colonies by way of Havre, in a small carriage quite muddy enough to have come all the way from Havre, although it had only made the journey from Saint Denis to Paris.

On his side Carlos Herrera had his passport signed at the Spanish Embassy, and made all his arrangements in the Quai Malaquais preparatory to his journey to Madrid. This was his reason: within a few days Esther was to become the owner of the small house in the Rue Saint Georges, she was to obtain in advance a bond of thirty thousand francs; Europe and Asia were sufficiently shrewd to sell it in her name and bring the money secretly to Lucien. Lucien, reputed to be rich through the generosity of his sister, would thus be enabled to pay the balance of the debt on the Rubempré estate. Nobody could find fault with his conduct in this respect. Esther alone had the power to be indiscreet, but she would rather die than betray the least sign of complicity. Clotilde had lately displayed a rose-colored scarf about her stork-like neck, and therefore the day was won in the Grandlieu mansion. The stock of the omnibus system already paid three hundred per cent. By disappearing for a few days, Carlos would disarm all suspicion. Human prudence had foreseen everything; a mistake was impossible. The pseudo-Spaniard was to depart the day after that on which

Peyrade had met Madame du Val Noble on the Champs Élysées. But on that very night at two o'clock in the morning Asia came to the Quai Malaquais in a cab, and found the engineer of the machine smoking in his room, absorbed in a review of the scheme we have described, like an author scanning a proof sheet of his book, seeking for some error. A man such as he could not repeat an omission like that of the porter in the Rue Taitbout.

"Paccard," whispered Asia in her master's ear, "recognized Contenson yesterday at half-past two in the Champs Élysées, disguised as a mulatto servant to an Englishman, who for the past three days has been walking up and down the Champs Élysées, in order to watch Esther. Paccard recognized him this morning by his eyes, as I did when he was disguised as a butcher's boy. Paccard drove our little lady in such a manner as to keep the rascal in sight. He is at the Hotel Mirabeau, and he has interchanged so many signals of intelligence with the Englishman that Paccard says that the Englishman can't be an Englishman."

"We have a gad-fly after us," said Carlos. "I shall not go until the day after to-morrow. Contenson is evidently the man who has spurred on the porter of the Rue Taitbout to follow us to our very door. We must make certain whether the sham Englishman is our enemy."

At twelve o'clock M. Samuel Johnson's mulatto was waiting gravely upon his master, who, faithful to his custom, always ate a sumptuous breakfast.

Peyrade wished to pass for an Englishman of the *drinking* species: he never rose from table till his second bottle was empty. He wore black cloth gaiters, extending as far as his knees and padded so as to increase the dimensions of his legs; his pantaloons were lined with thick cloth, his waistcoat was buttoned up to his chin; his blue cravat muffled his neck up to the cheeks; his head was covered by a small red peruke; he had increased his height by three inches: the oldest habitué of the Café David would have failed to recognize him. By his square-cut coat, black, ample and well brushed as an English coat always is, a stranger would have taken him for a British millionaire. Contenson had displayed the cool insolence of the confidential valet of a nabob: he was silent, surly, distant, uncommunicative, made foreign gestures and uttered ferocious exclamations. Peyrade was finishing his second bottle when a waiter introduced, without ceremony, into the apartment a man whom Peyrade, as well as Contenson, recognized as a gendarme in civilian's dress.

"Monsieur Peyrade," said the gendarme in a whisper to the nabob, "I have orders to take you to the Prefecture."

Peyrade rose without a word and went to get his hat.

"You will find a cab at the door," said the gendarme, on the stairway. "The Prefect wished to arrest you, but he has contented himself with requiring an explanation of your conduct through a constable whom you will find in the carriage."

"Shall I get in with you?" asked the gendarme of the constable, when Peyrade had taken his seat in the carriage.

"No," replied the officer. "Tell the coachman quietly to go to the Prefecture."

Peyrade and Carlos sat together in the same carriage. Carlos had a poignard within reach. The cab was driven by a confidential coachman, quite capable of allowing Carlos to slip out unnoticed, and of being amazed to find a corpse in the carriage when he came to his journey's end. A detective's body is never reclaimed. Justice permits this class of murderers to go unpunished; they are too difficult to trace. Peyrade cast his searching glance over the magistrate whom the Prefect of Police had commissioned to examine him. Carlos' appearance was satisfactory: a bald head, furrowed with wrinkles in the back; powdered hair; then, over sore eyes, bordered with red, and evidently in constant need of care, a pair of gold spectacles, very light and very bureaucratic, with two thicknesses of green glass. These eyes were certificates of some foul disease. A linen shirt, with smoothly ironed ruffles, a waistcoat of worn black satin, constable's trousers, black grogram stockings, and shoes tied with ribbons, a long black surtout, two-franc gloves, black and worn for ten days, a gold watch-chain. He was neither more nor less than the inferior magistrate whom men misterm *constable.*

"My dear Monsieur Peyrade, I regret that a man

like you should be the object of surveillance which you are careful to justify by your behavior. Your disguise is not to the Prefect's taste. If you think that you can escape our vigilance by this means you are mistaken. Doubtless you joined the route from England at Beaumont-sur-Oise?"

"At Beaumont-sur-Oise?" replied Peyrade.

"Or at Saint Denis?" suggested the pseudo magistrate.

Peyrade felt troubled. This new question required an answer, but every answer was dangerous. An affirmation would be mockery, a denial, if the man knew the truth, meant ruin.

"He's clever," thought Peyrade.

He tried to smile at the officer, and gave him this smile for an answer. The smile was accepted without protest.

"What was your purpose in assuming your disguise, in taking an apartment in the Hotel Mirabeau, and in dressing Contenson as a mulatto?" demanded the constable.

"The Prefect may do with me as he wishes, but I owe account of my actions to no man but my superiors," said Peyrade with dignity.

"If you wish me to understand that you are acting on behalf of the general police of the kingdom," replied the sham constable dryly, "we will change our direction and go to the Rue de Grenelle instead of the Rue de Jérusalem. My orders in respect to you are most specific. But take care; they are not nursing any deep grudge against you, and yet in a moment you would ruin yourself. For my part, I wish you no harm. But, out with it! Tell me the truth."

"The truth is this," said Peyrade, casting a scrutinizing glance at the eyes of his Cerberus.

The face of the pretended magistrate remained motionless and impassive; he did justice to his art; all truth appeared indifferent to him; he seemed to be annoyed with the Prefect for some whim. Prefects have their crotchets.

"I am madly in love with a woman, the mistress of that broker who is traveling for his own pleasure and for the displeasure of his creditors, Falleix."

"Madame du Val Noble," said the officer.

"Yes," continued Peyrade. "To be able to support her for a month, which will not cost me more than three thousand francs, I dressed myself as a nabob, and took Contenson for my domestic. This, monsieur, is so true that if you will leave me in the cab, where I will wait for you, on the word of an old Commissary-General of police, and go into the hotel, you can question Contenson. Not only will Contenson confirm what I have had the honor of telling you, but you will meet Madame du Val Noble's maid who is this morning to bring us a consent to my proposal, or the conditions of her mistress. You can tell an old monkey by his grimaces. I have offered a thousand francs a month, a carriage—that makes fifteen hundred; five hundred francs in presents, as much in entertainments, dinners, plays; you see that I am not a penny out of the way in telling you three thousand francs. A man of my age can easily spend three thousand francs on her latest whim."

"Ah! Papa Peyrade, do you still love women enough to—? But you surpass me there; I am sixty years old and I get on very well without them. Nevertheless, if everything is as you say, I suppose that your foreign dress was necessary for the gratification of your fancy."

"You see that Peyrade or Père Canquoëlle of the Rue des Moineaux—"

"Yes, neither of them would have suited Madame du Val Noble," interrupted Carlos, delighted to learn Père Canquoëlle's address. "Before the revolution I had for my mistress a woman who had belonged to the Jack Ketch of that time. One day, at the theatre, she pricks herself with a pin, and exclaims, as people did in those days, 'Ah! bloody!' 'Is it a reminiscence?' asked her neighbor. Well, my dear Peyrade, she left her husband on account of the joke. I imagine that you don't care to expose yourself to a similar insult. Madame du Val Noble moves in a fashionable sphere. I saw her at the Opera once and thought her very handsome. My dear sir, ask the coachman to drive back to the Rue de la Paix; I will go up to your room with you and see everything for myself. A verbal report will doubtless satisfy the Prefect."

Carlos drew from his side pocket a snuff box of black card-board, lined with vermilion, and offered it to Peyrade with a gesture of charming cordiality. Peyrade said to himself:

"These are their agents! Lord! if M. Lenoir or M. de Sartine should come to earth again, what would they say?"

"That's no doubt a portion of the truth, but it's not all, my dear friend," said the counterfeit officer, as he sniffed the last grains of his pinch of snuff. "You have been meddling in the love affairs of the Baron de Nucingen, and doubtless you purpose to catch him in some slip-noose; you have missed him with your pistol and now you wish to bring your heavy artillery to bear. Madame du Val Noble is a friend of Madame de Champy—"

"Ah, the devil! the game's up!" thought Peyrade. "He's more wily than I supposed. He's tricking me; he talks about letting me go, and yet he continues to pump me."

"Well?" demanded Carlos, with a magisterial air.

"Monsieur, it is true that I made the mistake of searching, on M. de Nucingen's behalf, for a woman with whom he was wildly in love. It is the reason of my present disgrace, for it seems that I have unintentionally touched upon very grave interests."

The petty magistrate was impassible.

"But after fifty-two years' experience I know the police well enough," continued Peyrade, "to keep myself well away from them since the scolding I received from the Prefect, who certainly was right."

"Then you would give up your caprice if the Prefect should require it? That, I think, would be the best proof of the sincerity of what you have told me."

"How he runs on! how he runs on!" said Peyrade to himself. "Who would have believed it? The agents of to-day are as good as those of M. Lenoir!"

"Give it up!" replied Peyrade aloud. "I shall wait the Prefect's orders. But if you care to come in, here we are at the hotel."

"Where does your money come from?" demanded Carlos point-blank, with an air of extreme sagacity.

"Monsieur, I have a friend—" said Peyrade.

"Tell that," answered Carlos, "to a judge in court."

This bold scene was, on Carlos' part, the result of one of those combinations whose simplicity could proceed from no brain except that of a man of his stamp. Very early in the morning he had sent Lucien to call upon the Countess de Sérizy. Lucien requested the count's private secretary to go to the Prefect on behalf of the count, and ask for information concerning the agents employed by the Baron de Nucingen. The secretary had returned, provided with a memorandum concerning Peyrade, a copy of the summary in the form of an indorsement:

"In the police since 1778, and come to Paris from Avignon two years before.

"*Without money and without morality. A depositary of state secrets.*

"*Lives in the Rue des Moineaux, under the name of Canquoelle, the name of a small estate in the department of Vaucluse, where his family lives. The family was, moreover, honorable. Has been recently inquired after by one of his grand-nephews, named Théodore de la Peyrade.* (See the report of an agent. Docket No. 37.)"

"He must be the Englishman whose mulatto servant is Contenson," Carlos had exclaimed when Lucien added some extra information given him by word of mouth.

In three hours' time this man, active as a Commander-in-Chief, had discovered, through the services of Paccard, an innocent accomplice well fitted to play the part of the gendarme, and had disguised himself as a constable. Three times in the cab he had been on the point of assassinating Peyrade; but he had made a firm resolution never again to commit murder with his own hands, and adhering to his principle he determined to rid himself of Peyrade by pointing him out as a millionaire to a few liberated galley-slaves.

Peyrade and his mentor could hear the voice of Contenson as he talked with Madame du Val Noble's waiting-maid. Peyrade made a sign to Carlos to remain in the ante-room, with an air that seemed to mean, "You are going to judge of my sincerity."

"Madame consents to all," Adèle was saying. "At this moment madame is visiting one of her friends, Madame de Champy, who has secured for another year a furnished apartment in the Rue Taitbout, which no doubt she will be glad to let my mistress have. It will be more convenient for madame to meet M. Johnson there, for the furniture is still in good condition, and monsieur can buy it for madame by making a bargain with Madame de Champy."

"All right, the leaves are there if the carrot's wanting," said the mulatto to the surprised maid; "but we'll share—"

"There's a negro for you!" exclaimed Mademoiselle Adèle. "If your nabob is a nabob, he'll not find it hard to present madame with the furniture. The lease expires in April, 1830; your nabob may renew it if he thinks fit."

"I am well satisfied," answered Peyrade in bad French, as he entered the room and tapped the maid on the shoulder. Then he made signal of inquiry to Carlos, who implied by a gesture of assent that the nabob should not depart from his rôle. At this juncture the scene was suddenly changed by the entrance of a person against whom both Carlos and the Prefect of police were powerless. Corentin suddenly appeared. He, finding the door open, had stepped in casually to see how Peyrade was acting his part as nabob.

"The Prefect invariably *sniffs* me out!" whispered

Peyrade in Corentin's ear. "He has discovered that I am playing nabob."

"We shall checkmate the Prefect," whispered Corentin in return.

Then, after a cold bow, he began to examine the magistrate surreptitiously.

"Stay here until my return; I am going to the Prefecture," said Carlos. "If you don't see me again, you are at liberty to carry out your whim."

After having whispered these words in Peyrade's ear so as not to disgrace the nabob in the eyes of the waiting-maid, Carlos made his exit, not caring to remain longer beneath the scrutiny of the newcomer, in whom he recognized one of those fair-complexioned persons whose blue eyes are at once terrible and cold.

"He is the constable that the Prefect sent after me," explained Peyrade to Corentin.

"He?" replied Corentin. "You have put your foot in it. That man has three thicknesses of cardboard in his soles, as you can tell by the position of his foot in the shoe; and then a constable has no reason to disguise himself."

Corentin hurried downstairs in order to verify his suspicions; Carlos was stepping into the cab.

"Hi! Monsieur l'Abbé," cried Corentin.

Carlos turned his head, perceived Corentin and sprang into his cab. Nevertheless Corentin had time to say, as the door was closing:

"That's all I cared to know."

"Quai Malaquais!" cried Corentin to the driver with a voice and look of devilish irony.

"Well," thought Jacques Collin; "it's all up with me. They are aroused. I must get the start of them, and above all find out what they want of me."

Corentin had seen the Abbé Carlos Herrera five or six times, and the aspect of this man could not be forgotten. Corentin had recognized first the squareness of his shoulders, then certain swellings on his face, and the three false inches obtained by an interior heel.

"Ah, ha! old man, they have been making game of you," said Corentin, perceiving that Peyrade and Contenson were alone in the bed-chamber.

"Who?" exclaimed Peyrade in a voice of metallic vibration; "I shall spend my last days in fastening him to a gridiron and broiling him alive."

"It's the Abbé Carlos Herrera, probably the Corentin of Spain. Everything's explained. He's an accomplished villain, who wished to make the fortune of a young man by coining money in a pretty woman's mint. It's for you to decide whether you care to tilt with a diplomat who seems to me most devilishly crafty."

"Oh!" cried Contenson, "he received the three hundred thousand francs the day that Esther was arrested; he was in the cab. I remember his eyes, his forehead and certain traces of small-pox."

"Ah, what a dowry my poor Lydie might have had!" exclaimed Peyrade.

"You can be a nabob still," said Corentin. "In order to keep an eye on Esther we must bind her fast to Madame du Val Noble; she was the real mistress of Lucien de Rubempré."

"They have bled Nucingen of more than five hundred thousand francs already," remarked Contenson.

"They need as much more," continued Corentin. "The Rubempré estate costs a million. Papa," he added, slapping Peyrade's shoulder; "you can have more than a hundred thousand francs to marry Lydie with."

"Don't tell me that, Corentin. If your plan fails, I don't know what I may be capable of—"

"You shall have them to-morrow, perhaps! The priest is very cunning; we must tame him. He's an arch-devil, but I have him fast; he's no fool and he'll surrender. Try to be as stupid as a nabob and fear nothing."

*

The evening of the day on which the real adversaries met face to face on a fair field, Lucien went to pass the evening at the Grandlieu house. The assembled company was numerous. In the sight of all her guests, the duchess detained Lucien long by her side and treated him with marked attention.

"You have been on a little journey?" said she.

"Yes, madame. In her desire to compass my marriage, my sister has made very great sacrifices, and I have been enabled to purchase the Rubempré estate and to remodel it entirely. I have found, in my Paris lawyer, a man shrewd enough to avoid the claims which the late rascally owners would have raised had they known the name of the purchaser."

"Is there a château?" asked Clotilde smiling.

"There is something which resembles a château, but the wisest plan will be to use its materials to build a modern house."

Clotilde's eyes shot flames of happiness across her smiles of content.

"To-night you will play a rubber with my father," said she to Lucien in a low voice; "in a fortnight I trust you will be invited to dinner."

"Ah, my dear sir," said the Duke de Grandlieu, "they tell me that you have bought the Rubempré estate; allow me to offer you my congratulations.

It is a fitting answer to those who accused you of being in debt. People such as we can have a public debt, like England and France; but, you see, people without money—beginners—can't indulge in that sort of thing."

"But, your lordship, I still owe five hundred thousand francs on my land."

"Then you must marry a girl who will bring them to you. But you will find it a difficult task to discover a bride with a fortune like that in our Faubourg, where men give small dowries to their daughters."

"Their name alone is enough," replied Lucien.

"We are but three for a game of whist—Manfrigneuse, d'Espard and I; will you make the fourth?" said the duke to Lucien, pointing toward the card-table.

Clotilde came to the table to watch her father play.

"Does she mean me to take this compliment to myself?" said the duke, patting his daughter's hands and casting a side-glance at Lucien, who remained quite serious.

Lucien, the partner of M. d'Espard, lost twenty louis.

"Dear mother," said Clotilde to the duchess, "he was clever enough to lose."

At eleven o'clock, after exchanging a few words of love with Mademoiselle de Grandlieu, Lucien drove back to his lodgings, and went to bed thinking of the complete triumph in store for him within a month, for he no longer doubted that he would be accepted as Clotilde's betrothed, and married before the Lent of 1830.

The next day, after breakfast, while Lucien was smoking his cigarette in company with Carlos, who had become very anxious, the servant announced that M. de Saint Estève—what an epigram!—would like to speak either with the Abbé Carlos Herrera or with M. Lucien de Rubempré.

"Was he told that I had gone?" asked the priest.

"Yes, monsieur," answered the groom.

"Receive him," said Carlos to Lucien; "but don't utter a single compromising word; don't let a gesture of surprise escape you—it's the enemy."

"You shall listen to me," replied Lucien.

Carlos concealed himself in a neighboring apartment, and looking through a crack in the door, he saw Corentin enter. Such was that great man's genius for transformation, that the priest could recognize his voice alone. On this occasion Corentin represented an old chief of division in the department of finance.

"I have not the honor of being known to you," said Corentin; "but—"

"Excuse me for interrupting you, sir," said Lucien; "but—"

"But, I wish to speak to you concerning your marriage with Mademoiselle Clotilde de Grandlieu, which will not come to pass," replied Corentin quickly.

Lucien sat down and did not answer.

"You are in the hands of a man who has the power, the will and the readiness to prove to the Duke de Grandlieu that the Rubempré estate will be bought with the price that a blockhead has paid for your mistress, Mademoiselle Esther," continued Corentin. "It will be easy to discover the minutes of the judgments in virtue of which Mademoiselle Esther has been prosecuted, and I have the means of loosening d'Estourny's tongue. The exceedingly adroit manœuvres employed against the baron will be brought to light.—Now, everything can be arranged. Give me a hundred thousand francs and you will be left in peace. This has nothing to do with me. I am merely the agent of those who are playing this game, nothing more."

Corentin might have talked for an hour; Lucien smoked his cigarette with an air of perfect indifference.

"Monsieur," he answered, "I do not wish to know who you are, for people who undertake such commissions as this are nameless so far as I am concerned. I have heard you quietly to the end; I am at home. You do not appear to be destitute of sense. Listen to my dilemma."

There was a pause, during which Lucien, with an icy stare, met the cat's eyes that Corentin directed toward him.

"Whether you found your assertions on facts entirely false, and I shall take no note of this," continued Lucien, "or whether your statements are correct, by giving you one hundred thousand francs,

I should give you the right of demanding of me as many hundred thousands of francs as your employer can discover Saint Estèves to send me.—But to cut short your estimable negotiation, learn that I, Lucien de Rubempré, fear nobody. I have no part in the practices about which you are talking. If the Grandlieu family stir up any difficulty, there are other young and aristocratic women whom I can marry; lastly, it is no reproach for me to remain a bachelor, especially when, as you believe, I am carrying on so prosperous a trade."

"If M. l'Abbé Carlos Herrera—"

"Monsieur," said Lucien, interrupting Corentin, "the Abbé Carlos Herrera is at this moment on his way to Spain. He has nothing to do with my marriage, and no concern in my interests. He is a politician, and has been kind enough to aid me for years with his advice, but he is obliged to render an account of himself to his Majesty, the King of Spain; if you have business with him I advise you to take a journey to Madrid."

"Sir," said Corentin shortly, "you shall never be the husband of Mademoiselle Clotilde de Grandlieu."

"So much the worse for her," replied Lucien, pushing Corentin impatiently toward the door.

"Have you reflected soberly?" asked Corentin coldly.

"Sir, I do not recognize your right to interfere in my affairs, nor to deprive me of a cigarette," said Lucien, tossing away his extinguished cigarette.

"Good-bye, sir," said Corentin. "We shall not see each other again.—But certainly there will come a time in your life when you would give half your fortune to have decided to stop me as I walked down your staircase."

In answer to this menace Carlos drew his hand across his throat.

"To work, now!" he cried, looking at Lucien who had grown pale after this terrible conference.

If, among the limited number of readers who study the moral and philosophical style of a book, there is a single person capable of believing in the satisfaction of the Baron de Nucingen, that one person would prove how difficult it is to subject the heart of a courtesan to any physiological maxims whatsoever. Esther had resolved to make the poor millionaire pay dearly for what that millionaire called his "tay of driumph." In the early days of February, 1830, the house-warming had not yet been given in the *leetle balace.*

"But," said Esther confidentially to her friends, who repeated the speech to the baron at the carnival, "I keep open house and I wish to make my husband happy as a *plaster cock.*"

This phrase became proverbial in the world of these women.

The baron gave himself up to lamentation. Like married men, he became somewhat ridiculous; he began to bewail his fate in the presence of his confidential friends, and his discontent was noised abroad. Nevertheless Esther continued conscientiously to play her part as the Madame de Pompadour of the prince of speculation. She had already given two or three receptions solely for the purpose of introducing Lucien into her house. Lousteau, Rastignac, Du Tillet, Bixiou, Nathan, the Count de Brambourg, the flower of rakes, were all constant guests at her salon. Finally Esther accepted as actresses for the piece which she was playing, Tullia, Florentine, Fanny Beaupré, Florine, two actresses and two *danseuses*, and besides these Madame du Val Noble. Nothing is more melancholy than the house of a courtesan without the salt of rivalry, competition among gowns, and diversity of faces. Within six weeks Esther became the wittiest, most amusing, loveliest, most elegant among those female pariahs who compose the class to which she belonged. Placed on her true pedestal, she tasted all the delights of vanity which seduce ordinary women, but always as a woman whom some secret thought has raised above her caste. She kept within her heart an image of herself in which she gloried even though it made her blush; the hour of her abdication was always present to her consciousness; and thus she lived doubly, while her inward life did not cease to pity her outer existence. Her sarcasm was impregnated with her inner disposition where there remained the deep loathing, which the angel of love dwelling within the courtesan, felt toward the infamous part, vilely played by the body in the presence of the soul. At once the spectator and the actor, the judge and the accused, she fulfilled the admirable fiction of Arabian fairy tales, where there is almost always a sublime being hidden beneath a degraded envelope, whose type, under the name of Nebuchadnezzar, appears in the book of books, the Bible. The victim who had been granted life only to the day of her infidelity, might well amuse herself at the expense of her executioner. Besides, the information which Esther had acquired concerning the secretly shameful methods to which the baron owed his colossal fortune, removed the last scruples from her mind, and she delighted to play the part of the goddess Ate,— Vengeance, as Carlos had called it.—Now she made herself charming, now detestable, to this millionaire who lived only in her. When at length the baron had reached such a stage of suffering that he resolved to desert Esther, she would rivet him to her more strongly than ever by some tender scene.

Herrera departed publicly for Spain, and went no further than Tours. His carriage had proceeded as far as Bordeaux, where a servant was left to play the part of his master and to await his coming, in a Bordeaux hotel. Returning by diligence in the guise of a commercial traveler, Carlos had secretly installed himself in the Rue Saint Georges, where, through the medium of Asia, Europe and Paccard, he directed his machinations with care, and watched everybody, especially Peyrade.

About a fortnight before the day chosen for her

fête, which was to be on the evening following the first ball at the Opera, the courtesan, whose wit had begun to render her redoubtable, sat in the Theâtre des Italiens, in the back of a box that the baron—obliged to furnish a box—had secured on the ground floor in order to conceal his mistress and avoid appearing by her side in public, at a few steps from Madame de Nucingen. Esther had chosen a position which enabled her to see Madame de Sérizy, in whose train Lucien was almost always to be found. It was the poor courtesan's happiness to be able to contemplate Lucien on Tuesdays, Thursdays and Saturdays as he talked to Madame de Sérizy. Toward half past nine o'clock Esther saw Lucien enter the countess' box. His brow was contracted and pale, and his face looked almost distorted. These signs of inward trouble were visible only to Esther. The knowledge of a man's face is, for the woman who loves him, what the wide sea is for a mariner.

"Heavens! what can it be? what has happened? Can he have need to speak with that angel of hell who is his guardian angel, and who lives hidden in a garret between the rooms of Europe and Asia?"

Filled with such cruel thoughts Esther scarcely heard the music. We may easily believe that she had no ear for the baron who sat holding his *anchel's* hand between his own, chattering to her in his Polish-Jew *patois*, which must be as painful to those who read as to those who heard it.

"Esder," said he, loosing her hand and pushing it from him with a slight movement of vexation, "you to nod lisden do me."

"Baron, you jabber love as you jabber French."

"Der tefil!"

"This is not my boudoir; I am at the Italiens. If you were not one of those safes manufactured by Huret or Fichet, and metamorphosed into a man by some strange whim of nature, you wouldn't make so much disturbance in the box of a woman who loves music. Of course I don't listen to you. You sit there bustling about my gown like a cock-chafer in a pile of papers, and you force me to smile from mere pity. You tell me, 'you are luffly; you are zweed enough to ead!'—You old sot! suppose that I were to answer, 'You are less displeasing to me to-day than yesterday; let us go home?' Why, by the way in which you breathe—for even if I did not hear you I couldn't help perceiving you—I see that you have overeaten enormously and that your digestion is beginning. Learn this of me,—for I cost you dearly enough to give you now and then a bit of advice for your money!—learn, my dear, that when a person has a troubled digestion like yours he is not permitted to say indiscriminately to his mistress at all times and seasons, 'You are luffly.'—An old soldier died of that lunacy in the *arms of Religion*, as Blondet said. It is ten o'clock. At nine o'clock you finished dining with Du Tillet and your pigeon, the Count de Brambourg. You have millions of truffles to digest; call again to-morrow at ten."

"How gruel you are!" exclaimed the baron, who recognized the perfect justice of this medical argument.

"Cruel!" repeated Esther without taking her eyes off Lucien. "Have you not consulted Bianchon, Desplein and old Haudry? Since you have discerned the aurora of your happiness, do you know the appearance you present to me?"

"Vat?"

"A fat countryman, swathed in flannel, who hour after hour walks from his arm-chair to his window to see whether the thermometer is precisely at ninety, the temperature ordered by his physician."

"You are eine ungradevul vooman!" exclaimed the baron, despairing of hearing music such as elderly lovers often hear at the Italiens.

"Ungrateful!" said Esther. "And what have you given me until now? A great deal of discomfort! Think a moment, papa; can I be proud of you? You are proud of me; I look well in your laces and your livery. You have paid my debts!—Well and good! But you have milked the public of millions enough—ah, don't make a face; I know all about you—to make this too trifling to think of. Yet it is your best title to glory. A woman from the streets, and a thief; nothing could make a better match. You have built a magnificent cage for a paroquet that pleases you. Go and ask of some Brazilian macaw whether he owes a debt of gratitude to the keeper who has shut him in his cage.

Don't look at me like that; you look like a heathen priest. You show your red and white macaw to all Paris. You say, 'Is there anybody else in Paris who owns such a paroquet as this? How he chatters! how cleverly he hits on the right word!' Du Tillet enters; he says to him, 'Good morning, you young rascal.' You are happy as a Dutchman with a unique tulip, as an old nabob living in Asia on an English pension, who has just bought of a commercial traveler the first Swiss snuff-box that has the advantage of three openings. You wish for my heart; wait, I will show you the means of gaining it."

"Dell me, dell me! I vill to everyding vor you. I luff to pe plackguartet by you!"

"Be young, be handsome, be like Lucien de Rubempré, who stands there near your wife, and you shall have *gratis* that which you can never buy with all your millions."

"I leaf you, vor ubon mein vort, you are egsegraple zis efening!" said the lynx, drawing a long face.

"Good-night then," replied Esther. "Bid *Chorches* raise the head of your bed very high and let your feet slope downward for to-night. Your complexion looks apoplectic. Now, dear, never say that I take no interest in your health."

The baron was standing with his hand on the door-knob.

"Come here, Nucingen!" said Esther, calling him back with a haughty wave of her hand. The baron bent over her with canine servility.

"Do you want me to be kind to you and give you *eau sucrée* to drink at my house to-night, while I caress you, you fat monster?"

"You preak my heard."

"'*Preak your heard,*' that's described in a single word, *gife!*" replied she, mimicking the baron's pronunciation. "Send Lucien to me. I want to invite him to our Balthasar's Feast; I'm sure that he will not refuse. If you succeed in this small negotiation, I'll tell you so sweetly that I love you, my fat Frederick, that you will believe me."

"You are eine enghandress," said the baron, kissing Esther's glove. "I vould gonzent to have you rail ad me vor ein hour eef zere were zurely eine garesse ad ze ent."

"Go. If I am not obeyed, I—" said she, menacing the baron with her finger as mothers do to children.

The baron raised his head like a bird caught in a trap, as it looks imploringly toward the hunter.

"Oh, God! What can have happened to Lucien?" said she to herself. When left alone she no longer restrained the tears which fell fast from her eyes. "He has never been so sad before!"

This is what had happened to Lucien that very evening. At nine o'clock, according to his usual custom, Lucien had driven out in a cab on his way to the Grandlieu mansion. Reserving his saddle horse and his driving horse for the morning, as all young men do, he had hired a coupé for his winter evenings, and had selected from the stock of a fashionable livery stable one of the most magnificent, drawn by magnificent horses to match. For a month past everything had smiled on him: he had dined thrice at the Grandlieu table; the duke had been most cordial; his stock in the omnibus system, sold for three hundred thousand francs, had enabled him to pay another third toward the purchase of his estate; Clotilde de Grandlieu, who now made the most careful toilettes, had at least ten pots of paint on her face when he entered the parlor, and she openly avowed her love for him. Several persons of distinction talked of the marriage of Lucien with Mademoiselle de Grandlieu as a probable event. The Duke de Chaulieu, former ambassador to Spain, and, for a brief moment, Minister of Foreign Affairs, had promised the Duchess de Grandlieu to beg of the king the title of marquis for Lucien. After taking dinner with Madame de Sérizy, Lucien had gone that evening from the Rue de la Chausée d'Antin to the Faubourg Saint Germain to make his daily visit. Arrived there, his coachman called, the gates were opened, and the cab stopped at the door of the house. As he stepped from his equipage, Lucien noticed four carriages in the court-yard. Immediately upon perceiving M. de Rubempré, one of the footmen, who opened and closed the door of the peristyle, advances, walks out upon the porch and stands before the door like a soldier at his post of duty.

"His grace is not at home!" says he.

"Madame la Duchesse is receiving," observed Lucien to the valet.

"Madame la Duchesse is out," replied the valet with gravity.

"Mademoiselle Clotilde—"

"I believe that Mademoiselle Clotilde does not receive, sir, in the absence of Madame la Duchesse."

"But there are people here," replied Lucien, thunderstruck.

"I do not know," answered the footman, endeavoring to be at once uncommunicative and respectful.

There is nothing so terrible as etiquette for those who admit it to be the most formidable law of society. Lucien was at no loss to understand the full significance of this scene, disastrous for him: the duke and the duchess were unwilling to receive him. He felt the spinal marrow freezing within the rings of his vertebral column, and a few drops of cold sweat stood out upon his forehead. This conversation had taken place in the presence of his own valet, who held the handle of the carriage door and was waiting to close it. Lucien nodded his readiness to depart, but as he was stepping into the cab he heard a scuttling noise, such as people make when they descend a staircase, and then the successive cries of the footman: "The servants of his lordship, the Duke de Chaulieu! The servants of Madame la Vicountess de Grandlieu!" Lucien said but a word to his valet, "To the Theâtre des Italiens; be quick!" In spite of his haste the unfortunate dandy could not avoid the Duke de Chaulieu and his son, the Duke de Rhétoré, with whom he was obliged to exchange salutes, for they did not say a word. A great catastrophe at court, the fall of a redoubtable favorite is often consummated on the threshold of a cabinet by the words of a doorkeeper, with the face of a plaster cast.

"How can this disaster be instantly made known to my counsellor?" Lucien had asked himself on his way to the Italiens. "What can be happening?"

He became lost in conjectures. This is what had taken place: That same morning, at eleven o'clock, the Duke de Grandlieu had said to Clotilde as he entered the little parlor where the family breakfasted in the absence of company, "My child, until further orders have nothing to do with M. de Rubempré."

Then he had taken the duchess by the hand and had led her into the embrasure of a window to say to her in a low voice a few words which made poor Clotilde change color. As Mademoiselle de Grandlieu watched her mother listening to the duke, she saw a startled look of surprise come over her face.

"Jean," the duke had said to one of his domestics, "here, take this short note to his lordship, the Duke de Chaulieu; ask him to give you an answer, 'yes' or 'no.'—I am inviting him to dine with us to-day," he added, turning toward his wife.

The breakfast had been profoundly sad. The

duchess seemed thoughtful; the duke appeared angry with himself, and Clotilde could scarcely hold back her tears.

"My child, your father is right; obey him," the mother had said to her daughter in a compassionate voice. "I cannot say, like him, 'do not think of Lucien;' no, I understand your sorrow.—Clotilde kissed her mother's hand.—But, my angel, my advice to you is: Wait without taking a single step; suffer in silence, since you love him, and trust in the fond care of your parents! Noble ladies, my child, are noble because they know how to do their duty on all occasions with nobleness."

"What is it about?" asked Clotilde, pale as a lily.

"Things too grave to speak of in your presence, dear heart," answered the duchess; "for if they are false they would sully your thoughts to no purpose, and if true, you must never know them."

At six o'clock the Duke de Chaulieu had found the Duke de Grandlieu awaiting him in his study.

"Advise me, Henri—these two dukes called each other familiarly by their first names. It is one of those shades of etiquette invented in order to mark the degrees of intimacy, to repel the advances of French familiarity, and to humiliate pride of others—advise me, Henri. I am in such a quandary that I can take counsel only of an old friend who knows the world, and you know it by heart. My daughter Clotilde is in love, as you have heard, with that little Rubempré, to whom they have half obliged me to promise her hand. I have always opposed the match, but the truth of the matter is that Madame de Grandlieu could not defend herself against Clotilde's love. When the fellow had bought his estate and had paid three-quarters of the purchase-money, I could no longer make any objection. And then last night I received an anonymous letter—you know such things should be taken with a grain of salt—in which I was told that the fellow's fortune comes from a dishonest source, and that his story, that the funds necessary to the purchase of his property came from his sister, was all a lie. The letter ended by advising me, in the name of my daughter's happiness and of my family's honor, to make inquiries and pointed out to me the means of enlightening myself. Here it is, read it."

"I share your opinion of anonymous letters, my dear Ferdinand," replied the Duke de Chaulieu, when he had read the letter to the end; "but distrust them as he may, a man ought to make use of them. These letters are precisely like spies. Close your doors to this fellow, and proceed with your investigation. Ah! I know exactly what you want. Your lawyer is Derville, a man in whom we have entire confidence; he has the secrets of many a family, and can keep this one as well. He's a man of integrity, a man of weight, a man of honor; he's adroit and cunning, but he has only the shrewdness that belongs to business; you should employ him only to obtain proofs of which you must be the judge. We have at the ministry of foreign affairs, through the police of the kingdom, an extraordinary man, whom we often employ to discover state secrets. Apprise Derville that in this affair he will have a lieutenant. Our detective is a *gentleman* who will present himself decorated with the Legion of Honor; he will have all the air of a diplomat. This fellow will be the huntsman, and Derville will simply assist in the chase. Your attorney will tell you whether the mountain bringeth forth a mouse or whether you ought to break with young Rubempré. In a week you will know what course to take."

"The young man is scarcely enough of a marquis at present to take offence because he finds me 'out' for a week," remarked the Duke de Grandlieu.

"Certainly not if you give him your daughter," replied the ex-minister. "If the anonymous letter is right, how can it inconvenience you? You will send Clotilde on a journey with my daughter-in-law Madeleine, who wants to go to Italy."

"You solve my difficulty! and yet I scarcely know whether I ought to thank you—"

"Wait for the outcome."

"Ah!" exclaimed the Duke de Grandlieu, "what is the gentleman's name? I must tell Derville. Send him to me to-morrow at four o'clock; I shall have Derville; I will introduce them to each other."

"The real name," said the ex-minister, "is, I believe, Corentin—a name that you must be ignorant of; but this gentleman will come to your house under his ministerial name. He is called M. de Saint something—ah! Saint Yves! Sainte Valère!—either of them will do. You can trust him; Louis XVIII. trusted him completely."

After this conference the major-domo received orders to close the door to M. de Rubempré; a command which was fulfilled.

*

Lucien was walking up and down the foyer of the Italiens like a drunken man. He saw himself the talk of all Paris. In the Duke de Rhétoré he had one of those pitiless enemies on whom a man must smile without the possibility of revenge, since their attacks are conformable to the laws of the world. The Duke de Rhétoré knew the scene which had just taken place on the porch of the Grandlieu mansion. Lucien, who felt the necessity of telling this disaster speedily to his intimate privy-counselor, feared lest he might compromise himself still further by going to Esther's house, where he would be apt to meet acquaintances. So great was the confusion of his mind that he forgot Esther's presence in the theatre; and in the midst of his perplexity he was obliged to talk with Rastignac, who, not having heard the news, congratulated him on his approaching marriage. At this moment Nucingen advanced with a smiling face and said to Lucien:

"Vill you to me ze kintness of goming to zee Montame te Jamby, who vishes to eenfite you herzelf to our house-varming."

"Gladly, baron," answered Lucien, to whom the financier appeared like a protecting angel.

"Leave us," said Esther to M. de Nucingen, when she saw him entering with Lucien; "go and see Madame du Val Noble, whom I see sitting with her nabob in a box in the third tier. He is very much like the nabobs in the Indies," she added, casting an intelligent glance toward Lucien.

"And he," said Lucien, smiling, "bears a terrible resemblance to yours."

"And," added Esther, answering Lucien by another look full of meaning, while she continued to talk to the baron, "bring her and her nabob hither; he is very anxious to make your acquaintance; they say that he is immensely rich. The poor woman has already sung countless elegies to me. She complains that her nabob is immovable; if you rid him of his money bags, he'll have less ballast."

"You zeem to dake us vor roppers!" said the baron as he went out.

"What is the matter, my Lucien?" whispered Esther in her lover's ear, which her lips touched as the door of the box closed.

"I am lost! I have just been refused admittance to the Grandlieu house, under the pretext that nobody was at home. The duke and duchess were there, and five fine carriages were waiting in the courtyard."

"What! your marriage broken off?" said Esther, in an agitated tone, as if she could see a distant Paradise.

"As yet, I do not even know the conspiracy against me."

"My Lucien," she answered in a strangely

fascinating voice, "why are you sad? You will make a better marriage, later.—I will win two estates for you."

"Give a supper to-night so that I can speak secretly with Carlos, and above all invite the sham Englishman and Madame du Val Noble. This nabob is the cause of my ruin; he is our enemy; we must get him in our power and then we'll—"

But Lucien stopped with a gesture of despair.

"What is it now?" asked the poor girl, who felt as if she were seated on live coals.

"Oh! Madame de Sérizy sees me!" exclaimed Lucien, "and to complete my misfortunes, the Duke de Rhétoré, one of the witnesses of my discomfiture, is with her."

It was true. At that very moment, the Duke de Rhétoré was playing upon the sorrow of the Countess de Sérizy.

"You allow Lucien to show himself in Mademoiselle Esther's box?" the young duke was saying as he pointed out the box and Lucien. "You, who take an interest in him, should warn him that this kind of thing must not be. He can sup at her house or perhaps even—but, upon my word, I am not astonished at the coolness of the Grandlieu toward this fellow: I just saw him refused admittance, on the porch."

"Those women are very dangerous!" said Madame de Sérizy, who held her lorgnette leveled against Esther's box.

"Yes," said the duke, "as dangerous for what they can do as for what they would like—"

"They will ruin him!" said Madame de Sérizy, "for I am told that they are as expensive when a man does not pay them as when he does."

"Not for him!" replied the young duke, feigning astonishment. "They are far from costing him anything; they would give him money were he in want. They all run after him."

About the corners of the countess' mouth there came a little nervous twitch, which could not be included within the category of her smiles.

"As you will," said Esther; "come to supper at midnight. Bring Blondet and Rastignac. Have at least two amusing people, and let us not be more than nine."

"Some method must be found to induce the baron to summon Europe, under the pretext of giving directions to Asia, and you must tell her what has happened to me so that Carlos may know it before he has the nabob in his clutches."

"It shall be done," said Esther.

Thus Peyrade was probably to be beneath the roof that covered his adversary. The tiger was coming into the lion's den, and the lion was well guarded.

When Lucien re-entered Madame de Sérizy's box, instead of turning her head toward him, of smiling upon him, and of arranging her gown so that he might sit by her side, she paid not the least attention to the new-comer and continued to gaze across the theatre, through her lorgnette; but Lucien perceived by the trembling of her cheeks that the countess was a prey to one of those terrible fits of agitation which are the expiation of unlawful love. He advanced, nevertheless, to the front of the box, near her, and stationed himself in the opposite angle, leaving a small empty space between the countess and him; he leaned against the railing of the box, rested his right elbow upon it, and his chin upon his gloved hand; then he posed as for a three-quarters portrait, waiting for her to speak. When the middle of the act came, the countess had not uttered a word. She had not even looked at him.

"I do not know," she said at length, "why you are here; your place is in Mademoiselle Esther's box."

"I go thither," said Lucien, who went out without looking at the countess.

"Ah! my dear," said Madame du Val Noble, as she entered Esther's box in company with Peyrade, whom the Baron de Nucingen did not recognize, "I am delighted to present to you M. Samuel Johnson; he is a warm admirer of M. de Nucingen's talent."

"Really, monsieur?" said Esther, smiling toward Peyrade.

"Oh! yes, very great," said Peyrade in bad French.

"Well, baron, here is French that is as like yours as Bas Breton is like Burgundian. It will amuse me immensely to hear you talk about money-matters. Do you know what I demand of you, monsieur nabob, in return for making the acquaintance of my baron?" said she smiling.

"Oh! I thank you, then you will present me to *monsir le beronnette.*"

"Yes," she replied, "you must do me the pleasure of supping with me. There is no pitch which attaches men to one another like champagne; it seals every matter of business, especially the deepest. Come to-night, you will find good company—and, as to you—my little Frederic," she added in the baron's ear, "you have your carriage; hurry to the Rue Saint Georges and bring Europe to me; I must have a word or two with her in regard to my supper. I have secured Lucien; he will bring a couple of wits with him.—We'll make the Englishman pose as a laughing stock," whispered she to Madame du Val Noble.

Peyrade and the baron left the two women alone.

"Ah! my dear, you will be clever if you ever succeed in making that brute a laughing stock," said La Val Noble.

"If it were impossible, you would lend him to me for a week," answered Esther laughing.

"No, you would never keep him half a day," replied Madame du Val Noble. "My bread is too hard; it breaks my teeth. As long as I live I hope never to have another Englishman's happiness in my keeping. They are all cold-blooded egoists, pigs in men's clothes."

"What, no tenderness?" asked Esther smiling.

"Not an atom, my dear. The monster has never called me by an endearing name."

"Never?" said Esther.

"The wretch invariably calls me 'madame,' and at the times when all men are more or less tender, always keeps perfectly cool. Love! heavens and earth! For him it's like shaving. He wipes his razors; he puts them into the case, he looks at himself in the glass and seems to be saying: 'I have not cut myself.' He treats me with a respect that drives a woman wild. This villainous stink-pot milord amused himself with making poor Théodore hide, and leaving him standing in my dressing-room for half a day at a time. Then he tries to cross me in everything. And close-fisted!—As Gobseck and Gigonnet together. He takes me out to dinner and doesn't pay for the carriage that brings me home, if I have not ordered my own."

"What does he give you?" said Esther.

"Oh, my dear, absolutely nothing. Five hundred francs a month, no extras, except my carriage. And what is that? A carriage such as grocers hire to go to the mayor's office on their wedding day or to drive to church or the *Cadran bleu*. He pesters me with his respect. If I pretend to be nervous and unwell he is quite indifferent, and says, 'I want milady to do exactly as she pleases, for nothing is more detestable, ungraceful, than to say to a pretty woman, 'you are a bale of cotton, a piece of merchandise. Eh! Eh! You belong to a member of the society of temperance and anti-slavery.' And my prize stands there pale, self-contained, cold, thus giving me to understand that he respects me as he would respect a negro. It has nothing to do with his heart, but rather with his abolitionist opinions."

"He couldn't be more odious," said Esther, "but I would ruin such a beast."

"Ruin him?" objected Madame du Val Noble. How could I unless he loved me? But even you would scarcely care to ask him for a penny. He would listen to you gravely and would answer you with those Britannic formalities, which make you long to box his ears, that he was paying dearly enough for the trifling difference that love made in his poor life."

"To think that in our sphere we can meet with men such as he!" exclaimed Esther.

"Ah, my dear, you have had the chance yourself! Take care of your Nucingen."

"But your nabob has a purpose."

"That is what Adèle told me," replied Madame du Val Noble.

"Now, my dear, perhaps he intends to become hateful to a woman so as to be sent away after a time," suggested Esther.

"Or perhaps he wants to make some business venture with Nucingen, and chooses me because he knows how intimate you and I are; that's what Adèle believes," continued Madame du Val Noble. "That is why I introduced him to you this evening. Ah! If I could be certain what his plans are, what a neat arrangement I might make with you and Nucingen!"

"You don't fly into a passion?" said Esther, "you don't tell him his business from time to time?"

"You might try it, you are very clever;—but, in

spite of all your attractions, he would kill you with his icy smiles. He would answer you: 'I am on the side of anti-slavery and you are free.'—However amusing you might be, he would look at you and say, 'Very good,' and you would see that in his eyes you were nothing more than a Punchinello."

"How about anger?"

"The same thing! It would amuse him. You might cut into his left breast without hurting him a particle; his heart must be made of tin. I told him so. His answer was, 'I am quite content with this physical arrangement.'—Always polite, my dear; his very soul is gloved. I am going to suffer this martyrdom for several days longer in order to satisfy my curiosity. Had it not been for that, I should have had his ears boxed long ago by Philip, who has not his equal at fencing. There is nothing else that—"

"I was just going to suggest it!" exclaimed Esther; "but first you should find out whether he knows how to box, for among these old Englishmen that saves them from attacks of malice—"

"That man has not his equal! If you saw him waiting for my orders, asking at what hour he may present himself so as to surprise me—when everything was arranged beforehand!—and employing all the outward formulæ of respect, such as *gentlemen* use, you would say, 'This woman is worshipped,' and there's not a woman living who wouldn't say as much."

"And yet people envy us, my dear!" said Esther."

"True!" exclaimed Madame du Val Noble. "We

have all learned, more or less, in our lives how little men care for us; but, dearest, I have never been so cruelly, so deeply, so thoroughly hurt by brutality as I am by the respect of this gross wine-bibber. When he is drunk he goes away, so as not to be unpleasant, as he said to Adèle, and so as not to 'belong to two powers at once, wine and woman.' He monopolizes my carriage and makes use of it far more than I. Oh! if we could only make him roll about under the table to-night!—But he drinks ten bottles and is merely intoxicated; his eye looks clouded, but he can see clearly."

"He's like people who live in a house with windows dirty on the outside," said Esther; "they can see everything that goes on without. I know this peculiarity among mankind; Du Tillet has this quality in a superlative degree."

"Try to have Du Tillet and add Nucingen; if they could drag him into some of their combinations, I should be revenged! They would reduce him to beggary! Ah! my dear, to fall to a hypocrite of a Protestant after poor Falleix, who was so amusing, so kind-hearted, so droll. How we have laughed together. They say that brokers are always stupid;—his wit was never lacking but once—"

"When he left you without a penny? That taught you the pains of pleasure."

Europe, under M. de Nucingen's escort, put her viper-like head in at the door and, after having heard a few sentences which her mistress whispered in her ear, she disappeared.

At half past eleven o'clock that night, five carriages were waiting, in the Rue Saint Georges, before the door of the illustrious courtesan; one belonged to Lucien, who came with Rastignac, Blondet, and Bixiou, another to Du Tillet, a third to the Baron de Nucingen, the fourth to the nabob, and the fifth to Florine, who had been carried off by Du Tillet. The threefold windows were hidden by magnificent curtains of Chinese silk. The supper was to be served at one o'clock. The candles burned brightly; the little parlor and the dining-room, displayed all their splendor. Everything promised one of those nights of debauch such as these three women and these men alone could undergo. The company was to play cards, for there were nearly two hours to while away.

"Do you play, milord?" asked Du Tillet of Peyrade.

"I have played with O'Connell, Pitt, Fox, Canning, Lord Brougham, Lord—"

"Rattle off at once the names of an infinity of lords," said Bixiou.

"Lord Fitz-William, Lord Ellenborough, Lord Hertfort, Lord—"

Bixiou looked at Peyrade's shoes and bowed.

"What are you looking for?" asked Blondet of his friend.

"A spring to press and stop the machine," said Florine.

"Do you play for twenty francs the hand?" asked Lucien.

"I play for all you care to lose," replied the nabob.

"Is he good at the game?" said Esther to Lucien.

"They all take him for an Englishman!"

Du Tillet, Nucingen, Peyrade and Rastignac sat down at the whist table. Florine, Madame du Val Noble, Esther, Blondet and Bixiou grouped themselves about the fire to talk. Lucien passed the time in turning over the leaves of a magnificent volume of engravings.

"Madame, dinner is served," said Paccard, dressed in a resplendent livery.

Peyrade, placed at Florine's left, was flanked on the right by Bixiou, who had received instructions from Esther to thoroughly intoxicate the nabob by constant challenges to drink. Bixiou possessed the faculty of drinking indefinitely. Never in his whole life had Peyrade viewed such splendor, tasted such dishes, nor seen such beautiful women.

"To-night," thought he, "is worth the three thousand francs which La Val Noble has cost me already. Besides I have just won a thousand."

"Here is an example to follow, nabob," exclaimed Madame du Val Noble, who was sitting beside Lucien, as she pointed out the magnificence of the dining-room with a gesture.

Esther had placed Lucien by her side, and held one of his feet pressed between both of hers, beneath the table.

"Do you hear?" demanded La Val Noble, looking at Peyrade, who seemed blind to his surroundings. "This is the manner in which you should arrange a house for me. When a man returns from the Indies, with millions, and wishes to do business with Nucingens, he should rise to their level."

"I belong to the society of temperance."

"Then you shall drink with a will!" said Bixiou. "For it's hot in the Indies, isn't it, uncle?"

Bixiou's joke during the supper was to treat Peyrade as one of his uncles returned from the Indies.

"Montame ti Fal Nople has tolt me zat you hat blans?" asked Nucingen, examining Peyrade with attention.

"This is what I've been waiting for," said Du Tillet to Rastignac, "a chance to hear these two jabberers together."

"You will see that they will end by understanding each other," said Bixiou, who guessed what Du Tillet would say to Rastignac.

"*Sir beronette*, I have thought of a little speculation, Oh, very comfortable.—Very profitable indeed, and rich in its percentages."

"Do listen to him," said Blondet to Du Tillet. "He will not talk for an instant without bringing in Parliament and the English government."

"It is in China—opium."

"Yez, I know," replied Nucingen quickly, with the air of a man who owns his commercial world; "but ze Enclish cofernment has daken gondrol of ze obium trate ant vould nod allow us."

"Nucingen got ahead of him on the mention of the government," said Du Tillet to Blondet.

"Ah! you have traded in opium?" exclaimed Madame du Val Noble; "now I understand why you are so stupefying; it has stuck to your heart."

"Vy!" exclaimed the baron to the supposed opium-merchant, as he pointed toward Madame du Val Noble; "you are like me; millionaires can nefer make vomen to luff zem."

"I love dearly and often, milady," answered Peyrade.

"Always for temperance's sake," said Bixiou, who had succeeded in persuading Peyrade to finish his third bottle of Bordeaux, and was now inducing him to broach a bottle of port wine.

"Oh!" exclaimed Peyrade, "it is very fine Portuguese wine made in England."

Blondet, Du Tillet and Bixiou exchanged smiles. Peyrade had the power of disguising everything about him, even his mind. There are few Englishmen who will not assure you that gold and silver are better in England than elsewhere. The chickens and the eggs coming from Normandy and expressed to the London market enable Englishmen to maintain that the London chickens and eggs are superior —*very fine*—to those of Paris, which come from precisely the same districts. Esther and Lucien remained stupefied before this masterpiece of costume, language and audacity.

The company drank and ate so much and so heartily that amid stories and laughter, it came to be four o'clock in the morning. Bixiou thought that he had borne off one of those victories so pleasantly

HOW MUCH LOVE COSTS OLD MEN 385

described by Brillat-Savarin. But at the moment when he said to himself, as he filled his uncle's glass: "I have conquered England," Peyrade answered the brutal scoffer with a "Never say die, my boy," in excellent French, which was heard by Bixiou alone.

"Ho, there! you people! He's as much English as I am!—My uncle is a Gascon! I could never have had another kind."

Bixiou was alone with Peyrade, and so nobody heard this revelation. Peyrade fell from his chair to the floor, whence he was immediately lifted by Paccard and carried to an attic room, where he was laid, wrapped in a profound sleep.

At six o'clock in the evening the nabob was awakened by the application of a damp cloth rubbing his face, and found himself lying on a wretched springless bed, face to face with Asia, who was masked and covered with a black domino.

"Ah! ha! Papa Peyrade, let's come to terms," said she.

"Where am I?" said he, looking about him.

"Listen to me. It will make you sober," replied Asia. "If you don't love Madame du Val Noble, you do love your daughter, don't you?"

"My daughter?" cried Peyrade, reddening.

"Yes, Mademoiselle Lydie."

"Well?"

"Well, she's no longer in the Rue des Moineaux; she is kidnapped."

Peyrade sobbed like a soldier dying of mortal wounds on the field of battle.

"While you were counterfeiting the Englishman, somebody else was counterfeiting Peyrade. Your little Lydie supposed that she was following her father. She is in a safe place. Oh! you'll never find her, unless you make good the harm you have done."

"What harm?"

"Yesterday the door of the Duke de Grandlieu was closed to M. Lucien de Rubempré. This result is due to your intrigues and to the man whom you set upon our trail. Not a word. Listen!" said Asia, as Peyrade opened his lips. "You shall never have your daughter, pure and without spot," she continued, emphasizing the ideas by the accent which she placed upon each syllable, "until the morrow of that day on which M. de Rubempré comes forth from Saint Thomas Aquinas' married to Mademoiselle Clotilde. If within ten days Lucien de Rubempré is not received on the same footing as formerly, in the Grandlieu house, you shall die a violent death, for no precaution can ward off the blow which threatens you. Then when you feel the touch of death upon you, you shall have leisure before you die to ponder over this thought: 'My daughter will live impure for the rest of her days!' Although you have been stupid enough to fall into our clutches, you still have wit enough to meditate upon this communication of our government. Don't squeal, don't say a word. Go to Contenson's lodging and change your costume; return home, and Katt will tell you that, at your bidding, your little Lydie went out and has not returned. If you make a complaint, if you take any steps, they will begin by taking that revenge on your daughter to which I told you they would resort; she is promised to De Marsay. With Père Canquoëlle, there's no need of pretty speeches nor of gloved hands, is there? Go down stairs and think twice before you meddle with our business again."

Asia left Peyrade in a pitiable state; every word had fallen like a blow from a hammer. Two tears were in the detective's eyes and two wet streams ran down his cheeks.

"They are awaiting M. Johnson for dinner," said Europe, showing her head at the door a moment later.

Peyrade did not answer; he walked down the stairs and through the streets until he came to a cab stand. He hastened to Contenson's lodging and undressed himself, but he did not say a word to his friend. Dressed once more as Père Canquoëlle, he reached his dwelling at eight o'clock. He climbed the stairs with a beating heart. When the Flemish woman heard her master, she said to him so naturally: "And mademoiselle—where is she?" that the old detective leaned against the wall for support. The blow was too great for his strength. He entered his daughter's room and fainted from the violence of his grief when he saw that the room was empty and when Katt recounted to him the circumstances of an abduction as craftily planned as if he himself had been its author.

"Now," thought he, "I must yield; later I will have my revenge. Now to see Corentin!—For the first time we have met our match. Corentin shall leave the pretty boy free to marry empresses if he will. Ah! I understand how my daughter fell in love with him at first sight. Oh! the Spanish priest was a good judge.—Courage, Papa Peyrade. Disgorge your prey!"

The poor father did not suspect the awful blow in store for him.

When he had reached Corentin's house, Bruno, the confidential servant, who knew Peyrade said: "Monsieur is away."

"For long?"

"For ten days."

"Where?"

"I don't know."

"My God, I am going mad! I ask where? As if we were apt to tell servants," thought he.

*

Some hours before the time when Peyrade was awakened in his attic in the Rue Saint Georges, Corentin, newly arrived from his country place at Passy, presented himself at the door of the Duke de Grandlieu in the costume of a valet belonging to some aristocratic family. In a buttonhole of his black coat the ribbon of the Legion of Honor was displayed. His appearance was that of an old man, with powdered hair, very wrinkled and pale. His eyes were covered by eyeglasses with tortoise-shell rims. In a word he had the air of some ex-chief of the Police Department. When he had given his name, M. de Saint Denis, he was conducted into the duke's study, where he found Derville reading the letter which he himself had dictated to one of his agents, a secretary. The duke took Corentin aside to explain to him everything that Corentin already knew. M. de Saint Denis listened calmly and respectfully, and amused himself meanwhile studying the grand seigneur, penetrating to the bed-rock, clothed though it was with velvet, and bringing to light his true life, then and always absorbed in whist and the consideration of the house of Grandlieu. *Grands seigneurs* speak so unaffectedly to their inferiors, that Corentin had not asked many questions of the duke in his humble manner before he drew upon himself a torrent of impertinence.

"If you will trust me, monsieur," said Corentin to Derville after having been formally presented to the attorney, "we leave to-night for Angoulême by the Bordeaux diligence, which makes the journey quite as quickly as the mail; we shall not need to delay there more than six hours in order to obtain the information that his lordship wishes. If I have rightly understood your lordship, will it not suffice to ascertain whether the sister and brother-in-law of M. de Rubempré have been able to give him twelve hundred thousand francs?" said he, addressing the duke.

"You have understood perfectly," replied the peer of France.

"We can be here again in four days," continued Corentin, looking at Derville, "and neither of us will be obliged to leave his business long enough to give rise to any inconvenience."

"That was the sole objection I had to make to his lordship," said Derville. "It is four o'clock; I return to say a word to my head clerk, to pack my valise, and after dinner, at eight o'clock I shall be— But can we secure places?" asked he of M. de Saint Denis, interrupting himself.

"I will answer for them," said Corentin; "at eight o'clock be in the waiting-room of the Principal Department. If there are no places, I shall have some made, for this is the manner in which his lordship the Duke de Grandlieu must be served."

"Gentlemen," said the duke with infinite grace, "as yet I do not thank you.—"

Corentin and the attorney, who took this phrase as a permission to depart, bowed and went out. At the moment when Peyrade was questioning Corentin's servant, M. de Saint Denis and Derville, seated within the *coupé* of the Bordeaux diligence, looked about them in silence as they passed the outskirts of Paris. The next morning, on the way from Orleans to Tours, Derville, who was greatly bored, became talkative and Corentin deigned to amuse him, although with some reserve, and allowed the lawyer to suppose that he belonged to diplomatic circles and that he was expecting to become Consul-General under the protection of the Duke de Grandlieu.

Two days after their departure from Paris, Corentin and Derville stopped at Mansle, to the great astonishment of the attorney, who supposed that he was on his way to Angoulême.

"In this little town," said Corentin to Derville, "we shall meet with trustworthy information concerning Madame Séchard."

"You know her then?" asked Derville, surprised to find Corentin so well informed.

"I loosened the driver's tongue when I learned that he was from Angoulême. He told me that madame lives at Marsac, and Marsac is but a league away from Mansle; I thought that we should be better situated here than in Angoulême, to learn the truth."

"Moreover," thought Derville, "as his lordship told me, I am simply the witness of investigations made by this confidential agent."

The landlord of the inn of Mansle, called "La Belle Étoile," was one of those big, bloated men whom a stranger expects never to see again, yet who still stand on their door-steps ten years later, with the same quantity of flesh, the same cotton cap, the same apron, the same knife, the same greasy locks, the same triple chin, and who are stereotyped in the books of all romancers from the immortal Cervantes to the immortal Walter Scott. Do they not all boast of their kitchen's excellence, are they not ready to do everything to serve you, and do they not give you at length a bony chicken and vegetables cooked in rancid butter? They all praise their delectable wines and force you to swallow the vintage of the neighborhood. Since his early youth Corentin had learned to draw from an innkeeper things more substantial than doubtful dishes and apocryphal wines. Thus he pretended to be easily satisfied and told his fat host that he relied entirely upon the discretion of the best cook in Mansle.

"I have no trouble in being the best, for there is no other," replied the landlord.

"Give us our dinner in a private room," said Corentin, winking at Derville, "and above all don't forget to light a fire; it takes the stiffness out of a man's fingers."

"It was none too hot in the coupé," said Derville.

"Is it far from here to Marsac?" asked Corentin of the innkeeper's wife, who had descended from the upper regions upon hearing that the diligence had set down travelers before her door.

"Are you going to Marsac, sir?" demanded the hostess.

"I don't know," replied he, somewhat dryly. "Is the distance from here to Marsac great?" he asked once more after he had given his hostess time to observe his red ribbon.

"If you drive, it's a matter of half an hour at the most," replied the landlady.

"Do you think that M. and Madame Séchard are there in winter?"

"Doubtless. They stay there the year round."

"It is five o'clock; we shall find them still up at nine?"

"Oh! until ten; they have company every evening—the curé, M. Marron the doctor—"

"They are excellent people?" said Derville.

"Oh! monsieur, nobody better!" replied the landlady; "honest, upright people, and not ambitious; why, though M. Séchard is comfortably off, he would have had millions, people say, if he had not allowed himself to be cheated out of an invention which he discovered in the manufacture of paper, and which has filled the pockets of the Cointet brothers."

"Ah! yes! the Cointet brothers," said Corentin.

"Hush," said the innkeeper, "what do these gentlemen care whether M. Séchard has or has not the right to the patent of an invention for making paper? These gentlemen are not stationers.—If you intend to pass the night at my house,—the Belle Étoile"—continued the host, turning toward the two travelers, "here is the book; I beg of you to register your names. We have a brigadier of police who has nothing to do and who spends his time in meddling with our business—"

"The devil! I supposed that the Séchards were very rich," said Corentin, while Derville wrote his name and his profession as lawyer at the Tribunal of First Instance of the Seine.

"There are people," replied the landlord, "who say that they are millionaires, but you might as well try to keep a river from flowing as to keep tongues from wagging. . M. Séchard has put two hundred thousand francs aside for a rainy day, as they say, and that's a large sum for a man who began life as a common workman. His savings have perhaps amounted to as much, for he has succeeded in drawing from ten to twelve thousand francs from his estate. This is on the supposition that, for ten years, he has been too stupid to put out his money at interest! But call it three hundred thousand francs, if he has exacted usury, as people suspect, and you have it all. Five hundred thousand francs is a long way from a million. If my fortune were only the difference I should not be at the Belle Étoile."

"What," said Corentin, "have not M. David Séchard and his wife property amounting to two or three millions of francs?"

"But," exclaimed the innkeeper's wife, "that's what they ascribe to the MM. Cointet who robbed him of his invention, and never gave him more than twenty thousand francs.—Where do you suppose honest people like them could have picked up millions? They were in great embarrassment during their father's life. Without Kolb, their administrator, and Madame Kolb, who is as devoted to their interests as her husband is, they would have had scarcely enough to live upon. What did they have then, including La Verberie? a thousand crowns a year!"

Corentin took Derville aside and said to him: "*In vino veritas!* Truth lies beneath the corks. For my own part, I regard an inn as the official register of a district; the notary is not a whit better informed than the tavern keeper of what is going on in a small community. You see, we are supposed to know Cointet, Kolb, etc. An innkeeper is the living catalogue of everything that takes place; he acts as the police without suspecting it. A government should support two hundred spies at the most. For in a country like France there are ten millions of honest detectives. But we are not obliged to rely upon this report, although in this little town, people would be apt to know something of the twelve hundred thousand francs that have disappeared to pay for the Rubempré estate.—We shall not stay here long."

"I hope not," said Derville.

"This is the reason why," continued Corentin. "I have discovered the most natural method in the world to make Séchard and his wife tell the truth. I count upon you to support, with your legal authority, the little ruse which I shall make use of to enable you to hear a clear and concise statement of their fortune.—After dinner we shall leave you to pay a visit to M. Séchard," said Corentin, turning to the landlady, "you will make sure to get our beds ready; we wish to have two apartments. There must be room at the 'Belle Étoile.'"

"Oh! monsieur," said the woman, "we have found the ensign."

"Oh! puns are used in all the departments," said Corentin, "you have no monopoly on them."

"Your dinner is ready, messieurs," said the landlord.

"Where the devil could this young man have found his money? Was the anonymous letter right? Was it the money of some pretty woman?" said Derville to Corentin as they sat down to dinner.

"Ah! that would be the subject of another inquiry," said Corentin. "Lucien de Rubempré lives, so the Duke de Chaulieu told me, with a converted Jewess, who passes herself off for a Dutch woman, named Esther van Bogseck."

"What an odd coincidence!" exclaimed the lawyer; "I am investigating the inheritance of a Dutchman named Gobseck; it's the same name with a change of consonants."

"Ah!" remarked Corentin, "I shall give you information concerning their affiliation upon my return to Paris."

An hour later these two agents of the noble house of Grandlieu started for La Verberie, the house of M. and Madame Séchard. Never had Lucien felt emotions so stirring as those which came over him at La Verberie, as he compared his own destiny with that of his brother-in-law. The two Parisians were destined to find the same spectacle which, but a few days before, had struck Lucien's imagination. Everything breathed calm and plenty. At the time when the two strangers were about to arrive, the drawing-room of La Verberie was occupied by a company of four persons: the curé of Marsac, a young priest of twenty-five, who had become, at Madame Séchard's request, the instructor of her son Lucien; the village doctor, M. Marron by name; the mayor of the commune, and an old colonel retired from the service, who cultivated roses on a small estate across the street from La Verberie. Every winter evening this company assembled to play an innocent game of cards at one centime a point, to borrow newspapers or to return those which they had read.

When M. and Madame Séchard bought La Verberie, a handsome house built of sandstone and covered with tiles, its dependencies proper consisted of a garden of two acres. As time went on, consecrating her economies to this single purpose, Madame Séchard had extended her garden as far as a small watercourse, and sacrificing the vineyards which she purchased, she converted them into lawns varied by clumps of trees. At the time of this story, La Verberie, surrounded by a park of some twenty acres, passed for the most important estate in the neighborhood. The house of the late M. Séchard and its dependencies furnished for cultivation rather more than twenty acres of vines, bequeathed by him to his son, beside five farms yielding an annual revenue of some six thousand francs, and ten acres of meadow land situated on the other side of the watercourse, directly opposite the park of La Verberie, and Madame Séchard counted upon adding to them the following year. Already throughout the neighborhood people dignified La Verberie by the title of chateau and called Eve Séchard the Lady of Marsac. In satisfying his vanity, Lucien had only imitated the peasants and workers in the vineyards. Courtois, the proprietor of a picturesque mill a few gunshots away from the fields of La Verberie, was, people said, negotiating for its sale to Madame Séchard. This probable acquisition would give La Verberie the proportions of an estate of the first rank in the department. Madame Séchard, who gave much to charity with as much discernment as generosity, was esteemed as well as beloved. Her beauty, become magnificent, had reached the height of its development. Although nearly twenty-six years old, she had retained the freshness of youth, thanks to the repose and abundance that life in the country bestows. She was a loving wife and respected in her husband a man whose modest talents suffered him to renounce the turmoil of a life of glory; in short to describe her it is perhaps enough to say that in all her life she had never felt a single heart-beat that was not inspired by her children or by her husband. The tribute which this household paid misfortune was, as may be imagined, the deep sorrow caused by Lucien, in whose life Eve Séchard felt that there were mysteries and dreaded them all the more because during his last visit Lucien brusquely cut short every question of his sister by telling her that ambitious men owed account of their actions to themselves alone. In six years Lucien had seen his sister thrice and he had not written her more than six letters. His first visit to La Verberie had taken place after the death of his mother, and his last had for its object the demand of the falsehood so necessary to his career. This had occasioned between M. and Madame Séchard and their brother a serious scene, which left hideous doubts in the heart of this sweet and noble life.

The interior of the house, transformed as completely as the exterior, was comfortable without any appearance of luxury. The reader can judge of this by a rapid glance about the room in which the company were gathered at this moment. A pretty carpet from Aubusson, twill hangings of gray cotton with green silk trimmings, paintings representing the forest of Spa, a table of carved mahogany, covered with gray cashmere and green embroidery. Flower pots filled with flowers, in spite of the season, offered a picture very pleasing to the eye. The green curtains, the ornaments on the mantelpiece, the frames of the mirrors, were free from that bad taste which spoils everything provincial; in short, all things, fitting and neat to the smallest details, gave repose to the soul and the eye by that poetry which a loving and intelligent wife can introduce into her household.

Madame Séchard, still in mourning for her father, was sitting near the fireplace, working over a piece of embroidery, aided by Madame Kolb, the housekeeper, to whose care she intrusted the details of the household. Just as the carriage reached the outskirts of Marsac, the accustomed company of La Verberie was increased by the arrival of Courtois, the miller, a widower, who wished to retire from business and was anxious to sell his property at a round price. Madame Eve seemed desirous to buy it, and Courtois knew the reason why.

"A carriage is stopping here!" said Courtois, hearing the rumbling of wheels at the door, "and to judge from the rattling it comes from the neighborhood."—

"It must be Postel and his wife on their way to see us," said the doctor.

"No," said Courtois, "the carriage comes from the direction of Mansle."

"Montame," said Kolb, a large and stout Alsatian, whom we know—see *Lost Illusions*—"here ees ein zolicetor vrom Baris who veshes do speak do mennesir."

"A solicitor?" cried Séchard. "The very name gives me the colic."

"Thanks," said the mayor of Marsac, Cachan by name, who for twenty years had been a lawyer in Angoulême, who had once been employed in prosecuting Séchard.

"My poor David will never change, he will always be absent-minded," said Eve, smiling.

"A solicitor from Paris," said Courtois; "then you have business in Paris?"

"No," said Eve.

"You have a brother there," remarked Courtois.

"Take care lest it be about old M. Séchard's property," said Cachan. "The old gentleman always did business in an odd fashion!"

Corentin and Derville entered, and after bowing to the company and repeating the names of the different guests, they requested a private conversation with Madame Séchard and her husband.

"Certainly," said Séchard. "But is it on business?"

"Only in regard to your father's property," replied Corentin.

"Then kindly allow the mayor, who is an old attorney of Angoulême, to be present at the conference."

"You are M. Derville?" asked Cachan, looking at Corentin.

"No, monsieur, that is he," replied Corentin, pointing to the attorney, who bowed.

"But," said Séchard, "we are quite private here, we have no secrets from our neighbors. There is no need of adjourning to my study, where there is no fire. Our life is perfectly open."—

"But your father's," said Corentin, "has harbored some mysteries, which perhaps you would not care to make public."

"Is it, then, anything to be ashamed of?" asked Eve, alarmed.

"Oh, no! It is a youthful peccadillo," said Corentin, setting one of his thousand professional snares with the utmost coolness. "Your father gave you an elder brother."—

"Ah! the old fox!" cried Courtois; "he loved you little enough, Monsieur Séchard, and yet he never let you know it, sly old dog! Ah! now I understand what he meant when he said: 'You will see strange things when I am dead and buried.'"

"Oh! Don't be alarmed, sir," said Corentin to Séchard, examining Eve with a sidelong glance.

"A brother!" exclaimed the doctor. "That cuts your inheritance in two."

Derville made a pretence of looking at the handsome before-letter proof engravings which were hung upon the panels of the drawing-room.

"Don't be alarmed, madame," repeated Corentin, seeing the surprise which appeared upon Madame Séchard's beautiful face. "This was merely a natural son. The title of a natural child is not that of a legitimate son. This child is in terrible poverty; he has a right to a sum based upon the size of the inheritance—the millions left by your father."—

At this word *millions*, there was an exclamation of the most complete unanimity throughout the room. At this juncture Derville ceased to examine the engravings.

"Old Séchard, millions?" said the fat Courtois. "Who told you that—some peasant?"

"Sir," said Cachan, "you do not belong to the Treasury, therefore you could not have been told how—"

"You need not be afraid," said Corentin; "I give you my word of honor that I am not a real estate agent."

Cachan, who had just motioned to everybody to keep quiet, made a visible gesture of satisfaction.

"Sir," continued Corentin, "were it but a million, the portion of an illegitimate child would still be considerable. We do not come to bring suit; on the contrary, we come to make a proposal to you. Give us a hundred thousand francs and we leave you."

"A hundred thousand francs," cried Cachan, interrupting Corentin. "But, sir, Séchard senior left twenty acres of vineyard, five small farms, ten acres of pasture at Marsac and not a penny with it."

"Nothing in the world," exclaimed David Séchard, intervening between the disputants, "would induce me to tell a lie, Monsieur Cachan, and still less were it to favor my own interests. Monsieur," said he to Corentin and to Derville, "my father left us, besides his estate"—

Courtois and Cachan motioned in vain to Séchard to be silent.

He continued:

"Three hundred thousand francs, which brings the amount of his property to about five hundred thousand francs."

"Monsieur Cachan," said Eve Séchard, "what portion does the law give to a natural child?"

"Madame," said Corentin, "we are not unreasonable; we simply ask you to give us your word in the presence of these gentlemen that you have not received more than three hundred thousand francs in cash from the inheritance of your father-in-law, and we shall certainly come to an understanding."

"First, give your word of honor," said the old attorney of Angoulême to Derville, "that you are a lawyer."

"Here are my credentials," said Derville to Cachan, handing him a paper folded in legal form, "and this gentleman is not, as you might think, a general inspector of real estate. You need not be disturbed," added Derville. "It was simply that we had the most powerful motives to learn the truth concerning the Séchard succession and now we know it."

Derville took Madame Eve by the hand and led her very courteously to the other end of the drawing-room.

"Madame," said he in a low voice, "if the honor and the future of the house of Grandlieu were not at stake in this question, I should not have lent myself to the stratagem invented by this decorated gentleman; but you will excuse it, it helps to uncover the lie by the aid of which your brother has abused the justice of a noble family. Take good care not to spread the report that you have given your brother twelve hundred thousand francs to enable him to buy the estate of Rubempré."—

"Twelve hundred thousand francs!" exclaimed Madame Séchard, growing pale; "where can my unhappy brother have got them?"

"Ah!" said Derville, "I fear that the source of this fortune cannot be honest."

The company could see tears gather in Eve's eyes.

"Perhaps we have rendered him a great service," said Derville, "in preventing him from plunging deeper in a lie which may prove dangerous."

Derville left Madame Séchard seated, still pale and with the tears yet upon her cheeks, and bowed to the company.

"To Mansle!" said Corentin to the small boy who drove the carriage.

The diligence from Bordeaux to Paris, which passed Mansle in the night, had a single empty place; Derville begged Corentin to allow him to profit by it, pleading the importance of his business, for at bottom he distrusted his companion, whose diplomatic dexterity and self-possession appeared to him the results of habit. Corentin remained for three days at Mansle, unable to get away; eventually he was obliged to write to Bordeaux and to engage a place from there to Paris, which he was unable to reach until nine days after his departure.

❋

During this time, Peyrade went every morning to Corentin's house, both at Passy and in Paris, to find out whether he had returned. On the eighth day he left at both houses a letter written in a private cipher, in order to explain to his friend the nature of the fate that hung over him, the abduction of Lydie, and the hideous destiny to which his enemies devoted her. Attacked, as he had long been accustomed to attack others, Peyrade, deprived of Corentin, but assisted by Contenson, still remained disguised as a nabob. Although his unseen enemies had discovered him, he judged with wisdom that he might gain some light by standing his ground on the battlefield. Contenson had set all his acquaintances upon Lydie's trail and he hoped to discover the house in which she was concealed; but day by day the impossibility of ascertaining the slightest information grew more and more evident and added to Peyrade's despair. The old detective had himself surrounded by a guard of twelve or fifteen of the ablest men in the secret service. All the approaches to the Rue des Moineaux and the Rue Taitbout, where the nabob was living with Madame du Val Noble, were watched with scrupulous care. During the last three days of the fateful delay granted by Asia to re-establish Lucien on his old footing with the Grandlieus, Contenson did not stir from the side of the veteran of the former lieutenant-generalcy of police. Thus the poetry of terror which the stratagems of hostile tribes spread throughout the heart of the American forests, the poetry which Cooper has used so well, clung to the most trivial details of Parisian life. The passers-by, the shops, the cabs, a person standing at a window, all lent to the men-numbers, to whom old Peyrade's life was intrusted, the vast interest which, in Cooper's novels, is offered by the trunk of a tree, a colony of beavers, a rock, a bison's skin, a motionless canoe or leafy branches overhanging the water.

"If the Spaniard has gone, you have nothing to fear," said Contenson to Peyrade, pointing out to him the undisturbed tranquillity which they enjoyed.

"And if he has not gone?" replied Peyrade.

"He took one of my men behind his calash; but, at Blois, the agent was obliged to get off, and could not regain the carriage."

Five days after Derville's return, Lucien received, in the morning, a visit from Rastignac.

"My dear boy," said the dandy, "it gives me great pain to fulfill a duty which has been intrusted to me on account of our intimacy. Your hopes of marriage are at an end and they can never again be renewed. You can nevermore set foot within the Grandlieu threshold. To marry Clotilde, you must wait for her father's death, and her father has become too much of an egoist to die soon. Old whist players remain long upon the very brink—of a card table. Clotilde is going to Italy with Madeleine de Lenoncourt-Chaulieu. The poor girl loves you so deeply, my boy, that the family have been obliged to have her watched; she wished to come and see you, she had even made her little plan of escape. That must be a consolation in your sorrow."

Lucien did not answer; he looked at Rastignac.

"After all, is it a misfortune?" continued his compatriot; "you will easily find another girl as noble and more fair than Clotilde. Madame de Sérizy will arrange a marriage for you out of revenge; she cannot abide the Grandlieus, who have never consented to receive her; she has a niece, little Clémence de Rouvre."

"My dear Rastignac," replied Lucien at length, "since our last supper, I have not been on good terms with Madame de Sérizy; she saw me in Esther's box, a scene followed, and since then I have left her to go her own way."

"A woman of forty odd does not quarrel for long with a young man as handsome as you are," said Rastignac. "I know something about these setting suns; they last for ten minutes on the horizon and for ten years in a woman's heart."

"For a week I have been waiting for a letter from her."

"Go there!"

"It would be wise."

"At least come to see La Val Noble. Her nabob is returning to Nucingen the supper which he received of him."

"I am invited and I shall go," said Lucien seriously.

On the evening following the confirmation of his misfortune, of which intelligence had been immediately given by Asia to Carlos, Lucien, with Rastignac and Nucingen, made their appearance at the house of the false nabob.

At midnight, Esther's former dining-room united almost all the actors of this drama, yet its deep interests, which lay beneath all these tempestuous existences, were known only to Esther, Lucien, Peyrade, the mulatto Contenson, and to Paccard, who had come to serve his mistress. Unknown to Peyrade and to Contenson, Asia had been requested by Madame du Val Noble to come to her cook's assistance. As he sat down at table Peyrade, who had given five hundred francs to Madame du Val Noble to furnish a handsome supper, found within his napkin a scrap of paper on which he read these words written in pencil: *The ten days expire the instant that you sit down at table.* Peyrade handed the paper to Contenson, who stood behind him, saying to him in English: "Did you tuck my name there?"

Contenson read this *Mene, Tekel, Phares* by the light of the candles and put the paper into his pocket; but he knew well how difficult it is to verify writing in pencil and especially a sentence written in capital letters, that is to say with lines mathematically arranged, since the capital letters are composed entirely of curves and straight lines, in which it is impossible to recognize the habits of the hand, as in the handwriting known as "running."

The supper was without gaiety. Peyrade was a prey to visible preoccupation. Of the young *high livers*, accustomed to enliven a supper, Lucien and Rastignac alone were present. Lucien was very sad and dreamy, while Rastignac, who had lost two thousand francs before supper, drank and ate with the sole idea of making them good after supper. The three women, struck with this cheerlessness, looked at one another. Melancholy despoiled every dish of its savor. Like plays and books, suppers must take their chances.

At the end of supper, the guests were served with ices called *plombières*. As everybody knows, this kind of ice contains tiny comfits of fruit placed upon its surface, and is served in small glasses without any pretence to pyramidal form. These ices had been ordered by Madame du Val Noble of Tortoni, whose celebrated establishment is at the corner of the Rue Taitbout and the Boulevard. The cook had the mulatto called to pay the caterer's bill. Contenson, to whom the boy's importunity seemed unnatural, went down-stairs and silenced him with these words:

"You don't come from Tortoni?"

Then he returned to the dining-room instantly.

But Paccard had already profited by this absence to serve the ices to the guests. Scarcely had the mulatto reached the door of the apartment when one of the agents who were guarding the Rue des Moineaux called from below:

"Number twenty-seven."

"What is it?" answered Contenson, hurrying down the flight of stairs.

"Tell papa that his daughter has returned, but in such a state! My God! Tell him to hurry; she is dying."

Just as Contenson re-entered the dining-room, old Peyrade, who had drunk deeply, was swallowing the little cherry of his *plombière*. Madame du Val Noble's health was being toasted; the nabob filled his glass with "wine of Constance," and emptied it. Troubled as Contenson was by the news which he was about to deliver to Peyrade, he was struck, as he entered, by the rapt attention with which Paccard gazed at the nabob. The two eyes of Madame de Champy's valet looked like two fixed flames. This observation, in spite of its importance, was not enough to delay the mulatto, and he bent over his master at the moment when Peyrade replaced his empty glass upon the table.

"Lydie is at home," said Contenson, "but in a sad condition."

Peyrade gave vent to the Frenchest of French oaths in a southern accent so pronounced that deep amazement appeared on the faces of the company. Perceiving his error, Peyrade threw off the mask, by saying to Contenson in good French:

"Call a cab! I come instantly."

Everybody rose from the table.

"Who then are you?" cried Lucien.

"Yez!" said the baron.

"Bixiou told me that you could play the Englishman better than he, and I wouldn't believe him," said Rastignac.

"It is some discovered bankrupt," said Du Tillet aloud. "I suspected as much!"

"What a singular place Paris is," said Madame du Val Noble; "after having failed in his quarter of the city, a merchant reappears as a nabob or a dandy in the Champs Elysées without the slightest hesitation. Oh! I was born under an evil star; failure follows me like a gad-fly."

"They say that every flower has its own," said Esther quietly; "mine, like Cleopatra's, is an asp."

"Who am I?" said Peyrade, at the door. "Ah! you shall know, for if I die I shall come out of my grave nightly to clutch your feet."

As he said these last words, he looked at Esther and at Lucien; then, profiting by the general astonishment, he disappeared with extraordinary dexterity, for he wished to rush to his house without waiting for a cab. In the street, Asia, enveloped in a black cloak, with a hood such as women wore to balls at that time, touched the detective's arm on the steps of the porte cochère.

"Send for the sacraments, Papa Peyrade," she said to him, in the same voice which had already prophesied misfortune. A carriage stood by, Asia stepped into it and the carriage disappeared as if it were borne away by the wind. There were five carriages about the door; Peyrade's men could discover nothing.

On arriving at his country house, situated in one of the most retired and smiling spots of the little town of Passy, the Rue de Vignes, Corentin, who passed for a tradesman with a hobby for gardening, found the cipher of his friend Peyrade. Without wasting an instant he stepped into the cab which had brought him, drove directly to the Rue des Moineaux and found Katt alone. He learned from the Flemish woman the story of Lydie's disappearance, and pondered in amazement over the lack of foresight which Peyrade and he had displayed.

"*They* don't know me yet," he said to himself. "Those people are capable of anything; I must learn whether they kill Peyrade, for if they do I shall not show myself."

The more infamous a man's life is, the more tightly he clings to it; it becomes a protestation, a revenge never forgotten for an instant. Corentin descended the stairs and hurrying to his house disguised himself as a little poverty-stricken old man, with a little straggling beard, wrapped in a little coat, worn to a greenish hue, and returned afoot, spurred on by his friendship for Peyrade. He wished to give orders to his most reliable and efficient Numbers. As he made his way along the Rue Saint Honoré, from the Place Vendôme to the Rue Saint Roch, he walked behind a girl dressed as if for the night, with her feet encased in slippers. This girl, wrapped in a white night-dress, with a night-cap on her head, sobbed as she walked, and groaned involuntarily; Corentin made a few steps past her and recognized Lydie.

"I am the friend of your father, M. Canquoëlle," said he in his natural voice.

"Ah! then there is some one in whom I can trust!" said she.

"Pretend that you don't know me," continued Corentin, "for we are pursued by cruel enemies and forced to disguise ourselves. But tell me what has happened."

"Oh! sir," said the poor girl, "my story tells itself, but I may not tell it.—I am dishonored, lost, though I cannot explain how."

"Where do you come from?"

"I don't know, sir; I ran away so hurriedly, I have passed through so many streets and turned so many corners, thinking that I was followed. And when I met an honest man I asked my way to the Boulevards in order to get to the Rue de la Paix. At last, after I had walked for—what time is it?"

"Half-past eleven!" said Corentin.

"I escaped at nightfall; then I have been walking for five hours!" exclaimed Lydie.

"You will find rest, you will find your good Katt."

"Oh! monsieur, there is no more rest for me! I don't wish to rest anywhere but in my grave; and I shall await my time in a convent, if they think me worthy to enter."

"Poor little girl, you did all that you could."

"Ah, sir, if you knew what vile creatures I have been thrown among."

"They must have put you to sleep?"

"Ah! that was it," said poor Lydie. "A little more strength and I shall reach the house. I feel faint and my ideas are not very distinct. Just now I thought that I was in a garden."

Corentin carried Lydie in his arms; she lost consciousness and he bore her up the stairway.

"Katt!" he cried.

Katt appeared, crying for joy.

"Don't rejoice too soon!" said Corentin sententiously; "the girl is very sick."

When Lydie had been laid upon her bed, and when by the light of the two candles which Katt had lighted, she recognized her chamber, she grew delirious. She sang snatches of sweet tunes, and then of a sudden, screamed horrible phrases which she had heard! Her lovely face was streaked with tints of violet. She mingled the remembrances of her pure life with those of the ten days of infamy. Katt wept. Corentin paced up and down the room, stopping by moments to examine Lydie.

"She is paying her father's debt!" said he; "can there be a Providence? Oh! I have been right to have no family. A child, I'll swear to it, is a hostage to misfortune, as some philosopher says."

"Oh!" said the poor girl, raising herself upon her elbow, and letting her lovely hair fall backward, "in place of being laid here, Katt, I ought to be laid upon the sand at the bottom of the Seine."

"Katt, instead of crying and looking at your child, which will not cure her, you ought to go and find a

THE DEATH OF ESTHER

doctor; first the one at the mayor's office and then MM. Desplein and Bianchon. We must save this innocent creature."

Corentin wrote down the addresses of these two celebrated physicians. At this moment a familiar step climbed the staircase; the door opened. Peyrade, his face purple and covered with sweat, his eyes almost bleeding, breathing like a porpoise, sprang from the parlor door to Lydie's room, crying:

"Where is my daughter?"

Peyrade saw a melancholy gesture of Corentin; his look followed the gesture. Lydie's condition can only be compared to that of a flower lovingly reared by some botanist, which has fallen from its stalk and been trodden beneath the hob-nailed boots of a peasant. Transport this image into a father's heart and you can understand the blow that fell upon Peyrade. Big tears welled up in his eyes.

"Somebody is crying; it is my father," said the child.

Lydie could still recognize her father; she raised herself from her bed and fell down at the old man's knees, just as he sank into an arm-chair.

"Pardon, papa!" said she in a voice which pierced Peyrade's heart at the moment when he felt as if a hammer beat against his skull.

"I am dying. Ah! the villains!" were his last words.

Corentin went to his friend's assistance; and saw him breathe his last.

"Death from poison!" said Corentin to himself.

"Ah! here's the doctor," he exclaimed, hearing the rumbling of a carriage.

Contenson, who appeared with his face cleansed from its black disguise, stood as though transformed into a bronze statue, when he heard Lydie say:

"Then you won't pardon me, father? It was not my fault!"

She did not know that her father was dead.

"Oh! how his eyes stare at me!" said the crazed girl.

"I must close them," said Contenson as he laid the dead Peyrade upon the bed.

"We are acting like fools," said Corentin; "let us carry him to his room. His daughter is half-mad; she will become wholly so, if she sees that he is dead, for she will think that she has killed him."

Lydie watched them bear away her father, and sat still as if she were dazed.

"There lies my only friend!" said Corentin, who seemed deeply moved when Peyrade was laid upon the bed in his own room. "In all his life he had but one avaricious thought and that was for his daughter! Let it be a lesson to you, Contenson. Every station of life has its honor. Peyrade did wrong to meddle with private affairs; our business is with public matters. But, come what may, I swear," said he, while his accent, look and gesture struck Contenson with dread, "to revenge my poor Peyrade! I will unearth the authors of his death, and those of his daughter's shame!—And by my own selfishness, by the few days which yet remain to me and which I risk in this revenge, every man among them shall end his life at four o'clock in the morning, in excellent health, clean shaven, in the Place de Grève!"—

"And I will aid you!" said Contenson, much moved.

Nothing is more affecting than the sight of passion in a cold, calculating, methodical man, who for twenty years has never been seen to display the slightest indication of sensibility. His the bar of iron, in fusion, which melts everything with which it comes into contact. Contenson's very entrails were stirred within him.

"Poor Père Canquoëlle!" continued he, looking at Corentin, "he has often paid for my dinner—and —none but vicious people would do a thing like this —he often gave me ten francs to play.—"

After this funeral oration, Peyrade's two avengers, hearing Katt and the physician from the mayor's office upon the staircase, went into Lydie's room.

"Go to the Commissioner of Police," said Corentin, "the public prosecutor would never find warrant for a prosecution, but we must have a report left at the Prefecture; that, perhaps, may be of some use. —Sir," said he to the physician, "you will find in that room a dead man; I do not think that his death was natural. You will make an autopsy in the presence of the Commissioner of Police, who will come at my request. Try to discover traces of poison; you will be assisted in a few moments by MM. Desplein and Bianchon, whom I have summoned to examine the daughter of my best friend, for her condition is worse than her father's, though he is dead."

"I have no need of these gentlemen's assistance in the practice of my profession," said the doctor.

"Ah! good!" thought Corentin. "Don't let us interfere with you, sir," continued he aloud. "To be brief,—this is my opinion: those who have killed the father have also dishonored the daughter."

At daybreak Lydie had at length succumbed to her fatigue: she was sleeping when the distinguished surgeon and the young doctor appeared. The physician entrusted with the autopsy had opened Peyrade's body and was searching for the causes of death.

"While you wait for your patient to awake," said Corentin to the two famous doctors, "would you aid one of your medical brethren in a demonstration which you will surely not find uninteresting? Your opinion will not be without weight in the legal statement."

"Your relative died of apoplexy," said the doctor; "there are proofs of a horrible cerebral congestion."

"Make an examination, gentlemen," said Corentin, "and look to see whether, in the catalogue of poisons, there are not any which produce the same effect."

"The stomach," said the doctor, "was completely filled with matter, but so far as I can see, without the apparatus for a chemical analysis, there is no trace of poison."

"If the characteristics of cerebral congestion are perfectly evident, that," said Desplein, pointing to the great quantity of ill-digested food, "is, considering the subject's age, a sufficient cause for death."

"Did he eat here?" asked Bianchon.

"No," said Corentin, "he came here hurriedly from the Boulevard and found his daughter dishonored.—"

"There is the real poison, if he loved his daughter," said Bianchon.

"What poison is there which could produce that effect?" demanded Corentin, without abandoning his idea.

"There is but one," said Desplein, after a careful examination. "It is a poison of the Javanese archipelago, taken from a species of bush which as yet is little known. It is akin to strychnine, and serves to poison that most dangerous weapon, the Malay creese—at least, so they say."

The Commissioner of Police arrived; Corentin informed him of his suspicions, and requesting him to write out a report, he stated in what house and with what persons Peyrade had taken supper; next he advised him of the plot formed against Peyrade's life and the cause of Lydie's condition. When he had concluded, Corentin stepped toward the apartment of the poor girl, where Desplein and Bianchon were examining the patient; but he met them at the door.

"Well, gentlemen?" inquired Corentin.

"Place the girl in an asylum; if she does not

recover her reason in childbirth, that is if she becomes pregnant, she will be a maniac and melancholy to the end of her days. For her cure there is no other resource than the sentiment of maternity, if it wakens.—"

Corentin gave forty francs in gold to each doctor, and turned to the Commissioner of Police, who pulled him by the sleeve.

"The doctor maintains that the death is natural," said the officer, "and it will be all the more difficult to make a report since Père Canquoëlle is the subject: he meddled with many people's affairs and we should never know whom we might fall foul of—men like him often die *per order*.—"

"My name is Corentin," said Corentin in the commissioner's ear. The commissioner betrayed a gesture of surprise.—

"Make a note of these facts," continued Corentin. "It will be very useful later, and don't send it unless under the heading of confidential information. The crime cannot be proved and I know that the preparations would be cut short at the very first step.—But some day I will deliver up the guilty to Justice. I am going to watch them and catch them with the blood still on their hands."

The Commissioner of Police bowed to Corentin and went away.

"Sir," said Katt, "mademoiselle, will do nothing but sing and dance; what can I do?"

"Something has happened then?"

"She has learned that her father is dead.—"

"Put her in a cab, and take her with all gentleness to Charenton; I am going to write a line to the Director-General of the Police of the Kingdom, so that she may be suitably cared for. The daughter at Charenton, the father in the Potter's Field!" said Corentin. "Contenson go and get the cart for the dead poor. Now you have two men to settle with, Don Carlos Herrera!"

"Carlos?" ejaculated Contenson; "he is in Spain."

"He is in Paris!" said Corentin peremptorily. "He has within him the genius of Spain in the time of Philip II., but I have traps for everybody, even for kings."

✽

At nine o'clock in the morning of the fifth day after the disappearance of the nabob, Madame du Val Noble was seated at the foot of Esther's bed and was crying there, for she felt herself upon the brink of penury.

"If I had an income of but a hundred louis! With that, my dear, a woman could retire into some little village somewhere and be able to marry.—"

"I can get it for you!" said Esther.

"How?" exclaimed Madame du Val Noble.

"Oh! very simply. Listen to me. You are bent upon suicide; play that comedy well; you will summon Asia and offer her ten thousand francs for two black pearls, contained in very thin glass. They hold a poison which kills in one second; you will bring them to me; I'll give you fifty thousand francs.—"

"Why not ask for them yourself?" said Madame du Val Noble.

"Asia would not sell them to me."

"It is not for you?" said Madame du Val Noble.

"Perhaps."

"You, who are living in the midst of pleasure and luxury in a house of your own! on the eve of a fête, which people will talk about for ten years to come, and which costs Nucingen twenty thousand francs! The guests, they say, will eat strawberries in the month of February—asparagus, grapes, melons.— There will be three thousand francs' worth of flowers in your rooms."

"Is that all? There are three thousand francs' worth of roses on the staircase alone."

"I have heard that your gown costs ten thousand francs."

"Yes, my gown is made out of point lace from Brussels; and Delphine, his wife, is furious. But I wished to look like a wife myself."

"Where are the ten thousand francs?" said Madame du Val Noble.

"It is all my money," said Esther, smiling. "Open my dressing-case; they are beneath my curl-papers.—"

"When people talk of dying, it is seldom that they kill themselves," said Madame du Val Noble. "If it were to commit—"

"A crime? out with it!" said Esther, finishing the sentence which her friend hesitated to complete. "You need not fear," she continued; "I don't wish to kill anybody. I had a friend, a woman who was very happy; she is dead; I shall follow her—that is all."

"Are you mad?—"

"Why are you surprised? We had promised this to each other."

"You must protest that note!" said her friend, smiling.

"Do what I say and go away. I hear a carriage coming, and it is Nucingen. That man will go mad with his happiness. He really loves me. Why is it we never love those who love us. They do everything to please us."

"Ah," said Madame du Val Noble, "that is the story of the herring, the most loving of fish!"

"Why?"

"No one has ever learned."

"Away with you, my pet! I must ask for your fifty thousand francs."

"Then—adieu."

For three days past Esther's behavior toward the baron had changed completely. The monkey had become a cat and the cat was turning into a woman. Esther lavished the riches of her affection upon this old man, and had made herself irresistible. Her conversation, divested of malice and bitterness and full of tender insinuations, had brought conviction into the mind of the fat-witted banker. She called him Fritz; he thought that he was loved.

"My poor Fritz, I have tried you in the fire," said she. "I have tormented you; your patience has been sublime. You love me, I recognize it, and you shall have your reward. You please me now, and I know not how it is, but I prefer you to a young man. Perhaps it is the result of experience.—In the end a woman comes to believe that pleasure is the soul's fortune, and that it is no more flattering to be loved for pleasure than to be loved for one's money. Young men are too egotistical; they think more of themselves than they do of us; while you think of nothing but me. I am all your life; I wish nothing more of you; my only desire is to prove to you the extent of my disinterested affection."

"I have gifen you nodding," answered the delighted baron. "I eentent to make ofer to you do-morrow an ingome of dirdy tausent vrancs.—Eet ees my vedding cake."

Esther embraced Nucingen so tenderly that he grew pale.

"Oh!" said she, "don't think that it is your thirty thousand francs that makes me thus; it is because now I love you, my fat Frédéric.—"

"Och, mein Gott, vy tid you broof me—I zhould haf peen so habby vor dree months."

"Is it in three per cents or in fives, my pet?" said Esther, passing her hands through Nucingen's hair and arranging it according to her fancy.

"Een drees—I haf guandities."—

The same morning the baron brought a duplicate of the entry in his ledger; he came to breakfast with his dear little girl, in order to receive her orders for the morrow, the glorious Saturday, the great day!

"Dake zis, meine leetle vife, meine only vife," said the banker joyously, his face radiant with happiness; "here ees someting to bay for ze exbenses of your dable for ze resd of your tays."

Esther took the paper without the slightest emotion, folded it, and laid it in her dressing-case.

"Now you are happy, monster of iniquity," said she, gently tapping Nucingen's cheek, "at seeing me at last accept something from you. I can't tell you the truth about yourself any more, for now I share the fruits of what you call your business. That's not a gift, my poor boy; it's a restitution.

Now don't put on your Stock Exchange expression; you know very well that I love you."

"Meine peaudiful Esder, meine anchel of luff," said the banker, "to not dalk any more een zis vay. I zhould not gare eef ze whole vorld zhould gall me ein ropper, eef in your eyes I vas an honesd man. I luff you more ant more efery tay."

"I intend that you should," said Esther; "I will not say another word to hurt your feelings, my pet elephant, for you have become simple as a child. Lord, you fat rascal, you never had any innocence. The little that you had when you came into the world must have reappeared on the surface; but it had sunk so deep that it never reappeared until after sixty-six years and then it was drawn up by love's hook. This phenomenon occurs among old men. And this is why I have come to love you; you are young, very young.—No one but I shall have ever known this, Frédéric.—I alone.—For you were a banker at fifteen. I suppose that you lent your college friends one bank note on the condition that they should give you two in return."

Seeing him smile she leaped into his lap.

"Do what you will, rob men, lead the way, I'll help you. Men are not worth the trouble of loving them; Napoleon killed them like flies. What do the French care whether it is to you or to the budget that they pay their contributions? They are not in love with the budget, and good Lord,—get to your work; I have thought it over; you are right. Shear the sheep. It says so in the gospel according to

Béranger. Kiss your *Esder*. Ah! do say that you will give that poor Val Noble all the furniture in the Rue Taitbout apartments! and then to-morrow you will offer her fifty thousand francs. That will look very well. Listen, my darling; you killed Falleix. They began a hue and cry after you. This generosity will appear Babylonian,—and all the women will be talking about you. Oh! you will be all that is great and noble in Paris; and the world is so constituted that it will forget Falleix. Thus, after all, 'tis but money placed at interest."

"You are right, meine anchel, you know ze vorld," said he, "you zhall pe meine gounseller."

"So you see," replied Esther, "how careful I am of my friend's interests, of his reputation and of his honor. Go and come back with the fifty thousand francs."

She wished to rid herself of Nucingen in order that she might summon a stock-broker and sell the bond that same afternoon at the Exchange.

"Ant vy ad vunce?" demanded he.

"Why, my pet, you must offer them, in a little satin box, under a fan. You will say to her, 'Here, madame, is a fan which I trust may please you.' People think you are but a Turcaret; you will surpass Beaujon."

"Jarming! Jarming!" exclaimed the baron; "zen I zhall pe glever! Yez, I zhall rebeat your vorts."

As poor Esther sat down, exhausted by the effort she had made in playing her part, Europe entered.

"Madame," said she, "a messenger sent from

the Quai Malaquais by Celestin, M. Lucien's valet."—

"Let him come in! No.—I will go into the other room."

"There is a letter from Celestin for madame."

Esther sprang into the antechamber; she looked at the messenger and saw nothing suspicious in his appearance.

"Tell *him* to come down!" said Esther feebly, as she sank into a chair, when she had finished reading the letter. "Lucien wishes to kill himself," she added in Europe's ear; "show *him* the letter."

Carlos Herrera, still dressed as a commercial traveler, came downstairs without hesitation, but when he perceived a stranger in the room his glance fell instantly upon the messenger.

"You told me that there was nobody," whispered he to Europe.

Then with extraordinary prudence, he passed at once into the parlor, casting a searching look at the messenger. Trompe-la-Mort did not know that for some time past the famous Chief of the Secret Service, who had arrested him in Madame Vauquier's boarding house, had a rival, thought by many more fit than he for his position. This rival was the messenger.

"They are right," said the sham messenger to Contenson, who was waiting for him in the street; "the man you described is in the house; but he is not a Spaniard, and I will burn my hand off if our bird isn't hidden beneath his cassock."

"He's no more priest than Spaniard," said Contenson.

"I'm sure of it," said the agent of the Secret Service.

"Oh! if we were right!" said Contenson.

Lucien had in fact been away for two days, and his enemies had profited by his absence to set this trap; but he returned the same evening, and Esther's anxiety was calmed.

The next morning, just as the courtesan was returning to bed after her bath, her friend arrived.

"I have the two pearls," said the Val Noble.

"Let me see them," said Esther, raising herself and burying her pretty elbow in a pillow trimmed with lace.

Madame du Val Noble held toward her friend two black balls like gooseberries. The baron had presented Esther with a pair of small greyhounds of a famous breed, which will eventually bear the name of a great poet of our era, who has brought them into fashion. Proud of the gift, the courtesan had kept for them the names of their ancestors, Romeo and Juliet. It is superfluous to speak of the charm, the whiteness, the grace of these animals, made for the drawing-room, whose behavior had something of English discretion. Esther called Romeo; Romeo ran toward her. His legs were so lithe, so slender, so strong, so nervous that they looked like rods of steel. He looked at his mistress. Esther made a gesture as if to throw him one of the two pearls in order to arouse his attention. "His name destines him to die thus!" said Esther, tossing the pearl which Romeo crunched between his teeth.

The dog did not utter a cry; he rolled over quite dead. The deed was done while Esther was still saying the words of her funeral oration.

"Ah, angels of Heaven!" exclaimed Madame du Val Noble.

"You have a cab; carry away the late Romeo," said Esther; "his death would make an uproar here; I shall have given him to you, and you will have lost him. Advertise. Hurry; to-night you shall have your fifty thousand francs."

This was said with the perfect insensibility of a courtesan, and so quietly that Madame du Val Noble exclaimed involuntarily:

"You are indeed our queen!"

"Come early, and look your best!"

At five o'clock in the evening Esther dressed herself in a bridal costume. A lace gown covered her white satin skirt; she wore a white girdle, and shoes of white satin. Over her beautiful shoulders was thrown a scarf of English lace. Her hair was intertwined with real white camelias, in imitation of the head-dress of some young girl. She displayed upon her neck a collar of pearls, the gift of Nucingen, bought for thirty thousand francs. Although her toilette was completed at six o'clock, she closed her doors to everybody, even to Nucingen. Europe knew that Lucien was to be introduced into the bed-chamber. Lucien arrived on the stroke of seven, and Europe found means to lead him unperceived to

Esther's room. When Lucien saw Esther, he said to himself:

"Why should I not go and live with her at Rubempré, far from the world, and never again return to Paris? I have had five years as earnest of the future, and this woman will never deceive me. Where can I find a masterpiece like her?"

"My dearest, you whom I have made my god," said Esther, kneeling on a cushion before Lucien, "bless me."

Lucien wished to raise Esther and embrace her, saying, "What is this pleasantry, my love?" He tried to grasp her waist, but she disengaged herself with a movement that expressed as much respect as horror.

"I am no longer worthy of you, Lucien," said she, suffering the tears to roll down from her eyes. "I beg of you to bless me, and swear to me that you will endow two beds at the hospital, since another's prayers in church will never buy my pardon from God. I have loved you too well, Lucien. Tell me that I have made you happy, and that sometimes you will think of me.—Tell me!"

Lucien saw that Esther was deeply in earnest; he stood, thoughtful.

"You wish to kill yourself," said he at length, in a voice which denoted deep meditation.

"No, my love; but to-day, as you know, marks the death of the pure, chaste, loving woman you have known—and I fear that I shall die of sorrow."

"Poor child, wait!" said Lucien. "For two days

past I have been making every effort, I have even been able to reach Clotilde—"

"Nothing but Clotilde!" ejaculated Esther, with an accent of concentrated rage.

"Yes," he replied; "we are in communication.— Tuesday morning she leaves Paris; but on her way to Italy, I shall have an interview with her at Fontainebleau."

"Ah, heavens! what would you men have for wives? Sticks of wood!" cried poor Esther. "Answer me this: If I had seven or eight millions, would you not marry me?"

"Child! I was going to tell you that if all is over for me, I do not wish another wife than you."

Esther lowered her head to conceal her sudden paleness and the tears which she wiped away.

"You love me?" said she, looking at Lucien with deep sadness. "Let my blessing go with you. Don't compromise yourself. Go out by the side door, and act as if you were coming from the antechamber to the drawing-room. Kiss me on the forehead," she said.

She took Lucien in her arms, pressed him frantically to her heart, and said, "Go, go—or I live."

When the dying woman appeared in the drawing-room, there was a cry of admiration. Esther's eyes had cast aside the depths of thought in which her soul was plunged. The blue black of her fine hair was set off by the camelias. In a word, every effect which this splendid courtesan had sought to produce had been obtained. She had no rivals. She seemed like the supreme expression of the boundless luxury by whose creations she was surrounded. She was sparkling with wit. She led the orgy with that cold and calm power which Habeneck displays in the Conservatory at those concerts in which the first musicians of Europe rise to the sublimities of execution in their interpretations of Mozart and of Beethoven. She noticed, nevertheless, with consternation that Nucingen ate little, drank nothing, and did the honors of the house. At midnight, nobody was in possession of his faculties. Glasses were broken past repair; two hand-painted curtains of Chinese silk were torn. For the second time in his life, Bixiou was intoxicated; nobody could stand erect; the women went fast asleep on divans. The guests could not carry out the jest which they had carefully arranged beforehand, of conducting Nucingen and Esther to their bed-room, ranged in two rows, with candelabra in their hands and singing in unison the *Buona sera* of the *Barbier de Sèville*. Nucingen gave his arm to Esther. Drunk as he was, Bixiou perceived them, and still found strength to say, as Rivarol did in regard to the last marriage of the Duke de Richelieu, "The Prefect of Police must be warned; danger is impending." The jester thought to jest; he was a prophet.

*

M. de Nucingen did not return to his house until Monday toward mid-day; but at one o'clock his broker informed him that Mademoiselle Esther Van Bogseck had sold, since Wednesday, the thirty thousand francs a year in bonds, and that she had lately realized the price.

"But Monsieur le baron," said he, "M. Derville's head clerk happened to come to my house as I was speaking of this transfer; and after he had seen Mademoiselle Esther's real name, he told me that she was the heiress of a fortune of seven millions."

"Pah!"

"Yes, she is probably the sole heiress of Gobseck, the old discounter. Derville is going to verify the facts. If your mistress' mother is the beautiful Dutch woman, she inherits—"

"I know eet," said the banker; "she haz tolt me ze zdory of her life. I vill wride eine line do Terfile."

The baron sat down at his desk, wrote a brief note to Derville, and despatched it by one of his servants. Then leaving the stock exchange at three o'clock, he went straight to Esther's door.

"Madame has left orders that she is not to be disturbed for any reason whatsoever; she is in bed and asleep."

"Ah, ze tefil," exclaimed the baron, "Irobe, zhe vould not pe zorry to learn zat zhe has pegome enormouzly rech. Zhe eenhereds sefen millions. Olt Copseck ees teat and leafes his sefen millions, ant your misdress ees his zole heiress, her modder peing ze own niece of Copseck, who, pesides, has mate ein vill. I coult nefer imachine zat ein millionaire like him zhoult leaf Esder in boferdy."

"Ah, then your reign is over, you old mountebank!" said Europe, eyeing the baron with an effrontery worthy of a servant in Molière. "You old Alsatian crow, she loves you about as well as you love the plague. Lord of heaven! Millions! She can marry her love. Oh! how happy she will be!"

And Prudence Servien left the Baron de Nucingen completely thunderstruck, to rush and announce, she first of all! this stroke of fortune to her mistress. The old man, intoxicated with joy more than mortal, and believing in the security of his happiness, felt his love drowned in cold water at the very instant that it attained its highest degree of incandescence.

"Zhe dezeivet me," he cried, with tears in his eyes. "Zhe dezeivet me! Oh, Esder; oh, mein life. Vool zat I am. To zuch vlowers efer grow vor olt men? I can puy eferything excebt youth! Oh, mein gott! vot zhall I to? Vat vill habben? Zie gruel Irobe ees right. Esder, once rech, esgabes me. I might as vell go ant hang myzelf.—Vat ees life widout ze define vlame of loff zat I have dasded? Oh, mein gott!"

The baron snatched away the tuft of false hair that for three months past he had mingled with his gray hairs. A piercing cry uttered by Europe made Nucingen shudder to his very entrails. The poor banker arose and walked with his legs reeling like those of a drunken man from the cup of disenchantment which he had emptied, for nothing intoxicates like the strong wine of misfortune.

From the door of the bed chamber he could see Esther lying rigidly upon the bed, her face discolored with the poison, dead! He walked to the bed and fell upon his knees.

"You are right; zhe hat zait zo! Zhe diet of me!"—

Paccard, Asia, all the household, ran thither. It was a scene of excitement and surprise, not of affliction. Everybody felt some uncertainty. The baron became a banker once more; his suspicions were aroused, and he was so imprudent as to ask where were the seven hundred and fifty thousand francs. Paccard, Asia and Europe looked at one another in so singular a manner that M. de Nucingen made his escape at once for fear of robbery or murder. Europe, who caught sight of a sealed package, whose softness betrayed the presence of bank notes, beneath the pillow of her mistress, at once set about "laying out the body," as she called it.

"Go and inform Carlos, Asia! To die before knowing that she had seven millions! Gobseck was the uncle of our late mistress!" cried she.

Europe's manœuvre was understood by Paccard.

The second that Asia turned her back, Europe unsealed the package on which the poor courtesan had written: "To be given to M. Lucien de Rubempré." Seven hundred and fifty notes, each of a thousand francs, gleamed before the eyes of Prudence Servien, who exclaimed:

"Why not be happy and honest for the rest of our days!"

Paccard made no objection; the thief within him was stronger than his devotion to Trompe-la-Mort.

"Durut is dead," answered he, taking the bank notes; "my shoulder has not been branded yet. Let's fly together, divide the sum so as not to put all our eggs into one basket, and then we'll marry."

"But where can we hide?" said Prudence.

"In Paris," answered Paccard.

Prudence and Paccard descended the stairs immediately with the speed of two honest people turned thieves.

"My child," said Trompe-la-Mort to Asia, when she had uttered the first few words of her recital, "find a letter written by Esther, while I write a will in proper form, and you will carry to Girard copies of the testament and of the letter. But in order to save time, I must slip the testament beneath Esther's pillow before the officers come to seal up her belongings."

He drew up the following testament:

"Having never loved any person in the world excepting M. Lucien Chardon de Rubempré, and having resolved to put an end to my life rather than return to the life of vice and infamy, whence his charity has rescued me, I give and bequeath to the aforesaid Lucien Chardon de Rubempré everything that I possess on the day of my decease, on condition that a foundation be made in the parish of St. Roch for the continual saying of masses for the repose of her who has given him all, even her last thought.

"ESTHER GOBSECK."

"That is like enough to her style," thought Trompe-la-Mort.

At seven o'clock that night, the testament, written and sealed, was placed by Asia beneath Esther's pillow.

"Jacques," said she, rushing upstairs with precipitation, "just as I left the room the officers of justice arrived."

"Do you mean a Justice of the Peace?"

"No, sonny. There was indeed the Justice of the Peace among them, but he was accompanied by gendarmes. The Public Prosecutor and a Judge of the Probate Court are with him; the doors are guarded."

"This death has stirred up a very sudden commotion," remarked Collin.

"Europe and Paccard have not yet reappeared. I'm afraid the birds have flown with seven hundred and fifty thousand francs," said Asia.

"Ah! the wretches!" said Trompe-la-Mort; "with their vile schemes, they'll ruin *us!*"

Human justice and the justice of Paris—that is to

say, the most suspicious, the most acute, the cleverest, the most learned justice of this world—too acute even, for at every instant she is interpreting the law—at length laid her hand on the machinators of this horrible plot. The Baron de Nucingen, recognizing the effects of poison, and not finding his seven hundred and fifty thousand francs, at once suspected one of the two odious personages whom he detested, Europe or Paccard, to be guilty of the crime. In his first burst of mad rage, he rushed to the Prefecture of Police. It was an alarm-bell, which collected all of Corentin's numbers. The Prefecture, the criminal bar, the Commissioner of Police, the Justice of the Peace, the Judge of the Probate Court—everybody was aroused. At nine o'clock at night, three physicians, who had been summoned, assisted at the autopsy of poor Esther's body, and the investigation began.

Trompe-la-Mort, warned by Asia, exclaimed: "They don't know that I am here. I can get a breath of air."

He raised himself by the frame of his garret window, and with matchless agility sprang out upon the roof, whence he began to study the surroundings with the matter-of-fact coolness of a mason laying tiles.

"Good," said he, as he saw a garden in the Rue de Provence, separated from them by five houses. "That's what I want."

"Your game is up, Trompe-la-Mort!" The sudden cry came from Contenson, who stepped from behind the chimney. "You will explain to M. Camusot what mass you were about to celebrate on the roof, Monsieur l'Abbé; and above all, why you were trying to escape."

"I have enemies in Spain," said Carlos Herrera.

"Escape to Spain by your garret," retorted Contenson.

The counterfeit Spaniard seemed to yield; but suddenly propping himself against the support of the window, which was raised considerably above the surface of the roof, he seized Contenson and hurled him backward with such violence that the detective fell headlong into the gutter of the Rue Saint Georges. Contenson died on his field of honor; Jacques Collin returned quietly into his garret and went to bed.

"Give me something which will make me very ill without killing me," said he to Asia, "for I must be in the agony of death so that I can give no answer to their *inquisitiveness*. Fear nothing; I am a priest, and a priest I shall remain. I have just rid myself, most naturally, of one of the few who can detect me."

At seven o'clock the night before, Lucien had set off post-haste in his carriage, with a passport which he had secured that very morning for Fontainebleau, and spent the night at the last inn in the direction of Nemours. Toward six o'clock the next morning, he walked on alone through the forest, and went as far as Bouron.

"It was in that fatal spot," thought he, as he sat

down upon one of those rocks which command the lovely landscape of Bouron, "that Napoleon hoped to make one mighty effort, on the day before his abdication."

At daybreak he heard the noise of a post-chaise, and saw a carriage pass him in which he could distinguish the servants of the young Duchess of Lenoncourt-Chaulieu and the waiting maid of Clotilde de Grandlieu.

"There they are," thought Lucien. "Now for a successful comedy, and I am saved. I shall be the duke's son-in-law whether he will or no."

An hour later the closed carriage, containing the two women, rolled toward him with that unmistakable gliding rumbling which heralds the approach of a fashionable traveling carriage. The two ladies had given orders for the carriage to stop on the hill overlooking Bouron, and the valet on the dickey told the coachman to halt. At this moment Lucien advanced.

"Clotilde!" he cried, tapping at the window.

"No," said the young duchess to her friend, "he must not get into the carriage; we must not be alone with him, my dear girl. Have one last conversation with him, I consent to it; but it shall be on the high road, where we will go afoot, followed by Baptiste. The day is fine, we are warmly dressed, and have nothing to fear from the cold. The carriage shall follow us—"

The two women stepped out.

"Baptiste," said the young duchess, "the postilion

will drive on very slowly; we wish to walk for a short distance, and you will accompany us."

Madeleine de Mortsauf took her friend's arm, and allowed Lucien to talk with Clotilde. They walked along together thus as far as the little village of Grez. It was then eight o'clock, and there Clotilde bade Lucien good-bye.

"So, my friend," said she, ending this long conversation with dignity, "I shall never marry anybody else. I prefer to believe in you rather than in other men; than in my father or my mother. Did woman ever give a stronger proof of attachment? Now try to dispel the fatal cloud which hangs over you."

The sound of galloping horses approached, and to the great astonishment of the two ladies, a company of gendarmes surrounded the little group.

"What do you want?" demanded Lucien, with all the arrogance of fashion.

"You are M. Lucien de Rubempré?" said the Public Prosecutor of Fontainebleau.

"Yes, sir."

"You will sleep to-night at the Force," continued he. "I have a warrant of arrest against you."

"Who are these ladies?" exclaimed the brigadier.

"Ah! yes;—your pardon, ladies. May I see your passports? For according to my information M. Lucien has acquaintances who, for his sake, are capable of—"

"You take the Duchess de Lenoncourt-Chaulieu for a woman of the streets!" said Madeleine, casting a look well worthy of a duchess upon the Public Prosecutor.

"You are handsome enough to be a duchess," replied the magistrate, tactfully.

"Baptiste, show our passports," answered the young duchess, smiling.

"Of what crime does this gentleman stand accused?" said Clotilde, while the duchess was endeavoring to push her into the carriage.

"Of complicity in robbery and murder," replied the brigadier of gendarmes.

Baptiste lifted Mademoiselle de Grandlieu in the carriage, for she had fainted dead away.

At midnight Lucien entered the Force, a prison situated on the corner of the Rue Payenne and the Rue des Ballets, where he was placed in a solitary cell. The Abbé Carlos Herrera had been confined there since his arrest.

www.ingramcontent.com/pod-product-compliance
Lightning Source LLC
Chambersburg PA
CBHW031305150426
43191CB00005B/81